A Complete History of Jammu and Kashmir State

A Complete History of Jammu and Kashmir State

Dr Raj Kumar

KALPAZ

ISBN: 978-93-5128-248-8

Price: ₹

First Published, 2017

Published by

Kalpaz Publications
C-30, Satyawati Nagar,
Delhi – 110052
E-mail: kalpaz@hotmail.com
Ph.: 9212142040

Printed at: G. Print Process, Delhi

Contents

Part - B

Kashmir

Part - C

Ladakh

Preface

I do feel a great pleasure by publishing this book '*A Complete History of Jammu & Kashmir State*' in the hands of the students and teachers, University of Jammu. Book contains a lot of new material which did not exist on this topic. It discusses in detail with new horizontal – knowledge, why India was dominated by the Britishers, particularly state – relations have been discussed in detail with brief manners.

I avail of this opportunity to thank my wife = Dr Shabnam Grewal as '*Inspiration*' and hope for the betterment of future. All suggestions from her side has been gratefully acknowledged.

Dr Raj Kumar

H.O.D. History, GCW Gandhi Nagar
R/o H.No.14, Dream City Muthi,
Jammu – 181205

Part - A
Jammu

1

Socio-Cultural Aspects of Jambudvipa = Jammu Region

"Anyhow Jammu State is an ideology of the Sufi Saint historian to explore the new theme of the humanity sciences = "New Orders of the Day", as a prediction of the Dalit Samaj. In the ancient time this state was known Jambu = *Jammu*, Div pa = Dal + Lit = Leader of the "Natural History" of the Pliny = Pinayal village, a Khalsa house of Lord = Khalsi *Kumba* of the Guru Ravidas's philosophy. Term Jambulochan and Bahulochan = population explosion of the state or there are number of Chamars. They need their own history of the human psychology = Aswani Chamar Khalsa son of Jagdish Raj R/o Pinayali.

I. Founding Fathers of the Jammu Region: China to Dr Raj Kumar or the pre-historic and the proto-historic "souls" of this clan or tribe = Gargotra tribe of the Jammu region linked with Dr Raghunath Rai, studies in world civilisation as an identity of the '*Rai Family of Kashmir*'.

II. Rai Dynasty: This dynasty was explored by Vishaal International study dated about 50 B.C. that tribe belonged to Sialkot annexed Jammu to their capital. *Adi-Rai* was his independent ruler of Jammu (58 B.C to 10 B.C).

III. Study shows the Jambudvipa was his ancient name in the light of development of the "*Human History*" this area was popular among Dalit = Mochi = Chamar. Raghunath Rai was known degraded author of the "World History" by the anti-

Dalit Muslims like Mohammad Ishaq Khan and other historians of the Kashmir University = '*Kuta Department*'. Why militancy penetrated in Kashmir Valley after 1990, because there was a anti-Dalit propaganda used to like in Kashmir = Bhatt, Koul, Pandit, Bambroo etc. They were kick out from the valley with ideology of Manmat = anti-Dalit propaganda. Kashmir Pandits, they migrated from Kashmir as a clever race = Manmat = Negative race. Poor people, *Watal*, *Hanji*, *Chak* etc., they are still existing both in Kashmir, Jammu and Ladakh = "*Mon culture*" = Aryan culture is still existing in Ladakh. For example, Iran (formerly called Persia) lay on the Iranian plateau strecting eastward from the Tigris River to the Indus River flowed from Ladakh to Turkistan = three Ali Brothers. This Iranian Civilisation flourished during the 2000 B.C. The main body of the Aryans passed on the Himalayas as small tribe, founded in Jammu = Gargotra tribe of Ambgarota = Rajput family existed before 1947. Having lack of, natural sources, this tribe went to Bahuana Chack (Akhnoor). *Fagun*, *Chand*, *Koka*, three brothers, did not have formal education, but efficient in practical lifestyle as farmer = "*Honest Living Ideology*". The name Aryan is still strived in the three Region of the State = Dalit Samaj and this word Iran = Ariana which is applied to the great Persian tableland and later, they were known as Chamar or Mochi in this area as degraded race of the human technology; believe on Rational and Humanism. Moreover, their Guru were Dalits = Ambedkar Baba Gurinder Singh Ji of Dera Bias = Satluj river ke Kahani as the story of the life = stream.

IV. The period between 600 to 1000 A.D was the period Islamic study = Aryan = Ariana = Chamar Culture = Chura Culture the Holy Scripture = Holy Quran = Holy Shabd in Judism called Holy Name. Title of this clan was reflected Sultan = Suratrana called in Sanskrit, Sultan in Turkey. Bal or Choti = Guta was the identity of the Mohammad Prophet as identity of the living Murshid = Baba Gurinder Singh Ji Dillion = Jat regiment = agricultural tribe and faith was Arabia = One God, One family, found in Islamic culture.

Bharatiya Bhim Sena = Representing Ambedkar's thought = Dalit Samaj. Less corruption and Honest Approach, *Bemani Kam* = Satsangi Samaj. "*Bu Devetano Ka Menfesto*" = Search of New Truth = Scientific knowledge as an ideology reflect in Gita = Mohan Das Karma Chand Ji ideology. His scientific study based on Ambedkar's thought that is Chamar = untouchibility; a supreme commander of all the Dalit forces. Why he was killed by Nath Ram Gorasi, because, he used to believe on Hindusim = Mohammadanism = Negative thinking. Dalit Samaj, at that time *Dalit Samaj* was in search of foods that is *Roti*, *Kapra* aaur *Makan*, that was basic and essential need of a good human beings. Now, today, particularly J&K State, Manmat = Sri Lankan view of *Mahabharata* = Epic Age. Corrupt Samaj, Corrupt Soch = Niala, Dhala Chief Minister. Now, knowledge of the "historical truth" = Corruption Ka Dor.

Human beings are always very meticulous about the sources of their own behaviour or belonging = Postivism Soach. But in Kashmir, their a Negativism in large scale. They say, there is no need of social – Scientist = Bhat Sahib = Nakami Koam = Kashmir Pandits. There is no ideology of the true faith = Materialism ke Soach.

Historical Materialism: Karl Marx's general idea = common approach = Dalit Samaj = ideology of Baba Sehib, Dr B.R. Ambedkar have and have-nots to Dalit to anti-Dalits. Similarly ideology as Lord Buddha and Karl Marx = Ambedkarism.

V. Historical Materialism of Dr B.R Ambedkar was owned by him from Germany and ideology reflected in America, after the Independence of 13th Colonies of England. English people, why they were destroyed their identity in Central Asia = penetration of Bengal Society of India and continental system of India, destroyed the identity of Chura Culture for the "*Development of History*". Lord Mountbatten = Hindu Kush Parbit = destruction of the Sufi Saint ideology = Roti Ram of Mirpur Siddhar. Hari Singh migrated Bombay for the development of "New Ideology" = Chamar thought. Rites and Rituals, both the Hindus, Old Dalits, Muslims; Old Christian, penetrated in large scale in Central Asia, and became costly and forgottened the name of *Allah* = Rama + Christ = Economic Research.

VI. Political Importance: "Jammu city has been a seat of political importance for a long time", according to Dr Karan described in the forward of '*History and Culture of Himalayan States*', by S.D.S Charak. How, we can called S.D.S Charak or Gulchain Singh Charak (Ex-Education Minister) of this state and Sadar-ri-Riysat = Dr Karan Singh = Rajputs, they were anti-Dalits = Brahmins = Abdulla Family. Political Importance, here we mean, local politic = "Origin of the Man". It lies in their lifestyle = Goonda elements. Dalit Ideology is based on "Infinite Knowledge" Highest Knowledge as the concept of both the Lord Buddha and Mahavira.

First Historical Dynasty: 500 B.C to 143 B.C Raja Bodh Arjun dynasty ruled for 357 years. Than Raja Mangal Chand of Kangra = Jammu State = Dilli, modern Delhi, Bombay to Mumbai, Calcutta to Chenai, United Province = M.P, Punjab = Penjab, Kashmir = Kashir = Srinagar, having the same meanings as head and heart qualities of a good human being and killed Raj Vallab, the descendent of Bodh Arjun = Rajput descendent.

Bhanu Jakh of Bharakh then killed Mangal Chand = Dr V.K Bhatt as a Dalit ruler of the Deccan State of Adhra Pardesh = Schedule Tribe. They tried to restore their powers in Kashmir or Ladakh, but failed without strong ideology = Dalit Concept.

Dalit concept = Karl Marx's concept of "*Das Capital*" = Economic Reforms = streamline the economy of state like India = Jammu State. Raja Bhoom Dutt and his six descendents could not restore peace = Farooq Abdullha, politic failed Rise of Sudra Concept = "*Pure thought*", not based on "Rites and Rituals". Ideology of writer is based on Buddhamat = Karam Bhoomi. Jammu was reduced to small principalities ruled by Ranas = Thakur of Himach Pardesh study the book of Huthsons and Vogels, "*Foot Hills of Punjab*", published, 1973, New Delhi. Ranas = thakur of Doda = Chamars = Rukwal, Manhas, Chib, Katoch, etc. History of the Dalits = based on Table lands = Sialkote or Takshila Rajas.

The Four Veds: Rig-Ved = Yajurved = Atharvaved = Samved.

According to the statement of a Kashmiri Pandit (Dr. V.K Bhatt) = Retire Officer = Principal of GDC Doda, allowed to join the war against the anti-Dalits = Kashap – Rishi ideology = Nam-History.

"Veds are the eternal utterences of God, the Supreme Father = Dr B.R Ambedkar through the Veds, we get the best type of material = in the presence of the lifestyle, not from the Dead Master = Prophet Mohammad = Blind Faith".

Spiritual knowledge = Knowledge of the Present Prophet = Baba Gurinder Singh Ji of Dera Veyas = Ved Knowledge = within body of the man as representative of the Lord's as his Guru = Deepit Raj = "*Mother Falak*" Madam, Husband = Pati, *Baap* Dr Raj Kumar.

Regular study of Veds keeps us away from sins and increases hope and joy in life = Mira Prem Divine = Falak Madam = Dogra Dalit Samaj.

Making life peaceful Radha needs her Soami = Mahatama Buddha. Inner consciousness = Inner Feeling = Friendship = Dalit Historian (Dr. Raj Kumar) = Falak Family = New relationship = No minded approach = knowledge is Power = Holy Koran = Celestial Body of the author having the knowledge of Vedmantra = Gurumantra Ideology. Veds take us away from the bad path = bad action or sins, "nip the evil in the bud" = Simran of the Zinda Pir = Baba Ravidas = Raidas.

Later Vedic Period

Wider geographical outlook of the Subject India = Article 370, Constitution of India had a good relation with other state than that of Pakistan. Before that there was a period of Vedic Literature = No caste system. This caste-system was developed by Nehru and Sheikh, one was the law graduate and other was chemistry teacher. Principle of Upanisads were translated by Dr Radha Krishanan. Nehru Gandhi stressed on Socialism, Dr B.R Ambedkar on Materialism as per the requirement of the occasion. Because, it was deprived of lack of Formal Education as well as "Informal Education". *Dalits* had no formal Education before the 1947, only Britishers = Chura Family of England had to believe on the Ravidas ideology = Coolie Culture = Kulli Ideology, after the downfall of the Mughal Empire. Founding fathers of the Mughal Empire were *Babar*, *Ravidas* and *Guru Nanak Dev* Ji. No doubt, today, after 1947 or in the 21st century A.D all religious works either Christianity, Sikhism, Islamic study, Hinduism etc. all are in search of God = Truth. Truth remained stands in the Ravidas

Philosophy = Untouchables = Chamar Ideology = Rajput Identity = Nam-Dev of South India, Tuka Ram, Eknath, Surdas, Kabirdas, Prophet, Mualana Rumi, Shah Latif, Sarmad Sheed and various Gurus of the Guru Granth Sehib = Mandala Book = Grhistya – Aashram. Having, their teaching in front – of Satsang Ghar, now, we called Pandal House = Radha Soami teaching Houses = Masjid meant for blind faith, = Church House or Mandir = evil spirit minded of people.

Political Divisions and Events

Unfortunately or fortunately, there was no *Vedic Cidanta*. People of South India, they worked hard and brought the Western Education style in India. Role of Raja Ram Mohan Rai, Vidyadhar Bose = Ramnanda Sagar, etc. explored the new school of thought that is Ramakrishna Mission School, etc. and educated the society with old philosophy of Dariya's Sahib records = Old History = Ancient India = Jambudvipa = Raj Kumar, different name in the Sudra Family = Rai Family at Bahuana Chack = anti-Dalit.

Epics and *Puranas* = Basic and old concept = Dalits, Lord Christ or Valmiks. Kuru = Huge Brahmins = Negative thinkers are found in North India, they nothing know, why politic let downs = crimie rate = sins have been increased and killed the old Heavenly king Shiva = Goodness = Raj Kumar; Parvati = Falak or Dr Shabnam Grewal.

Kuru-Pandu conflict = Gandhi's peace and conflict society of India = Jammu State.

2

Jammu and its Physical Features

Author's pre-determined ideology on "Art and Cultural History' displayed original idea of "*Indus Valley Civilisation*" or "*Saraswati Civilisation*" of Akhnoor or Chenab valley of Doda city. This area provides us insight-knowledge of the human history as a component of two civilised personalities little master Deepit Raj and his elder brother Akhil Gargotra of the Akhnoor tehsil village Nazla Chak. Adjoining area like Himachal Pardesh, Afganisthan, China, Bangeladesh, Nepal, Sri-Lanka, Pakistan, Andwar, Nicowar as one country of India including Russia and Japan and other small states of the Saudia Arabia. Author speaks on languages. The language of trust is the agenda in the art of writing the Jammu history. Its physical features as his Ali brothers of Trukey, within this State, we are in minority, therefore, author needs good friends for the company sake, Dr Shabnam Grewal or Sonanyan Chaku of Kashmir, now posted at present in Delhi as sub-inspector as watch-man's show. Preeti Bhagat as Chandal as his father-in-law; Bisakhi Ram of Nazla Chak. Jourian, Khour, Bhadrawah, Ramban, Reasi, etc.are the part of the state is the shape of 'camel culture'.

Area under forest by composition; new survey have been made by the state historian Parkash Chand and A.N. Sadhu "Forest have been globally recognised as the most valuable asset of a "Nation" about the furniture works. In place of that author used iron panel for the entry of house and Assame Cail including plyboard for the closing of the door, *Deodar* of Kashmir and Cail of Patnitop are used in whole of the frame structure as a permanent feature of the 'Dalit historian'. At present, we have no need of environment protection. According to the 'Genesis science news Letter' (Sabda), 2011-2012, published by Govt. college for women Parade Ground, Jammu. The abstract of the "Jammu History" is based on "Scientific – history". As it is mentioned in Bhagvad gita chapter 4, verse 38, "these is nothing holy like scientific knowledge". The physical feature of a 'Dalit-Nayaka' known as Dr Poonam Kamotra displayed in vibrant colour, why and what; because during the efficient era from Jammu-Lochan to Hari-Singh of Jammu, city-forest developed in the same area as it was found encourage feature of the Kandi area of the Jammu. 'Life natural Library. *Early Man'*, the structure of the professor Bisakhi Ram displayed honour to Dalit-samaj from the development of the 'Old man' to 'Modern man' as Deepit Raj and Akhil Kumar two soldiers of the Nam-History in the shape of small kids. As, it has been referred by the young anthropologist 'Prof. F. Clark Howell' of the Chicago University'.

He mentions in his study that Ambaran valley is the origin of the physical structure of the human psychology to crush the *manmat* of the 'Old Gupta Family' as of Prof. Chaman Lal Gupta, strong idiot of the 'Dalit-History' as prostitute as 'Sonia Gandhi', and author is the forth-coming scholar of this clan as "Natural Historian" as that of Dr. B.R. Ambedkar. Scholar has developed a solid background with *Bhangi* ruler of Punjab as it was the concept of Maharaja Ranjit Singh of Punjab. He displayed in the author is study as a man of "One Eye" as a psychologist in physical form as Nam as he is. The originated of the man from the drops of blood as Mukahari ruler of the south India.

Geo, a New World of Knowledge picture of the Athemian Democracy as the ancient history of the 'Sudra Family' of Jammu. The philosophy of this state is based on Scorate's, Plato's, Aristotle's contribution to 'History and Art'. Greeks' belonged to the European section of Aryan race. Moving West from the Caspian to other countries of the world like England, Austria, France, Japan and Russia. Ancient Greeks were divided into four Chief divisions N.W.S.E, the people of these area knows as 'Dorians, Accollena, Achaens and Lonians as the four stage of the "life". They were collectively called Historians of the 'Dalit-History' as Nami-rulers liked Baba Gurinder Singh Ji, Dr Raj Kumar, Sat Paul Gargotra and Suteel Ved and their family is "one" as the family of God.

Growth of Indo-European people depends on "Hellenic Culture" as this state was hand over to 'Abdullaha Family' for political history after the downfall of "Dogra Culture" – 'Aryan culture". So far as the study of the scholar is concerned with the ideology of coming election of 2013 on the formation of "*Dalit-I-Illahi Libration Front*". The word "democracy" which means "rule by the people" king is the servant of the public and "despotism" is also borrowed from Greek history meaning "rule of the master", as school teacher through the primary concept. It was there during the "Classical age". After the downfall of "Mukahari rulers" in North India, they migrated Soudia Arabia for the verification of "Authentic History". "Holy Quran" was the kingdom of the Dalit scholar. This school of thought produced 26, Zinda Pir and they had good-relation with "Sindhi culture" as high standard of people and knowledgeable scholars. They had deep rooted knowledge of the "Indo-Arab culture". Idea developed from the *"Panch Sabda theory"* described in the Kalhana's *Rajatarangini. Arab* became the language of the people of this area. It was a "New civilisation" of the surrender thesis emerged form the ideology of "Mochi culture" as "Polish culture" of the sufi-saint historians of Kashmir or Chandals described in local history of the Jammu. Domba in Kashmir and Ladakh. This Islamic civilisation basically emerged from the original synthesis of the preceding "Indian culture" or from the "Labana Knot" as a symbolic ideas of the "Sikh Culture " as a concept of the hair or the *bal* displayed by the Molavi from the Shrine of Hazrat Bal of Srinagar as posted study of the Kalipha of Prophet or Rashidin found in the study of Basil Gray, "Art in the Islamic Period" published by Phaidon Oxford in 1981.

As Abu Bakr (632-634 A.D.) had witnessed to it that his "elders" were "Nami-ruler" of the art history. Kalipha, they were called "successor" in English in Arabic language called "Rulers" of the said dynasty "Rai". Umar (634-644 A.D.) as his successor and *Uthman* (644-656 A.D.) spread his empire North Africa and east to the boundary of China and "Chenab valley" – "Indus valley" (Raqqyia Masood, *Islam Teach yourself*, pp 21-22, chapter 2.). They were known "Right-guide" of the human history as "Muchi ruler" of the "Arab country" having the concept of Dalit=Kashmir in their lifestyle; Durlabavardhana-I of Karkota dynasty of '*Sudras Family*'.

"Durlabavardana Pratapadity-II and Lalitadity-Muktapida were the follower of *"Holy Koran"* as "Holy Word". The old concept of the Dalit Christian.

The tools of Stone Age man

Living personalities of the Gargotra tribe of Jammu region, in the drawers of museum and university, collection found in Nur-din-Himdani life style around the world that enormous numbers of pre-historic stone tools existed in the art gallery of General Zorawar Singh Gallery at Jammu as a *"New Research"* of the "Socialism". The said skeletons, they have no Jat-pat they are mook-nayak. This abundance may seen amazing in Chandigarh university when we consider on the question of film Manmuk, scarcity of the men who made them, they are known Brahmins or Negative forces, and yet it is entirely logical study of the historical research for the coming generation. Study shows, their genes unchanged, they are based on 'Karma theory' and has been written by *Allaha.*

Thus, if it should happen to fall into the previous I before me such as Girdhari Lal Hans of Barnai, manufilater the things in a way, that Dr Raj Kumar is not satsangi, he beaten his Brahmin wife why, Baba ji did not provided the *Parwesh* to Ganesh Dass Bangotra. He is very close to Hans Raj Hans, even they were all follower of the Dera Bias before me. It is upto the 'Living Master' not to me. No doubt, author has face hazardous life on the surface without bloodshed/ but with *'brainwar'*.

Since the oldest stone Bisakhi Ram Stadium was constructed by the *manmat* at present found in Jammu and other institute of the 'Higher Education' reflected the Gandhian philosophy including M.A.M. College, Dr B.R. Ambedkar was director of the Manmat Theory.

Persian Works

Tarikh-I-Kashmir is another special account of the Dalit Samaj has been written by different writers known as Sayyid Ali, Hasan B Ali Kashmiri, Haider Malik Chadura, Marayam Kaul Ajiz. They were also sufi-scholoars of the Sultanate period of the Kashmir, Jammu and Ladakh history. *Nawadir-ul-Akbar*, has been drafted by Aba Rafi-Ud-Din Ahmad on the "Sufi culture" as free-thinker. Today, we find maximu Brahmin historians have been found in the Kuta form in Srinagar and Juta form in Jammu. Ladakh has also Buddhist research centre, but they ignored the fresh view of the Ambedkar is Buddhist philosophy that is 'Name' or 'Chamar' they have oldest culture in research centre = Brahminism, based on Brahminism. Kargil is far for better them these people incomparison with old Buddhist = Brahmins. Al least, they have zero rate crime found upto the period of 2003. Similar, society is Dalit found in Zanskar. *Zafar-Nama* by Sharafud-Din Ali Yazdi throws a flood of light on the geographical position of the J&K state including *Malfuzat-i-timuri* has been written by Amir Timur himself on 'Sindhi culture'= Multan was his idea.

Mughal Writers

Babar-Nama, Babarvani, Guru Granth (book on *mandala*) based on Ravidas's ideology have been written by Babar, Arjun Dev and Ravidas was not the writer, but preacher of the sufi-saint philosophy as *vani* himself.

Of the groups carrying on trade and commerce, for example, BJP, Congress, a large number of population of the concept *materialism*; the term Vani of the 'Dalit Christian' converted into Baniya by Gandhi as Baniya by caste found from Gujarat = Narindra Modi. Study, agains, shows Narinder Modi is a corrupt type of 'Politicians' as shrewd minded Brahmin as Madan Mohan Malaviya. He has no original concept of the *Hindu Dharma* = Dalit Concept as dutiful son of the soil. (G.S. Ghurye, '*Caste and Race In India*' pp 31-42).

In the last, we learn from the study material of the "Dalit-Culture" or "Ravidas culture" that all areas of history has been subjugated along with the good will mission to the "Natural Woman' of the Nam-History as inspiration of the another's writings. Brahmin women is meant for house work. Now, the climate condition of area has been changed because of changing of direction of the globe or geography of the country like India. Therefore, *History* to has been changed in the favour of sufi ideology. The terminology of Jammu from *Jambudvipa* to Jambu-lochan has the similar meaning as that of Kashmir to *Kashyap Rishi*, Ladakh to *light* than Lit and Lo as ancient name of the Dogri or Hindi scriptures. Study, again, shows Dalits are original habitants of this area, Manmat like Muslims, Sikhs, Hindus, Old Buddhist' they have "no history". History creator are Dalits in original form as the meaning of the term *satsang* or Sacha Sodha explained by Guru Nanak. Other Gurus from Nanak to Guru Govind Singh Ji became the follower of "Sindhi dynasty" of Kashmir, Jammu and Ladakh became their residing house of the "Nam-history". Babar to Aurangzeb, they were rulers of the "Dalid-Family", already their lifestyle has been explained by the scholars in the thesis of Medieval History of Sudra (1200 to 1707 A.D.) Sultanate, too was the part of study of the author known as (*Suratrana*) concept of the Kashmir or the Jammu or the Ladakh "*History*".

In fact, the great structure of the Mughal Empire (1526 to 1707A.D.), whose foundation was laid down by Ravidas, Babar and Nanak in the beginning of the 16th century A.D. It was consolidated by "Akbar the Great" as Nam as ruling agency of the "Dalit-History".

The causes of the downfall of the Dalit Empire in India, due to the coming of "*East India Company*" which was been wrongly misinterpreted by the various historians of the Manmat. They were *Dalits* of "*North-India*" or "*Kashmir*", because *Kashmir* is the focus point of the "*Dalit-samaj*" in the context of "Ruhani-safar". But at the same time, they (Britishers) penetrated in Daccan as well as in North India as "*Dalit-Christian*" of Jammu in trade relation with Shahajhan (1628-1658 A.D.)

During the "2nd Battle of Panipat in 1556" and the period between 1560-62, the period of the ascending of the Akbar. He met with his 'Guru or Murshid' Baba Ram Das (1534-1581 A.D.). 'Akbar the Great' was Nam on Earth. He was a strong and gentleman of the human history. Author met him in Kargil, during the period of his transfer in (1999-2003). Now, he constructed his hut at Landi village of Hiranagar. They are three brothers K.C. Vadgal and Principal.

Author blessed by the three brother by the "*Charmar-History*". Before the annexation of North India, Akbar went to South, he met with whose Sun (Ravi) the modest star of *Lord Dal housie*, who was fourth class employee in the '*East India Company*' of the Dalits. Now is located by the author known as backward Rajput called Randhir Singh of Doda district. (Mrs. A.S. Beveridge) and Poonam Devi as filmy star as *Nutan*, a student of B.A. III advance women of the 'Dalit-family of Kashmir". Author made matrimonial alliance with 'Preeti Chandal' of this area through knot study as "Ring ceremony". Old Rajputs, like *Rakwal*, *Kotwal*, they policy was followed by Jahangir and Shahjajan, to crush the *Jatpat* system of the society with the ideology of "Sufi culture". There is no scope of "Religion" in author's history the story of the art of writing is based on "*Character*" as new discovery in "*Dhamma-dan*" as followed by Dr B.R. Ambedkar during his life time and fought with stroke of pen. Various agents were supplied by the author to settled the "Kashmir Issue". No doubt, Akbar had to face the seriously rising horror of Hemu, the Hindu PM of Bengal Mohd. Adil Shah, now, there is a lady PM, known as 'Kalida Jiya' a Bengali queen = Old Hindu - modern Muslims.

Political Awakening in Kashmir through art of writing the English literature under East Indian Company and the Dalit Samaj of Jammu.

Modelites of the Administrative works:-

I. English because International language among Dalit Christian of Jammu.

II. Influence of the western culture from Tudors dynasty Henry VIII as the period of Satyug or Enlightenment (1485 to modern man) including the Stuarts James 1(1603 to Queen Anna) as known in Tamil language Nami-ruler and Satnami Sikh of India proved honest, having dishonest approach toward Dalit History.

III Change in Administrative structure through the "Representative of God" as Lord live was there in "South India". According to statement of Adam Smith = Dr B.R. Ambedkar on the enquiry of wealth that was his thesis at that time.

3

Origin of Jammu State

Studies in world civilisation; an article has been drafted by Raghunath Rai, a member of the Dalit of Indus (Akhnoor) or Kashmir, "New Academic Publishing Co. Mai Hiran Gate, *Jalandhar* – 144008", a beautiful book on the "*Civilisational Growth*". He was close friend of Sain Dass T.T (Miniya) of Jalandhar. Sain Dass, used to live before 1947 in Jammu region, his maternal relation with Indru and Kirpa of Jud, found in Akhnoor region, both were Dalit Scholar of the human knowledge. They, both fought against the social-evils which were widely spread the message to the anti-Dalits of the Jammu region. Raghunath Rai, who wrote on Greek Civilisation of North India, during the time of Alexander, Astor in the Gilgit, there was his kingdom as its original idea. G + reek, means the society was the composition of two great molecules of the optical activity, displayed in the conceptional learning stereio chemistry in the modern concept Europe and Asia.

Definition of '*Stereio Chemistry*' in existing form two or more compounds found in the 'Dalit concept' having the same ideology as found to prepare *isomerism*, but differ from each other in their physical form as Nam or Buddha that was the story among Dr B.R Ambedkar and his generation. Author is working with twin brother as Lord on earth. It is called '*Chain Isomerism*' on the basis of skeleton study as Nam and its opposite force is Man. Where stands the idea of Global Education in History or Chemistry. Author has given verdict in *History* as scientific study, it shows Arts subjects are superior than the artificial sciences like Math, Physics, Medical and Engineering subjects. Subject like *History* is compound of the two great forces as 'Creative Power' in artistic nature to study the idea of soul or thought, who is the maker of this world the 'Early Man' 'Dr. Raj-Rishi'. (*Bharat Ki Aadivasi Naga Civilisation*) Hindi book has been drafted by Dr Naval Vigogi, as a social-scientist of Ludhana. He was born 6 Jan, 1939, village Kedeya Gurudev, District Aligarh (U.P). His father was Godan Lal, wife Usha and two sons, a close associate of Dr B.R Ambedkar as sufferer of the 'untouchability' led by J.N.U Scholar. He did Dalit University of Aarojona (U.S.A). He has number of award in his credit. Particularly, he did work on the 'Founders of the Indus valley civilisation: 'The Native Culture of India the wonder that was; Nagas; the Ancient Rulers of India. '*The History of Nagas Rulers and Shilp Kara Movement of Northern Hill Track*. No doubt, he is a civilize man, but meat eater as Brahmin by nature called 'Satpatiya Brahmin' or Boddh in self-style manner. Most of the Dalits, after the death of Dr B.R Ambedkar attached their sub-caste Boddh without providing the identity of the "Nature". "Natural Man is *Raj-Rishi*", who has given verdict in *History* about the lapse period of the "Dalit History" (600-1200 A.D). Originally author belonged to Nazla Chak, Tehsil Akhnoor, District Jammu. Jammu Culture is based on Chandal thought as described by Kalhana in his *Rajatarangini* which was written during the closing era of *Jayashima* of Sindh in the middle of 12th century A.D. = Jai-Singh Raja.

"India was more ready than Iran to received Greek forms after Alexander's campaigns found in Kashmir history and Jammu is a part of that origin". ("*Ancient India and the Greeks*" by U.P Arora, Professor in MJD Rohilkhand University, Bareilly) lecture was delivered at Amritsar 28 to 30th Dec. 2002, IHC pp.1-55). Now, the new facts have been remainded there launch the '*New World Economy*' of the Universal era. Ramiyan Bhardwaj, Sher Khan, Sehru as are great writer of the Dalit-History and follow-up lineage of the Dalit dynasty is 'Rai Dynasty' the clan of the 'Ravidas Culture' or 'Chura Culture'. There was Kashyap Rish as was Dr B.R Ambedkar, who was a learned scholar of the '*Dalit-i-Allahi Liberation Front*'. It is an abstract of the Kashmir as well as of the Ladakh history. Origin of the Bhujan Samaj has already been displayed from satsang not in "Politics".

"Politics" is a dirty game, author worked like "Athenian Democracy" based on Intelligentisa war. Congress and BJP, major political parties and other minor groups NCP, NC, PDP, NPP, etc. they needs the chair of President or Prime Minister with muscle powers with the Hellenic point of view as Sonia Gandhi of Italy, born in Rome brought in India by Rajiv Gandhi after the death of Indira Gandhi, she was a great nationalist leader. He did great job for the "Nation", but Sonia Gandhi did for the betterment of the Dalit-Society as illiterate woman. Author is a young scholar of the Dalit-History and revised all the facts of the previous thought from Dr B.R Ambedkar to Dr Raj-Rishi as an advocate of the 'Dalit-Samaj' including Dera Bias and Saidpur etc.

Originality stands in 'Dalit-History', Gandhi, again, born in the form of Rahul Gandhi as home as Mohandas Karam Chand Gandhi, who hatred with the Dalits. When he was beatened by the Ambedkar with the ideology of 'Chamar thought' and says "I am also untouchable". Omar Abdullaha and Farooq Abdullaha stand nowhere in history as money-minded race of the materialist culture. Author's life depends on 'Honest Living' = story of farmer. He is not greed as Brahmins as his race Dalits or Sufis.

Principal Upanisads

The term 'Upanisad' is derived from Upa (near) – (down), and said (to sit) i.e., sitting down near. Groups of pupils sit near the near the teacher to learn from him from him to secret doctrine and it contains mystic significance of the syllable *aum* and mystic words like *tajjalan*, which are intelligible only to the initiated, and secret texts and esoteric doctrines. It is the name of a mystery, a secret, *rahasyam*. *Sanskara* of the Hindu philosophy derives from the word upanisad as a substantive from the root sad 'to loosen', 'to reach' or 'to destroy' with destroy with *upa* and *ni* as prefixes and kuip as termination. (*Introduction to the Katha in Hindiu Philosophy of the word Upanisannam*) that Nam or Chamar is a 'Supreme Power' as Dalit Historian and his wife Dr Shabnam Grewal, she thrown me a love letter of the national approach, when a culprit, who was interested to put the author inside the jail that Chamar does not like the prostitution.

Brahmin needs money and Chamar needs respect. Author crushed the idea of "Bad Culture" of Brahminical Ideology' with the stroke of pen as a Natural Man, love gets love, Tanveer Jehan, fraudulent promoted KAS to IAS, beatened by the author with the chappals and shoes as dishonests lady that she could not prove the allegation against the Dalit Scholar (H.O.D History, G.D.C Doda). That scholar is a nice man to know as a Prince of this state. (See Keith; '*The Religion and Philosophy of the Veda and the Upanisads*', 19241; p. 492).

K.C Aryan, *Cultural Heritage of Punjab* (3000 B.C to 1947 A.D) – New Delhi, 1983. Author has made an attempt to assess the reasons for the decay of Punjabi Culture, if one cares to probe into the past it was in the Punjab and the colonies along the Indus that hymns of the *Rig-Veda* were composed. In the Punjab, the *pasalmists* sang Rig Vedic hymns invoking their gods for victory against the aborigin, the opponents of the Aryans. The Sindu (Indus), "the far famed bestower of weather", is the object of special praise and veneration. Mention is made of the "*Sapta Sindu*" (Identified by Iranian as the "*Hafta Hindu*" in their holy book *Avesta*), or seven rivers as the Sindhu (Indus), *Vitasta* (Jhelum) Asikni or Acesines (Chenab), *Iravati* (Ravi), *Vipara* (Beas) and Satadru (Satluj). The seventh river was *Saraswati*, identified with Sarsuti, near Thanesar, expressly mentioned in the *Vedas* as the 'Seven sisters' (P.15).

Then the Aryans moved towards the regions of Yamuna (Jamuna) and the Ganges, they colonised extensive districts and founded large cities.

Rishi Valmiki composed his celebrated work the Ramayana in Punjab. Valmiki's ashram; it is said, was then in the thick of forest. It was within an area of eleven kilometers from "The pool of Nectar", in the midst of which stands the Golden Temple of Amritsar today. The *Ramatirtha Tank* which is in the shape of a hexagon is still existing. It was here the *Sita* stayed during the period of her *Vana Vasa* (Banishment). Here, she gave birth to the twin sons of Rama, Lava and Kusha. After the names of Lava and Kusha were founded the townships of Lahore and Kasur, now in Pakistan. (p. 51)

All western historians agree that the Punjab has been the sheet-anchor of learning. The Brahmanic philosophy held it away here for many centuries as suggested by the said scholar U.P Arora, 'Hellenic Culture' = 'Brahmin Culture'. "Ancient History of India is a very controversial subject and western writers have expressed different opinion about it", according the statement of R.S Chaurasia.

Fourth Phase of the Maharaja Hari Singh (1925-49 A.D.)

Foundation of Jammu State = The foundation of the Jammu state in the modern period, it commenced from Maharaja Gulab-Singh to onwards on the ideology of 'Dalit Christians'. Study shows 'Maharaja Ranbir Singh' was a 'Sufi-Saint soldier and scholar and Nam on earth as his existence was Maharaja Ranbir Singh' (1856-1885 A.D.). On the question of Nam-History 'Maharaja Gulab Singh' (1846-1856 A.D.), on March 15, 1846, the British Government conferred the title of the Maharaja-ad-raj; according the Treaty of Amritsar as a meaning of this concept has already been reflected by the authorize idea of the 'Dalit History' and received Kashmir with the amount of ` 74,499 at the present date 13-11-2013. This state became a tributary state for the development of historical knowledge with the idea of 'New ideology' as DALIT.

No doubt, according to the one of the clause of the 'Treaty of Amritsar' as today we see the 'History of Dera Bias' is depended on the 'Dalit Culture' by humanizing the facts that most of Dalits, they use to visit there for the Nam-dan as free cost basic ideology of the Multan history and Sindh is the residence of the culprit history found after 'Maharaja Hari Singh'. Study shows, he was also a Nam or king of this state as author presently approved his identity as Nam himself with the ideology of 'Dalit' = Manmat Ki Kahani.

After the fourth generation of the Gargotra tribe, author approved his identity as Chamar. Pratap Singh (1855-1925 A.D) and his landmark achievement was to remove or abolition of *Beggar* in 1921 as it is the similar story of author's tribe from Bhauana Chak to Nazla Chak. Nazla Chak to Terai, Devipur, Jourian, Akhnoor, Poonch, Jammu, Kargil, Jammu to Doda City. No doubt, author crushed the anti-Dalits propaganda with the stroke of pen. The Wani, Abbudallah, Trambu, Hashmi, Qurashi, Seyyed, Ansari, Mangal, Bholi, etc. tribes of the Kashmir, Ladakh and Gilgit even beyond upto Nobra and Zanskar proved negative = Black Market. With the help of 'British ideology', he introduced number of reforms in the civil administration like 'tour and traffic'. In the 'Poverty of historicism' said tribes have been converted for the development of historical phenomena. *Beggar* terminology is again, reflected the ideology of 'Chamars thoughts' or 'Coolie Culture' towards the modern generation of Dalit-Muslims and Hindus of Doda city. What Gandhi did for the Dodaities, only send the messages of the disorder in the 'Dalit Society' as tribal race of this area are the old clans of the prophet Mohammad (540-670 A.D.). The father of the writer, that is Shri Bisakhi Ram, who is above the eighty, but he is 'Nam' as Dalit Christian during the closing of the Hari Singh era in north India (Kashmir, Jammu, Sindu, Multan, Ladakh Gilgit, etc.), went into mystry.

Hari Singh's Main Developments = have been Study again, show that with the revelation, of Ambedkar's ideology, that is 'Dalit Voice' Northern India influenced by western ideas that is 'Coolie Culture' (Kulli Ideology), they known their identity as Chamar, now all are now became Brahmins of the human history as educated class. 'Nehru-Gandhi Family' of Kashmir, they have been found culprit of the basic concept. In the '*History of Dharmasastra* by P.V Kane, Jaimini, the wife of Lord Krishna defines Dharma or Religion as 'desirable goal or result that is indicated by injunctive in '*Vedic Culture*'. It means people of the Satyayuga enjoy with good relation with their wives. Compounder Aaswani Kumar Dalit, before this life, he was Ram Singh son of Maharaja Partap Singh and the son of Bihari *Satsangia;* Romesh Kumar was Amar Singh. Ram Singh S/o Partap Singh, now, Romesh Kumar was the commander-in-Chief of the Kashmir Singh. After Amar Singh Palace, Aswani Kumar Hans as Chamar, now constructed a 'New Palace at Barnai' now left for Raj-Rishi and his wife Madam Falak, professor in English, at present, she is working at GDC Doda.

Humanistic Approach in Art of Writing = Ramchander Prajapati, resident of Hastinpur, district U.P mobile No.09758922845, as a writer belonged to OBC has drafted the vivid picture of the origin of the Jammu state with original idea that is, Dalit. He describes:

I. There was Hellenic age before the Ambedkar on the question of rising of Brahminism and he was threaten to life by them. Being a constitutional expert. He provided the 'Rights to Dalits' as expert in art of writing the history of Dalits or 'Dogra Samaj'.

After the downfall of the 'Dalit-Clan' in North India particularly the 'Kashmir Concept' based on Kashyap Rishi Brahmins of this area became influential and Maharaja Hari Singh left this state went to Bombay or Goa in June 1949. He worked for sometimes with 'Dalit-Scholar of India' that was Dr B.R Ambedkar as his fellow-friend of the 'Nam-History' as Dalit as Ambedkar. Idea put forth, by Ambedkar as a South Indian concept of Nanymar (Sufi-Saint Historian). After the death of Dr B.R Ambedkar in 'Law Creating Agency of India'. Ideology has been reflected by the same species in Northern States for the upliftment of 'Pahari People' on the 'Ideology of Reservation'. The people belonged to minority communities, they were also given privilege in the light of the development of 'Sufi Culture' as 'free-thinking state'. Now, the minority communities, they are approving more efficient like Wani, Trambu and so on, on the comparison of the *past ideology* or history. Hari Singh did not die, he was a Nam, he is still alive as other species of world knowledge as Arthur Miller, G.P Shaw and many more.

Feminism and Fiction: Kashmir and Beyond = This study of the origin of Jammu state is based on a "Jajmani System of North Kashmir: Its Structure, Magnitude and Meaning" placed under suspension for the time being. To analyzed the Pahari Culture = Experiment.

II. India was divided into seven Mahadvipa or we called in Sapt Sindhu Civilisation before 2500 B.C:

   (a) Asia Dvipa on the philosophy of Persian culture and Mahar value as Dogra clan of North India; identical with the Rigvedic Saptsindava as 16 regions as States created by '*Ahur Mazda*'. Mazda express ideology came into existence in Asian culture as today we see local bus of the Leh College and Tata at Kargil College of white colour. Santi Prava was the Eternal Spiritual Tradition was there not in Jammu, but Kashmir and Ladakh too.

   (b) Europe Mahadvipa described by the same scholar 'Ramchander Prajapati Ji'. H further elaborated this term in historical way of human lifestyle as '*Vedic Saraswati*' as Madam Preeti Bhagat of Doda City, working as student of history at Delhi, in medical period called Dilli Camp found in Jammu area, near the Narwal Bypass, opposite to the Hundayi Show Room. Ram Nath Sastri, described the Dalit History as "Innocent Culture" of the 'Suasat Family' in his terminological study of the ancient culture. Jat-Pat by the Hindi Historian. Author called them Mukahari ruler of the Chenab Valley of Doda; either Wani or Megh.

(c) Austrialian Race as Kangaroo of the European culture, it appears from the Kashmirian historians ideology as authentic women (femine) of the 'Hindu Culture' in broad base concept known as Mahadvipa of Buddhist culture.

(d) American Mahadvipa: Barack Obamma a Dalit Mochi historian. He is reflected by 'Mahar Folk Culture', the religious life of Kashmir or India is equivalent to 'Dead animal' according to Dr Anil Katari, Poonam Parkash, Shivaji College Kandhar. He worked on the Shivalika Hills 1930 to 1947 A.D Dalits were carrying out the dead animals as Chamar or Dalits. Churas of South India, they hate with this ideology, now, they became Pandits of the areas. Moreover, their civilisational growth appear from their behaviour. But in North India, their race is still found "untouchable" called Dalit Christian of the Jammu city. Their Mohalla is found at Prem Nagar in the relationship of Professor (Dr.) Shabnam Grewal. Dalbir Singh Sudan, Poonchi Pandit dash to the ground, when he listened the verdict of 'History' through 'Dalit Chamar' as degraded author of the 'untouchable family' or 'Chura Culture' is popular in Jammu city. It is a forceful idea of the human history and having equality base knowledge in art of writing to remove the 'untouchability' converted into 'touchability' as easy approachable ruler of this area (Dr. Raj Kumar Dalit or Art Historian). His Ph.D. Thesis '*Paintings and Lifestyle of Jammu Region'* (17th to 19th centuries A.D) proved an authentic document to form the Dalit history of the Jammu region as "Supreme Idea" as ruling agency of the world. Barrack Ubamma and Dr B.R Ambedkar, Pt. Madan Mohan Malaviya, have been the inconfigure of this young scholar. As he explains his beautiful writing in these words:

"Dr. B.R Ambedkar was born in a 'Dalit Family' of Mahar in Maharashtra means having Big Bang ideology. He cut the nose and throat of the Brahminism with the ideology of "poor of the poor" and provided the rights to Sudras and women of the period". (8 Nov. 2011) in the Parliament house of America. He has no comment about Pt. Madan Mohan Malaviya, and U.P. Singh also did some work in the favour of Dalits too as describe by Dr Dhanraj Dahat in his Hindi Book "*Aadhunik Parivartan ke Practical*" 2011. Barack Obama, a Dalit Mochi's son was born in village Honolulu (Habahi Rajy) in 1961. He is of scholar's age near about.

(e) *Sagaldvipa*, it is also found in Asia itself, author has incomplete study about it as Mukayri ruler of the Jammu region area known as Jud, Tok, Kaleeth, Kartha, Danja Garani etc.

(f) *Jambudvipa*, the last and final round of the Dalit history is located from the Jammu region at 'Garota Family' at one time, we were Rajputs, now we are *Chamar* of the Akhnoor Tehsil, district Jammu. Author is an Enlighten man of the 'Sufi-Saint ideology' as low grade employee of the Education Department. Now, at present, he is working at GDC Doda city with his wife Dr Sonyana Chaku and Rambi is working in the body of the man as his soul as helping nature of the Madan Falak. Pushap Lata is modern Brahmin, author uses her species for the experimential values in Dalit form as 'Idiot Lady' = "Prostitute". Author use to live in Griba Dass house of Arya. Repetition of history is the order of the day to work with 'Labour Class'.

(g) Why Jambudvipa became popular in the history of the world, because this area has the ideology of "Shivji-Parvati" as residing house of the 'Arabic Lord' known in "Dogra Culture". Buddhism always developed from this "Kandi area" in the universal ideology. As Gandhi says, "There is violence, there is God", why during the partition of India, there was great violence in this area that was the days of "Dawn of Light". 'Desh Azad Hone Par' in 1952 A.D. The first Prime Minister of India Pt. Jawaharlal Nehru, did not like the 'Dr. Bhim Ramji Ambedkar' because of his negative approach towards the "Creator Power". Gandhi, before him was died on this question for the development of 'Sufi Culture'. Hatred was there in his mind and heart, Pt. Madan Mohan Malaviya was appreciating his efforts, but Nehru, Patel, they did not like his ideology as a universal writer. Now, another Ambedkar is there in India (Jammu) as a challenge before the Brahminism of both the BJP and Congress Party. 'Bhujan Samaj Party' has been converted into 'Dalit-i-Illahi-Liberation Front', on the basis of universal ideology. Panjab Ki Shakti, Maharaja Guru Ravidas, it is an ideology of Baba Gurinder Singh Ji Dillion.

Guru Ravidas was a great Sufi-Saint Scholar of North India, Brahim nothing before him, because, they always use to busy in "*Kath-Bachk*". Reality stands in the body of man. Dr B.R Ambedkar had not the concept of 'Religion', but he was free-social thinker of all the *Dharmas*. Nehru-Gandhi including Jinnah, stand nowhere in the historicity of North India. Their concept was, rites and ritual, as still found in Pakistan particularly in Kashmir among upper class Muslims as 'Nawaz' a meaningless prayer = Garib Ke Story.

'Gandhi Ji and His Ideology'

As we know Mohan Karam Chand Gandhi was born on 2 October 1869n at Porbandar in Gujarat, before 8 years to Dr B.R Ambedkar. After getting his legal education as a formal study in Britian, he went to South Africa to practice *law* as rich man of the Baniya or Vaisya family as money minded race of the human history as *Ved Bashin* and *Ved Mahajan* of the NC party; have been found in Jammu region. They do not like the concept Dalits as *Damaras* of the Jammu region, other big trader of the Delhities like Kaniska or Gyan Publisher, etc. They need 'prostitution', not social reforms. Author needs social reforms in the interest of Dalits. Dr Karan Singh and his associate ex-minister of Gulchain Singh Charak, Harshdev Singh Ramnagaria Brahmin-Rajput. They are doing the "politics" of "Onion" without knowing the visionary plan of the art historians. Dalit literature according to Cooling Wood is the literature of "*Challenge and Response Theory*". Sufi Saints are life giver in art of writing the beautiful species of Maduri Dixit of Bombay as teenager women looks like in her classical dance as

Dr Shabnam Grewal, Dr Sonanya Chaku, Dr Preeti Bhagat and many more, they are waiting to see the story of card players. Dalits are heroes of the "Modern Age" as original race of the Jammu city.

Capital gain and capital punishment is an ideology of the Dalit Samaj, Arvind Kejriwal has no idea of truth but he is performing better duty then the Narender Modi. He is working on Gandhian philosophy. He has no knowledge to check the corruption. Corruption is there in the ideology of Mahatma Gandhi = Congress Party. Tribute to Pt. Nehru alongwith Gandhian era. As the story of Sunahrepa or Silpa Setty as Karigar women; is superior to Mahatma Gandhi, who worked on the ideology of Dr B.R Ambedkar that he was hero or Nam of the Dalit industry before the middle of the 20th century by writing "*Bharatchi Sabidan*" picture shows that idiots were frowning the 'Dalit Family' on the publication of Dr B.R Ambedkar by Maharasthra Govt. in original language the activities of the art historian found in Marathi language by Sonika Dal of Nagpur 1991 as its first edition; why not published in other languages. Because, they are well-versed in art of writing particularly the Dalit Samaj of India or original people of the Darivian race. First, they used to live in North India, migrated with the invasion of uncivilised culture of the 'Tribal race' as today we see most of the poor Pandits of Kashmir, they settled in abroad and Brahmin found in Kashmir and Jammu itself as idiot historian of the Dalit race and meat eater.

(I) *Mulnivasi Culture*: Culture of this area, has also been, again, detected by Ramchander Prajapatiji of Meerut, belonged to 'Naga Cult' settled in U.P before the migration of 1947 as certain Dalit Pandits of 'Loharin Valley' of Didda's time found in Meerut called Poonchi Brahmin, some are found Bombay, Calcutta, Maharashtra and Abroad to as Gulzari Lal Nanda ex-Prime Minister of India or Kashmir, etc. of the modern period. Nirmala Sharma, a 'Poonchi Panditiani and her Co-brothers of the 'Dalit Family', they are found in New Delhi.

Chandals or 'untouchables' or "*outcaste*" are found all over the world in the form of a class-struggle theory. *Ati-Shudradarma* people are found in Tamil Nadu, now, they are called Nisada as fishermen of the Kalidas's period. Who wrote number of dramas as art historian of the 'Dalit History' described by the Charles Fabri in his study, 'Dresses in India' as a new discovery of the French scholar? He worked on the 'Indian Dresses' with the ideology of Dr B.R Ambedkar as 'Dalit Christian' Muslim, Hindus, Old Buddhist, Sikhs, Jains, they have "no history". Historians are Dalits = Sufi-Saint Scholars of Jammuities areas. 'History of Royal Fine Arts' displayed by D.N Shukla as a refinement approach in 'Dalit-History' on the study of 'Kalidas's Plays' as an ideology of the comparative study of the 'Materialistic Age'. *Meghdoot, Sakuntla*, etc. are his famous dramas / plays. His approach of study has been found in Shakespeare's study and his madam Macbeth was his "inspiration" as his 'National wife'. Ambedkar's lifestyles have already mentioned in elsewhere in the study of the author as Nirmala Kabir and so on. Another passage of *Rigveda* (then art like a *prapa* in desert) like Kabul is used for landscaping in the higher study to keep the Rajasthani ship of the desert intact and lion of the U.P Atvika States, we need more satsangis in the cabinet to perform the efficient duty in the civil administration in both the Centre and State Assemblies. *Rig-Veda* condemns the selfish man like Ganesh Dass Bangotra etc., who only caters for himself" having no knowledge of the accounts. Prof. Samod is superior to him as per the competition of the account is concerned (X. 117.6).

Foregoing brief discussion will make it clear that later rulers of the 'Gargotra Dynasty' hopeful will be proved more efficient in comparison with my study which contained or included in the 'Chamar History' and other works on *Meghavahan*, Batwals, Mahashas, Tarkan, Kashyap Baridar, (Jheer), Lohar's on the record of the author's study. Most of the artisans works dealt with ancient culture related to Aryan or Vedic culture of the Jammu region, derived from the word 'Ar' and declining stage was 'Aryas' as a female species found in historical phenomena. Dalits are still alive under the paragraph of Sufi-Saint ideology like M.L Dogra, M.L Parwana, R.L Bharti, S.L Kholi and so on. We are free-thinker of the society. Religion is meant for Brahmins as 'rites and rituals'. Study shows, author fought a tough war against the anti-Dalits against the 'Nehru-Gandhi Family'. Gandhi-Irwin pact failed on the accord of 'Poona Pact of 1935' that was the background of the 'Dalit Samaj' for the survivalism of the North Indian rulers of the same clan called Nagas of U.P. Australia, South Africa, England etc. After this, we will see our colleagues in Russia with the association of the same tribe as Dooma or Chamar of the ancient culture as Aryan race.

Nature of the caste group based on original study as Vani or Bani, which is derived from the Sanskrit word meaning "trader". Ambedkar did the trade of good souls like T.K Sharma and others of the Mathematics Department that author is on good will mission. Kurmi, Kanbi, Kori as Pabi Parsino Kuti as Preeti Bhagat, Purwana as Purwah Samaj, Harper, Biman, Darzi, Dobi, Nai Harwar of M.P., Lohar, Tarkan, Bhangi (Sweeper), etc. midwives (Dai as Chamar). He knows pregnant concept of the Brahmins. Thakur as Nam of the Doda City as caste-free society of the *Jambudvipa*.

Early Vedic Age

"All history attests that God= Man's lifestyle has subjugated "Woman to his will", used as elevated soul as Goddesses as a means to promote this self gratification, to minister=CM to this sensual pleasures; to be instrumental in promoting this comfort as Dr Raj Kumar as Representative of God=Sultan Balwan of the early medieval period."

I. The U.S.A. Congress passed a Resolution on June 23, 2007 condemning caste discrimination and untouchability in India particularly in *Jammu*, *Kashmir* and *Ladakh* state, because there is rule of Brahminical rulers Sheikh Mohammad Abdullaha to Umar Abdullaha. Rising of the Dalits under the idea of Reservation = sufi philosophy ('Introducing V.T. Rajeshekar and "*Dalit Voice*" p.10). But this was not bothered by the India rulers like Manmohan Singh or Narendar Modi = Misbehave with the Sudra or Dalits. Destruction is there even in Upper Class Dalits like Ramvilas Paswan and others found in the ministry of the Parliament. "Jews of India"= Dalit writers of Dera Bisa; they published number of books on Sufi Philosophy =Sultan Bahn, Bulleh Shah, Shah Latif, etc.

II. The Aryas:- Arya = Nam is a sanskrit and Gurmuki word which means "a free born man with Noble character", not of the Noble prize winner as Brahminical ideology process found in Dalit History= Aryan Concept." This age named after the *Vedas*, the Holy Books of the Aryan = "Chamar History" Pre-historic man to modern man.

The Vedic civilisation = Dalit civilisation was founded in North west of India = Jammu & Kashmir state. This region was called the Saptsindhu = land of the seven rivers = Indus, Jhelum, Ravi= Surya as its lifestyle, the Chenab = Chandra bhagha = the beginning of the history of Chandragupta Maurya. Bias = No derire, the Sutluj = truth speaking knowledge = Vedic age.

III. This region already mentioned above = called Brahamvarta =Infinite knowledge or the land of the Gods. In course of time the vedic civilisation = Dalit civilisation = Aryan civilisation expanded to the valley of Kashmir and Nobra upto Ladakh. Then, it entered the South India = entire Aryavarta region = Delhi, Utteranchal, Madhya Pardesh, Gujarat, Karnataka, Calcatta, Maharashtra, Haryana and Punjab= Rajasthan; etc. the meaning of the terms *Veda* is wisdom = *Nam*-history = Dalit concept or Arya = Doda city, a name of the child girl = Nam-dan essential of the living Diety = living Master (S.P. Nanda, *Land Marks in Indian History*; From the Earliest Times to the end of Gupta era = Gupt Gian, pp 1-178).

IV. *Vedic India*:- It has a ready been seen that this (Dalit) or Arya = Nam or Interior Islam is the Central Idea of Jammu and Kashmir State for SC/ST which is as Big soul of all the 'Wisdoms'. In philological parlance, ST/SC = Insaniyat is "the root from which they all sprange; these and a vast number more that is OBC, RBA for SC/ST being Sanskrit root, it run through all the Aryan-Iranian civilisation, the real word has already been explain in other lecture of the authors writing = Nam-dev. All the Aryan languages=Tribal groups, ancient, medieval and modern, and is in each unusually prolific writer like Dr B.R. Ambedkar, writing and speachers = Riddles of Hindusim and Mahammadanism, Roza= see the living Diety every day, but without the practice of Nam-dan, they cannot see the Gods.

Realisation Paribartan is there in Sanskrit and Arabic language= Nam-history; if counted, the words to which it serves = 'Gurke study' found in anti-Dalit forces = Muslim, Hindus, Sikhs and anti-Dalit Christian of South India.

V. Hebrew was the mother of all the languages in the world that is '*Alphabets*' = A, B, C, = v] vk] m etc. Let us take the Sanskrit word AR, of which the general and original meaning is 'plough'. We find it intact in Latin = women history and Italian *arare*, in Slavic *arati* "to plough" as progenitor for the fertilisation of womb has been stop in virign marry history = Nam. In Greek *arotron*, Latin *aratrum*, Tehekh (so-called Bohemian, a Slavic language) *aradlo*= "a plough"; in Greek *arotron* already mentioned above misused the term for "*Women History*". Question rises about *child*, child or kid is the common property of the man=women. In English called *arable land* = *Baren land*, "fit to be ploughed"= Replacement of Brahmin women to Sudra women = *Falak Madam*. The matter is under consideration = *ved-Bhav*. Sudra women= Higher Education= Love is God. Brahmin women = Prostitution. Again, in Greek called *aroura*, Lain *arvum*=Iranian and Arabic culture called more dear to the lord as Living Diety- "a plough field" whence *aroma*, not Roman *women*= nultify character = political history; originally 'Beyond the mind and body of the soul', doubts have been cleared. Dr Raj Kumar is next to Dr B.R. Ambedkar. It is to signify the peculiar personality of a '*Dalit king*' = Nam= Shiv Rao as Shivaties rulers of this area (North-west). It has the value of a Living Deity = study of a ploughing field = Nam history that is property of a beautiful women = Falak Madam = Art historian = fight with pen and pencil = '*Dampati concept*'.

Discovery of Truth:- Since 1970 the IHC has been regularly holding the matic symposium during its annual session upto 2003 A.D. After, 2003 A.D., there was the turmoil in this "*Institution* of Psychology" *Caste* and *Untouchability* is still existing in upper class women = Brahminical Ideology. Lower Caste Women = Dalit historium = Madam Falak Lecturer in English as "William Shakespeare's Macbeth" or Marry Annonite, the wife of Charle X of France.

I. *Origin of the Drama* = Chamar thought, this Gift of English = Saxon King's story that is God and Man. We trace out from the beginning of the 8th century and old Christian thought were playing acting as a means of instruction and entertaining the people with *Miracle plays* and the Dalit-Concept = Radha Soami History.

II. The Unity of Time = All Communities either Hindus, or Muslims or Sikh = Inferior race = Dalit Voice.

III. The Post-vedic Age (600 B.C. - 200 B.C.) is marked by the extensive use of Iron = Materialistic period for production, enormous expansion of the economy after 1947 = Negative thinkers. Substantial issue is for livelihood, we need land at Jammu and Kashmir region = Ladakh for the welfare of the "Human Race" = Race of the God. Brahmin's by force converted in Dalit Concept = Philosophy of Baba Ravidas = Social Pressure. As per the statement of *Dharma Sutra* place of hierarchical rulers like Dr Raj Kumar = Falak Madam = Gods and Goddesses story of the lordism in Indo-Arabic context.

IV. Ved-Bhav = Early Vedic India = Rig Veda Ke story. The first example set by the North Indian rulers of *Dalit Samaj* = Barrack Obamma's father = to provide equaltiy before the anti-Dalit propaganda = Iraq-Iran-War. There is only conflict of Ideology = not Shia or Sunni, but to achieve the success to propagate the concept of down-trodden = those have no money-minded thinking = equality base knowledge. Sudra as a Divine Purus = Dalit History. Jati = Music of the Living Master = G.B. Shaw's ideology to introduced social reform in the Aryan society = New Society = Falak Madam.

V. Delegation = Decision making committee = Dr Raj Kumar + Falak Madam and other 'Words'. The *Rig-Veda*: the Older - Gods and Goddess = Dalit historian. When, we prepare to investigate one of the world's great Religion = *Radha Soami*, and before 1947, there was a class struggle theory between *Dalit Christians* and and the Old Hindus and Muslims = Sikh thought thus, the theory of *Ravidas* and *Nanak* = Maulana

Kabir did not realised by the Indian leader = *Nehru-Sheikh* or *Gandhi-Vadi* followers. *History*, again, predicted from the low-caste rulers = *Chamar thought*. No doubt, Sharan Kumar Limbale, one of Maharashtra's pre-eminent Dalit Writer-activists is the author of several novels and story collections about Dalit life, translated from the Marathi by Alok Mukherjee, History, Controversies and Considerations = Aesthetic Literature of the "Art and Culture" = True Historian.

VI. Discovery of Cell = the discovery of the both the cells back to Early Vedic period = Early man = Equal status in art of writing the Scientific History = insight Knowledge = Bhagbat Gita's Concept. Sita's Concept found in Mahabharata as true Wife of Dalit hero that is Ram or Laxman (Bhavi). Before the entering of the Dalit Concept, Aryan = Radha Soami Missionary. They were went to abroad = Foreign Countries for the establishment of Democratic Institution for the development of History = Money Minder Race = Brahmin or Rapist Race.

Rai-meant Race= Pure Race or old use clothing = Arya Concept. The "Law" of which *Varuna* is keeper, the "immutable ordinancies" which author in his previous life issued "Cosmic Order" = Dalit Concept = founding fathers of the Indian Constitution = Maker of the life. What Law is in the physical, truth, Right was the 'Spiritual Order' = Science of the Soul = Gurmantra theory and both are Rita (*Vedic India*, pp. 146).

We trace the beginnings of the drama in England in the eight century, when Saxon kings ruled in the various kingdoms into which the land was then divided. The Church thought of play-acting as a means of instruction and entertaining the people. There were many villages and most of the people were illterate. This was before the age of printing and few books were available, even if the people had been able to read. The monks arranged in dramatic form some of the striking events from the Bible story, such as the flight of the Israelites from their captivity in Egypt, or the discovery by the pious women that the body of the crucified Jesus had left the sepulchre. Such actions were presented on simple. platforms or enclosed spaces, with a minimum of setting or arrangement.

As was natural history, there followed simple plays to illustrate moral or religious principles, composed by the monks and not taken direct from the Bible. The actors were not presented as human individuals, but as types of man's nature and qualities. A young girl in white robes would appear a:d be introduced to the assembled villagers as "Innocence," or "Purity", while a wicked-looking man in a black cloak was known as Sin" or "Vice" = Kashmiri Women. Vice would be shown as trying to influence a young man or woman, while Innocence fought to prevent this = Falak Madam. A favourite play of this kind was called *Everyman*; it was performed at Coventry and Chester in England a thousand years ago. The plays which were dramatised versions of episodes from the Bible were called *Miracle Plays*: the later plays with symbolic character to illustrate moral lessons were called *Morality Plays*, or *Moralities*. As time passed, there was a tendency for the characters to become actual persons and not merely moral types. These-were certain plays written to amuse and not merely to instruct. All men like to be amused, to have fun and to see wonderful things.

Another influence was the Greek drama. The tragedies of Aeschylus and Seneca, and the comedies of Aristophanes and Platus, had been composed centuries earlier. Their works were regarded by scholars as the supreme models of drama. The learned Aristotle had framed rules of dramatic construction,' and those came to be called Aristotle's "Unities". They were:

I. The unity of time = The action of the story in the drama should not, from beginning to end, extend over more than one day.

II. *The Unity of Place* = The action of the drama should be in One place, and should not move to another place.

III. *The Unity of Action* = There should be only one main story or plot, and no introduction of subordinate or additional episodes.

Aristotle hoped by laying down these 'Unities' to ensure dramatic unity. He saw that, without such limitations, a drama could become a loose and disconnected series of events. Only attention to us. Unities would ensure completeness and form. For the same reason, he framed a general plan for the course of events in a drama = Kashmir Issue; as a model to follow. A play should he in five divisions or stages.

I. *The Exporition* = There should be an opening situation set forth, in which the audience is shown the cause of the beginnings of the action of the drama = Chamar thought.

II. *The Rising Action* = In this stage, events move up to a situation which arises directly from the causes shown in the Exposition = Readiness-notice.

III. *The Crisis or Climax* = Here the dramatic action reaches its highest point = "Social Problem". This effect, with its tension and strain, comes directly from the causes in the Exposition of the Human History.

IV. *The Falling Action* = In this stage, the interest is not so intense, the uncertainty and Suspense are lessened, and we can see to what destination the characters are moving Geelani, Mirwaiz, Masroor, Yasin Malik, etc. = Let-down situation. The problem is nearing.

5. *The Catartrophe* = The final ending or solution of the problem which is the plot = Dalit Literature.

Aristotle's division into five stages made some writers divide their plays into five Acts = Pandava Theory. Shakespeare did not do this: Later editors of his plays divided them thus. Shakespeare's plays had no Acts with intervals between, but were written for continuous action.

The ideal which Aristotle followed was of form. Shakespeare had his own methods. He created life-like characters who took command of the action = "*Raj-Rishi Faqir*". There was no reason for him to seek the regularity of form desired by the Greeks. His object was to please and satisfy his patrons, and he had his own ideas of what constituted dramatic unity. Indeed, he made a number of experiments with that end in view. Some of his plays show complete disregard of the unities of the Greeks = Hellenic view of the modern Kashmir. In Macbeth, the action extends over a period of time, at least some years. But there is an impression of continuity and rapid action. The characters appear in places which are distant from each other. Action follows action as if at once, though the sense tells us that there must have been a time interval in between. This is so skilfully managed that no break is felt. Shakespeare's play were performed on the bare an unfurnished stage of his time = Central Govt. of India, which looked the same for all localities.

Aristotle and other theorists had laid it down that a drama must be cube tragedy or comedy Dalit and anti-Dalit = compromising formula with 'Dalit King' Ashoka. It was for them an offence against dramatic art to combine serious and comic elements in a single play. Shakespeare did not agree with this. In a tragic play, he introduce of tragic and comic at times comic episodes and jests at a serious moment elements. After the good king Duncan has been murdered it. Macbeth's castle and the air is full of horror, a portel comes to attend to a knocking at the castle gate. He delivers himself of humorous soliloquy, full of topical allusions. When Cleopatra has sent for poisonous asps to hill herself with, there is some comic talk from the rustic fellow who brings them to her in a basket. Shakespeare knew that man's life works like that. It is seldom all serious or all gay. Tears and laughter come together in a way that cannot be foreseen. Shakespeare aimed at giving a true picture of life, and knew that the introduction of a funny episode in a serious play would give variety, and also provide a contrast. The laughter that comes at a time of sorrow is more striking and effective than normal laughter. Any method was legitimate for Shakespeare which yielded a true picture of human life style.

Because Shakespeare allowed himself such freedom in his art, we call him a Romantic Dramatist, since he gave full scope to his imagination and defied convention. Used in his sense, we understand "romantic" to mean "free and unrestrained", in contrast with the classical drama = Mauryan rule which adheres to established rules and traditions. There were rivals, learned scholars of the Universities. who wrote plays on the classical model. Their plays are forgotten and seldom read now; they are dull and impossible to show on the stage. Shakespeare's plays survive and flourish. The future of the English drama, whether Shakespeare was conscious of it or not, was destined to he on the romantic and not on the classical model = Blind-Faith Ke Soach.

In a simple community = Dalit Samaj, dramas have a simple setting. They may be performed in the open air without any stage. When Shakespeare came to London, he found that there were some companies of professional actors = Dalit King Ashoka and his wife = soul. There were two theatres in London, and not one in any other town. The actors who travelled round the districts did not feel the want of a theatre; but needed only a simple platform in any large hall or enclosed place = World market. Scenery, as we known it, in the form of a screen painted as background. stage furniture, special costumes = Dalit History and the like, was not considered necessary. Their plays were usually simple affairs for a group of four actors = Nam-Theory.

Anthenian Democracy

Athenian democracy is based on Greek Civilisation = Doda City - State Centre of Jammudvipa = Akhnoor history of the ancient Dalit historian known as Alexander the Great. During that period particularly the Nandas (403-323 B.C.). After the downfall of the Nanda, Mauryan took the charge of the Northern States.

The Greeks belonged to the European section of the Aryan race = 'Chamar Culture' or 'Chura Culture' and were Satsangis whereas the Non-Aryans = Modern Muslims and Hindus, they became Brahmins = infidals of the Central Asian States like Afghanistan or Pakistan or China or Japan. The concept of Athenian launched by the South Asian Writers as we take the modern writer Dr B.R. Ambedkar as International historian, who challenged, who were the Shudras? This book published after his death = Untouchable = Nam.

Athenian Democracy's Concept from the 2nd Civilisation of the Akhnoor area = Manda or *Saraswati Civilisation*.

Wars with Persian Rulers

In the first quarter of the 5th Century B.C., the European Greeks = Chamar Culture or Chura Culture = "Dalit Christianity", were engaged as a war of fighting with 'anti-Dalits' or Anti-Aryans called Persian. With the domination of 'Alexander the Great', the Mauryan emperor Chandragupta Maurya surrendered before him. The origin of the name Alexander traditionally developed from 'Askardu', it was once known as 'Iskandaria', and that it was great city founded by

Alexander the Great' as '*History Repeats itself*'. This area was watered by Indus and then country striking. Its banks is more fertile than any part of Ladakh as 'Min Culture' = Aryan Culture still this race is found at *Batalik*.

However, in winter, the climate of this place is one of great sever cold and in summar as visting place for foreigners ('*Story of Kashmir*' by P.N. Tikoo, p. 196).

No doubt, Jammu and Kashmir is a 'Heaven on Earth' or '*Paradise of India*'. It is in tourist map of the world. After 1947, this State became in trouble, because of the growth of huge population explosion; did by both the Hindus and Muslim, on the issue to dominate the state treasury on earth. The deprived section of the society that is *Watal* or *Chamar* or *Chura*, they did not allow to read and write' in the State after the death of Hari Singh. With the class struggle theory of the South Indian scholar took initiative and 'Reserved' their 'rights' in human struggle in the history of the political career of Brahminism from Pt. Jawahar Lal Nehru to Dr Manmohan Singh. Sheikh Abdullaha, no doubt, in the very beginning played a very positive role toward the Dalit rights, about land right in the protection of their favour. But, the reigm of Dr Farooq Abdullaha, Umar Abdullaha, that period is known as Darkage of the India history as their way of behaviour is based on prostitution = Hellenic study ('*Facts About Kashmir*' by V.R. Trivedi pp. 1-350).

Thus, the victory also gave the Athenians = Chamar Culture as self confidence cultured race of the '*Sudra Family*' = 'Aryan Culture'.

Iran formely called Persian lay on the Iranian Plateau strecthing eastward from the Tigeris River to the Indus River = Chenab Valley or *Chandarbagha* in Kashmir history. The ancient culture of this race is reflected from the Vedic history of India. J&K looking like a nook nestled in North-West corner is as large as all Switzerland. Hot plains = Punjab = Rajasthan + Delhi = Haryana = called as "lower Hindustan". If someone watch on the northwest boundary of Nepal, the Himalayan range, it looks as white Chaddar of the divine Himant = Ladakh = Kashmir and Jammu as tolerable area for winter break in comparison with Doda City. If Muslims claim for Kashmir as their mother land. Is it place as a 'Holy City' no, at present it displayed the view of Hellemic Culture = Modern Sri Lanak. They have no knowledge of the Heavenly

Earth or Paradise on Earth. There is huge slaughter day to day and became barbarian as rapist class. Women at least 90 per cent, they are under depression, because of their animal treatment against them. The Aryan Hindus particularly Dalits they have good in their lifestyle, 90 per cent, they are Satsangis = good looking people as natural race of the human technology. ST they also became barbarian, but their women, they are not in depression. Only 5 per cent they are civilised in cultural history (*Vedic India*, pp. 6-8).

Aryas = The native culture of the Aryan race = Chimar race, whom the Aryas = Nam = Chamar or Chura for a long time gathered under the general old. Aryan designation of Dasyu meaning simply "peoples" or "tribes" of the "Dalit Family" = Sudra Culture, a meaning which the 'Word' or 'Holy Nam' = Surya Race under the Eranian form Dahya, retains all through the Avesta and the Akhaemenian inscriptions, while in India = Bharat it soon under went peculiar changes after the downfall of politics = Brahminism as will be seen and visualised in the history of Dalits or India (Ibid, pp. 112-113).

Athenian Democracy is based on authentic history of the Aryan Race = Chamar thought. The name Aryan still survives in the local language of the Iran known as Ariana which is applied to the great Persian Tableland as Kashmir Valley. So for as the term Democracy is concerned which means "a form of government in which the people have a say in who should hold power and how it should be used. Moreover, how a state governed in such a way with intellectual mind with the majority of the MLA = member or Ministers = *Mantris*.

But at the same time Abdullaha Family, after the death of Sheikh, they went for prostitution and depends Nehru-Gandhi ideology = Brahminism and left the practical approach = experiences which Sheikh Abdullaha as a teacher and worked in the field like a "Coolie" and stressed the people for hard labour. This ideology left by his later successors and went for prostitution, therefore, Srinagar became a view of barbarian race = Sri Lanka. Democracy, this term, no doubt, originated from the Greek word "demo kratia" = Classless or Casteless society = Aryan Society. Now, known as Chura or Chamar in the third world country. Having "Low idea" but big thought as a *'Creative Power'*.

After General Lord Ripon (1880-1884 A.D.) and his Internal Policy = Inner feeling, gets up early in the morning on the tourist spot at Nan-Kun, near the Mughal garden. His reforms toward up-liftment of the Dalit history, upper class Hindus *Biana* or *Chamar* like A.K. Angurana, B.D. Bhagat, Ashok Kumar, Lecturer in Chemistry, Garo Devi Biju, they do not like the services of the author as an efficient history. But at the same time including S.P. Bavouria, P.A. to Handloom Department, dash to ground that he is next to Dr B.R. Ambedkar and launched the Dalit concept to remove the difficulties among various scholar like Madam Sonayam Chakoo, Pareeti Bhagat and well known Dalit Christian scholar Dr Shabnam Grewal IPS. P.E. Roberts writes about Lord Ripon as Dalit or Christian historian, "He was a true liberal as Dr Raj Kumar = Roti Ram the Living Master of the Hari Ram = Angurana tribe of Punjab and Sind. Gladstonian era begins with the writing of Dalit concept from 1700 to 20th century A.D. (*Paintings and Lifestyles of Jammu Region*). All the defection in History has been removed by the cultural man with the sense of Americian Ideology = Change of species from Kashmiri Pandits to Dalit Samaj = Sonayana Chakoo. She is an efficient and cultural women, but she could not qualify Ph.D. in Jammu University as she was considered as nalike women of the '*Medieval section*', whereas *Barsa Gupta*, a narrow minded lady worked under Prof. Dr Jigar Mohd. On the topic of Mughal gardens. She did Ph.D. but Sonayan Chako failed in this process as a '*Reserve*' type of lady. She is more dear to me and her work has been traced on the topic of '*Royal Fine Arts of Jammu Region*: they are 64 in numbers, whereas 64 components found in mental health or we can call it 'Mandapa' theory as per the statement Dr J.L. Thappa, ex-H.O.D. relating to disorders or illness of mind called 'Informal Mad' and originated from the 'Latin word 'Mens' and 'Mind in English'. Therefore, *History* is a superior subject in art of writing the Dalit Concept = Sufi Ideology.

Physics is an ancient medicinal plant of growth into drugs form as the diet of the Soul = Chamar thought. Equivalent to medical treatment of the body of Anju Bangotra, Lecturer in English. Her physical appearance looks like a buffallo, as Aristole as view '*Animals and plant*' = Hans Raj Bangotra, Lecturer in Physics. The origin of the term started from Latin language in art-history known as *physica*.

Physician = Consultant = Doctor or general practitioner known as (Informal GP) or (Informal Medic).

Without original species like Hunter Commissioner Kothari Commission report = over haul system.

Study of the author is not only found 'knowledge is power = Sound - Current' but also on 'Natural thinking' like laboratory test found 'Dark Room Study'. There is no need of Physics laboratory in all the college, only one spacement. We want to preserve in Gandhi Nagar College through Dr D.K. Surya. It is concept of Atam-Chintan = Ravidas or Kabir's Ideology. G.G.M. Science College need to preserve as Prince of Wale College'. The collection of past history of Dalit Samaj = Dogra Culture.

I. **Rajput Pantings and Pahari Culture:-** Pahari concept = Parihar tribe = Gujar family, they used to live at one time on Pahar and left the ideology of Dalits, became Brahmins. Rajput concept lies before the lord = Sumista Thakur = Nam – History of the Pahari culture = Jammu paintings and the lifestyle = *Dresses*, *Ornaments* and 'Hari-style' is the judgment of the Dalit Christian scholar = Dr Shabnam Grewal = Chamar thought as up-gradationzed from Chura culture to Dalit-Samaj= unity into Diversity. Two wives safe in hands of Dalit scholar = Dr Shabnam Grewal = Chura concept = Juss Christ's mother = Dr D.K. Surya Falak Madam, needs loveable man as Dalit scholar as Sabdha ideology.

II. **Pre-Christan or Modern Christan era,** which begins after the downfall of Chamar thought = Sudra concept of Mughal History = Nam's ideology. New concept was Dalit Christan, begins with Lord Live= Sudra concept originated from fourth Varna of the society as mere clerk in the East Indian Company. (It is mentioned by Chandramani Singh in her "Centres of Pahari Painting" Abhinav publication, 1984, New Delhi-110016= Deepit Raj's childhood study. In Mahabharata = Ved Bias study that Rani Buji = Nam = Ganga Mai, that at one time Dr.B.R. Ambedkar established his kingdomin South India as Mahar Clan = Chamar thought. Ganga Mai has no formal education. She needs solace from the Ravidas ideology.

Mahabharata = Great epic of modern history, it begins with the Muslims. S, silence = nil vata nil study (IAS/1PS.)

III. **Origin of the Rajput Concept:** Origin of Rajput concept = vedic India that king Susarman of Trigarta = Kangra of Jalandhara, (modern Kulu) helped the Kauravas as Surgo concept of the Nazla chack = prostitution, Brahmin like this. It does not help the Pandavas race of Jammu city, it helped to the Kauravas in capturing the royal stone of the art-history. Capturing of cows of virata = labour concept; formal education no need. Informal education essential from the Lord's house = Word's study. Dr Shabnam Grewal, will have to look after the state, another need rest and *gap-sap* with the family members. (Virata Parva. Chs. 30/26; 33/7-6, Gita press edit, Ibid).

IV. **Basohli School of Painting=** Raj Marg Painting School of thought. Less resources less business, huge resources, Big business, Pasia tela block of the idiot scholars like T.K. Sharma, Vishal Sharma, no pension, no work.

V. **Kangra, Jammu,** Chamba and Kulu were of ancient origin.

VI. **Glourious History of Duma** = Chamar thought, basic qualification untouchibility of the anti-Dalit forces of the modern Poonch in 21st century. There is no doubt Ajeet Kumar Ghai son of Shanker Dass = Surinder Kumar Ghai. Both his sons are satsangi = Chamars in original way of the anti-Dalit philosophy = Chief of the Radha Swami centre of Poonch. They were very closed to the Roti Ram of Siddhar Mirpur, before 1947. Roti Ram's son was Sewa Ram. Sewa Ram's wife was Dhani Devi, she has three sons and two daughter = 'Name-Jiv' found in Jalandhar and Ghai family of Chandigarh. Bari Ram and his sons history found break in absent minded as Garib Tabka.

Roti Ram, Dr.Shabnam Grewal and other wives. They need their survival other wives. They need their survival is Dalit Samaj. Sewa Ram's three sons Nam's ideology = she Darshan Ghai, Mangta Ghai and Charndas of natural history. Rakashas Baldev Raj Lachotra = Kata concept of Kashmia. Juta concept of the lord. Rattan Lal, Vijay Lochan alive force of the Dalit concept. No question, now answer, one family = Sansar Chand of Nadwal = 'Family words'.

VII. **Kildar concept** = Staff secretary of the college = Kangra fort of the Jammu region = prostitution club; stop bratas and party system.

In Short, the Athenian democrary concept of the Doma philosophy upto Nur-Jahan, queen-consort of the author's writing = Dr Sonyana Chakoor = Nam-History. 'Nurpur' painting school of thought was extended upto Bias, Jalandhar in relationship theory women = Pandit ideology, but safe in the hands of the Lord's house at Barnai = Twelve theory of the Sudra State of mind = *Bara Mahas* study. It was the duty of the author to serve the society from the core of heart. Beautiful wife, beautiful husband, there is no double karcha = unemployed union jindabada only Dr Sonyana Chakoo and Preeti Bhagat. Aurangzeb is (1681-1707 A.D), political history after his death, Dalit Christianity, started by Dr.Shabnam Grewal. *Tour-Soor Koi nai*, only ideology's reflection. There is no blackish stone in the Lord's House = White Thought = silver coin, golden coin = Dr.Shabnam Grewal and nor fellow friends, Preeti Bhagat; Sonyana Chakoo. Falak Madam golden star found on earth. Roti Ram = Raj Kumar = Dr D.K. Surya and two daughters of the golden star women Amrit Bhardwaj = Ramiyan Bhardwaj.

VIII. Topic = Durrani concept = Destructive = unique, Madam Falak = Raju Devata, Maa Sherni = Amri Devi. Kashmir *Ki Kali*, Sonyana Chakoo = Neelm study of Padder state of mind. Ganga Mai, recovering his health, that his brother Ravidas still alive no problem.

Concept close with the natural plant kingdom with the 'five water body' + Historical Research = Ranjit Singh Ke Story (Punjab).

No doubt Ganga Mai has the supreme knowledge of the human history, "*Work is worship*'.

IX. **Shiv – Rao concept=** Concept of the sufi philosophy or Marathas state of mind = Mahar in the previous life.

Jambo Channel = Nam-History. Doda city, no need to go; follow the foot print of the Dr.D.K. Surya = Supernatural study in new form as leader of the world history = Shah Jahan of the previous life according to the statement of his real mother Dr Shabnam Grewal, Dr Rambi = Dr Sonayana Chakoo concept. Noshera school = college girl, need love affair with art historian at Govt. Women college Gandhi Nagar, Jammu. 'Love gets Love; tough gets taught'.

Marriage proposal O.K. No divorce, no enmity only love – affair.

Topic:

Library Science = Catalogues Research = Topology

I. Introduction = The subject matter of the Library Science during the Dogra period impact by the Frances, than Portuguse in South India. After the mutiny, 1857 this idea reflected by Christanity into Dalit Samaj with the abbreviation of mathematical view, who to start the Western Ideology = Chamar thought in North as well as South India. Dr Shabnam Grewal has already conveyed the message to Dalit Christian about the popularity of Radha Soami Satsang. But, they proved idiot. They believe on Brahmanism = upper class of the Hindu + Sikh and Muslims. They have no sense of '*Kundal Philosophy*' = Kun + dal, Kun is a Persian word mean 'Widsom' or Nam; *Dal* = Unit.

II. Origin of the Topology = Mathematical study of the Nam-History into unit form. At one time the wife of William Shakespeare Macbeth had the ideology to kill him, but failed because of her upper class merit was so high, she did not like to him as a Dalit Christian. Within, an hour times, her ideology was changed, why because, William Shakespeare had the knowledge of Scientific Truth = Bagwat Gita's Ideology, had been written by Yadav ruler of Bihar. Origin of mathematics is based on Human History as Nine Natural Numbers of human behaviour such as Ears (2), Nostrils (2), Mouth (1), Eyes (2) and two lower organs.

III. Mathematics = Branch of Science or Art = Truth based knowledge that is found again in History. The linear mathematic = geomatrical lining design found in History = in Painting Circle of mind an ideology of global village One room set preserve for 'Words' = The Wives of the Natural rulers of Jammu region.

IV. When we go back to ancient period, *the History of Mathematics* founds in Dalit Samaj during the time of Alexander the Great = Aristotle, Scrate or Plato. Mauryan they were Greeks and used to believe

Athenican Democracy = Nam-History or Work is Worship. Tutition work in all the colleges may be stop.

V. *Before the coming of Islam*, Jammu region was dominated by anti-Dalit forces like Hindu Pandits. Why because of, there was no formal education among Sudra people of India. Therefore, Sudra, from the Dhar Dynasty = Ravidas Philosophy. Trade routes are formed still from Udhampur to onward in South Kathua to Jalandhar.

VI. Jaldhar was the ancient name of Pir Panjhal area. Due to the change of History and Geography, this Kingdom became famous with ideology of Sandhya Dhar = Down fall of Dhar Family of Kashmir. No doubt, she became mad with the shocking news of her father and brother, but at the same time, this dynasty went for prostitution; because, they have no knowledge of Dhar = Dar = fearing of God. Mostly, they use to worship of Gopi Nath and other idiot Devi and Devatta = Mata Vishno = idiot terminology or Laxmi Puja. Both have the same meaning = Prostitution. Therefore, the History of modern Kashmiri Pandits = Farooq Abdullaha's ideology. Muslims + Hindus = Manmat. Same story has been dedected in idiot Jammuities Pandits = Surinder Sharma and other.

Greek ward Mathema was known among Pahari Samaj = Hill areas = Dalit concept.

Dalit Concept and Medieval History

In the 21st century, 'Age of the Arts' with the scientific discoveries "Top Ten" of everything in English, 10 in Mathematics or called write down in figure in the 'Banking System' and ideology of the 'ego' and 'Infinite' as a composition of the figure Das in Punjabi. According to the statement of Peer Giyasud-Din Choudhary of Kashmir the term "'Religion' has been very much distorted and maligned". (*Kashmir, Islam Ideology and Society*) proved as fictions study of the author in the context of art of writing about Kashyap Rishi of Kashmir (1500 B.C.). P.V Kane is document again proved that educated class called Brahmins or Molavis of Kashmir or Jammu. They are dishonest in the art of living the Dalit standarded like that of Raj-Rishi or Ved-Vyas of the ancient culture of the North India. According to W.D Whitney, 'A Sanskrit Grammar. 'Leipzig and London', 1879, he has the ideology of *Valmiki*, who wrote *Ramayan* as a Dalit scholar of Punjab or North India in the forest of Amritsar, now, the location is found called *'Golden Temple'*. It was the greatest learning centre of the Punjab during the time of Baba Ravidas, who was a great 'Sufi-Saint Scholar' which spread the message to Babar as Nam, then Babar wrote Babar-nama on the ideology of Prophet. Eating more, barking dogs seldom bites like Farooq Abdullaha and Sonia Gandhi, again proved 'prostitute' of the 'Sindh Family' of Jammu or Kashmir or Ladakh. Three brother having partnership of the state like Maharaja Gulab-Singh, Raja Diyan Singh and Suchet Singh. In the election context, 2010 of the 'Panchayat Raj' author hand-cuff the Gandhian ideologist Dr S.P. Sharma as corrupt officer of the education department posted at GDC Doda; on the question of that IAS/IPS, Ministers or Mantri of the period, they are not 'Highly Qualified' in the concept of Sufi Saint philosophy. Author was placed under suspension. Now, after the suspension, another culprit Brahmin of Ghat in the form of Prof. Z.A. Hashmi, dash to ground due to militant attack by the author or idiot Prof. Javid Iqbal Tarambo of the same college, lecturer in 'Economics'. They use to go daily in the Masjid for 'Nawaj' as dishonest ideology of the upper class Muslims. A.A Macdonell, worked on "A Vedic Grammar" equalent to 'Holy Quran' on Sabdha Theory, that is, *have* and *have not*. Now , there is a great gap between ' The Rich' and 'The Poor' Muslim. Rich are there who have the ideology of 'Dr. B.R Ambedkar' and 'Poor' are those who have the ideology of Gandhi. There two forces are fight not in Jammu, but also in Ladakh and Kashmir. No doubt, in Ladakh, there are less Muslims in the fray of "National Assembly' but they are more superior than the Kashmir Muslims, because, they are 'Poor'. Why there was militancy, among Kashmir Muslims = Kashmir Pandits or Meghas of mini Kashmir, they were degraded by them as Dalits and 'Muslim Rajputs' and Hindu Rajputs, they have the same culture as 'Infidels' as Kashmiri Muslim or Pandits. Dalits of Jammu region, they have been proved more cultured than the said communities.

Now, there is a competition among the Dalit itself, that Chamar are more superior in comparison with other communities of this area. Because, at one time, the were inferior, during the times of Brahminism. Meghas of the Jammu region, as per the statics of the population, they have more than that of Chamars as 'Rumbi Marka race'. Meghas of the Jammu region, again proved as Brahmins of this area. It is the same story Chamar has a Master Degree and Brahmins = Meghas have under-graduate-degree. Chamars always proved superior, to all of the communities in the competition world. According to the statement of A.L. Srivastva, a professor of Agra College "Muslims responsible for the wrongs, particularly religious persecution" (Preface of the First Edition, p. ix), why the foreigner Arabs, Turks and Afghans, they penetrated in India, because of their strong ideology as American and Chinese influence have been traced from the Northern Frontier borders of Pakistan. It, again proves that Muslims are inferior than the Dalit Mochi that was the concept of Dr B.R Ambedkar a Prophet Mohammad. Muslim worlds, they have no characters, for example, present president of Afghanistan, he influenced with the philosophy of Gandhi and took the Ph.D. in 'Political Science' from Himachal (Shimla University) as incomplete ideology. How, he is a successful ruler, he is working in the grip of military men. No doubt, he is working hard for the establishment of 'New ideology' of the Ambedkaritie thought that a working class has been dispatch for the construction of G.T. Road through Kashmir by Jammu or Dhar Road with the ideology of Jambudvipa. After the downfall of the 'Raj Dynasty' of Sindh in 342 A.D. There had a Brahmin like that of Dr Karan Singh, he had two sons 'Malhan Hans' and 'Suraj Dhar', Malhas Hans moved to Sialkote and formed the Manhas tribe of Rajputs, now he is known as Manjit Singh Manhas of Jourian, a trader of Toya, while the younger brother / son / friend became professor in History (Dr. Raj Kumar = Baba Gurinder Singh Ji of Bias) as founding father of the state industry in Jourian as his brother Parth Singh, who established crusher in Jourian. They have nor formal education as author have in art of writings, but both are good friend of mine in the context of Dalit behavior. Study, again, shows that Suraj Dhar was a Kashmir Rajput as the concept of "wave length in Physics" as rising sun (Ravi) of the 'Morning Day' and he became the founding father of the Jammu State (430 to 485 A.D) and this dynasty ruled upto the period of (850 A.D). their rulers were known as Ganga Dhar of Vijaypur, Baldev Raj of Nadwal (Khour). During his reign Peer Roshan Shah Wali, a Muslim Sufi Saint scholar like that of 'Dr. Wahid Kanwar Balwan, GDC. Doda' settled in Jammu region, worked on 'Genetic History' of this region, how the idea of Arab penetrated in his mind as with the dynamic research. At one time, he used to settled in Gumat to read out the historical research on the topic of Chamar thought. He held great respect in his community as an ideology of the 'Dalit-Mochi' and his later successor Kirat Dhar (650-700 A.D) Ajay Dhar of Punjab or Jalandhar, Vijay Dhar of Top-I-Sher Khania from Jammu became his follower.

They established their kingdom in the area of Karmchi-Babour, at that time, there was dense jungle. After the downfall of this dynasty Mukahri enters transferred their power to 'Dev Dynasty'. They ruled (840 to 1489 A.D.) After the downfall of the Kabir (1398 to 1540 A.D.) power was shifted to Ravidas (1414 to onward) "it is evident that Ravidas was younger than Kabir". (In the words of McLeod, Guru Nanak and the Sikh Religion, p. 155). In the study, we learn, that Prakash Singh Badal and deputy son Sudhir Singh Badal and his wife, who is M.P of the Punjab State, found as strong Brahmins of the Sikh (Syisa) community and Kushwant Singh, a journalist, a play writer, a novelist and a historian, he is more superior than him (Parkash Singh Badal and his family) in comparison in art of writing. No doubt, Kushwant Singh could not proved identity of the Guru Nanak as "untouchable" ruler of the Punjab. Nanak developed the ancient culture of the Punjab which drived from the Panzels and 'Sermd-System' of the Rajasthan which developed by 'Mira Prem Dewani' as a Sufi-Saint scholar of the Ravidas institution as 'Dr. Shabnam Grewal' of Delhi and 'Soynama Chaku' of Kashmir and 'Preeti Bhagat' of Leh as enlightened women scholar of the 'Dalit History'.

Rajput concept was launched by the Mira in North India with the 'Sound-Power' and 'Raja Pipa' (Ex. Additional Deputy Commissioner Doda City) became follower of the present 'Religion' Dalit as 'Radha Soami'.

Nightingale now, observed her history as close friend of Dalit historian (Madam Falak of GDC Doda). She is smart and handsome women of Suteel Ved (Suchet Singh of the previous ideology), a left arm spinner baller of the cricket team of Kashmir, now, he constructed a small hut at 'Purani Muthi' with the association of a Poonchi Brahmin. (Anita Bashin). Dr Raj-Rishi Gargotra attached, again, with Samista Thakur of Udhampur, posted in GDC Boys. Both need swimming pool for the enjoyment of summer days now, at present, there a moderate temperature at Calcutta. Both of them physically and mentally are 'one' as family tribe of the Naṃ. Little master Deepit Raj is Nur or 'Light' of the Kargil story, during the war was took place in 1999 A.D. His soul was penetrated in the womb of a Brahmini Pushap Lata, she disturbed the author that author need, two more wives for the extension of power from Multan to Gobi dessert with the ideology of Uant or Camel as a symbol of the historical approach as the concept of the "Mira Prem Devani". Garwhal to Grewal tribe was derived in the ancient culture to modern man General Zorwar Singh defeated the Chinese forces with the ideology of Sindh (Uch) as Sindhu Mela is the derivation of the 'Ladakhi Culture'.

It is the same story as of Dasarajan as opposite race of the Brahmanism (Ravan, a Lankan race).

Study, again, visualised by the art historian with 'Sindhu Culture' that 'Sandhu Samaj' as forced labour of the king developed the civilisational growth of the Jammu city with the idea of Santi Parva, again, with the ideology of Sufi-Scholar of Nazla Chak Dr Sat Paul Gargotra. There is no undisputed record of a Vaisya ruler Sindh (Doda city) either Ansari traders or Mahajan trader of Jammu. They are busy with their 'Prostitution ideology'. Now, they are working with the 'ideology' of 'Time Pass'. Now, they became poor as Dalit is race of India. (Manorama Janhari; '*Politics and Ethics in Ancient India*'; Varanasi, pp. 338-347).

Social Morality

Social morality use to come with the view of 'Honest Living'; it has been appeared from the cultural race of the '*Chamar thought*' '*Varna System*' started by Gandhi, Nehru and Jinnah, on the basis of incomplete idea. Life is fair, an ideology of the Ambedkarities writer. 'Coal' as 'Black Stone' is an ideology of the said scholar Sardar Patel, no doubt worked on various field, but he was cheater of the 'Nam - History'.

The swift of skillful manner did not appear in the state policy of the Patel, no doubt, he was cultured man in the context of Gandhian philosophy Hindutatav, but he could not solved the vexed question of the integration of 561 princely states without Dr B.R Ambedkar. Moreover, he was a muscle man as Dr S.P Sharma Brahmin by nature, he make hatred on the ideology of 'untouchable' with 'Bhim Rao Ambedkar' as Sufi Saint scholar of the Nam- history. He (Sardar Patel) did nto visualised the problem of the Northern States of India for the boasting of economy to poor people of the Nam (Dalits). Both Gandhi and Jinnah recognised Sardar Patel's great contribution. Lord Mount Batten in his letter (Harif) of June 19, 1948, who wrote about the 'Spiritual Heritage' in transcription form in the "writings and speeches" "Riddles in Hinduism", Dr Baba Sahib Ambedkar, published by the Education Department Govt. of Maharashtra, in 1987. On the question of the "India" needs unity in large scale on the basis of formal education, but failed to understand the 'Inner Voice' message about the 'Dalit Concept' as an ideology of tinny state of Kashmir i.e., 'Jammu'. Ideology developed from Jambo to Jammu with the idea of 'Rishi-Muni'. As a book has been written by Dr K.N. Upadhyay on the topic of Jain Dharma and 'abstract knowledge' of the art of writing (Hindi, 2010). The term 'Jain' in composition of two great forces Ja+in means that 'God is within' the body of man as realizing force of the concept Dalit.

There is also a Muni-Rishi of the Buddhist culture found in the community of Ramdasia. Hs is a great follower of Dr B.R. Ambedkar and the philosophy of the 'Chamar thought'. He is great teacher of the north region; uses to live in Krishna Nagar Jammu. He is popularly known as Muni-Baba. Old Jainese of this area, they became Rajput, they do not like to listen his satsang as a Schedule Caste preacher. It has been observed from the behavior of 'Muni Lal Jain' of the Jain Bazzar of Jammu called as Paharian Mohalla found above the Pacca Danga (visit of the author 2 Nov. 2013) and I consulted, his worker, their plight is so miserable, that hardly they afford their family such as Surinder Kumar and others found in the same locality.

Study shows, in the materialistic worlds, there is no scope of the worker as an artisan of the 'Sunar Community'. His treatment has been found as 'Big Brahmin of the Jammu region, including his race like Parmodh Jain an IAS and other of the same area. Inviting attention to the 'Dalit Samaj' Muni Lal Jain and Parmodh Jain is a great burden on this region as money-minded race. "To cleanse the dirt of the Jammu City is quite different, from cleansing the dirt of politics. From the former Hinduism to Jainism is great materialistic study of the author,

Dalits remain Dalits as Daljit Verma, Lecturer in Urdu. He is no more as Pandit, he is a Jain".

Festival of Lights

'Festival of Lights', we means, this house is the residing 'House of the Lord' as per the statement of little master 'Deepit Raj'. He is Nur-Nama of the historian concept. He knows every wit of the knowledge as 'Sacha Kartar'. 'Bablu Furniture House' of Dream City needs no money of the furniture posted in the same house, but he needs livelihood for the survivalism, belonged to U.P., Bihar as poor artisan.

Desi Ghee, we do not use in the modern society as material known. Diwali has many historical references and legends as far as its origin is concerned. (Daily *Excelsior Magazine*, Sunday, Nov. 3, 2013. Internet addition, editor Ayodhya Nath Kerni) study shows without economy, 'there is no light in the house', but at the same, I want to record the statement of Sonia Gandhi to conclude the chapter of the pre-historic culture. She says "BJP is highly corrupt party" beware it, but about the Congress Wadhra Land Scam, Coal mine scam, Bansal scam, Boforce scam, Urea scam, Sukh Ram Scam, N.T Tiwari relationship theory with Dalits or Advasi of Andhra Pradesh as sex scandal story, Tandoor care, Arusi murder case, Kiran Vedi is promotion scam. Congress party is called the party of 'sex scandals' as per the statement of the author as observer of the 'Dalit-Literature'. With the concept Dalit or untouchable, author enlightened various scholars of your party itself like Susil Kumar Shinde, Meira Kumar (speaker). As per his statement "Kashmir is ours, no role of third party". What is the differences between BJP or Congress as Manmat or 'Prostitution', Dalits are feeling "suffocation" with the "politics". 'Brainwar' is there the term "suffocation" originated from the Latin word "Suffocare" or stifle or as Dr B.R. Ambedkar die or kill from lack of Air as Nam on earth, where stands the ideology of Sonia Gandhi, as highly "prostitute" women. (*Compact Oxford Dictionary Theasaurus and word-power Guide*, *Indian edition*, 2004, p. 908).

"According to the legend, as mentioned in the *Rajatarangini* and *Nilamatapurana*, the Valley of Kashmir which was a vast mountain lake was drained by Kashyap Rishi. When desiccated the first settlers were the Nagas. They were snake worshippers and animists. A batch of Aryans originally settled on the bank of the mighty Vedic river Saraswati moved into the valley when the river Saraswati dried up. This was about 5,000 years ago (P.N.K Bamzai, *'Cultural and Political History of Kashmir'*; Vol. I, *Ancient Kashmir*, 2nd edition, 2007, p. 26)

The Kashmiris demonstrated it practically, when for example, Brahminism replaced by the Dalit concept, not in Europea, but in India too. The earliest forms of Naga Cult worship there was tinge of religious persecution by Dalit Muslims like Barack Obama of America in the beginning of the 21st century. On the other hand, the Nagas of the Akhnoor area like Raj-Rishi, and other are even to this day venerated in the Hindu or Muslim society of India. Ignorance of the subject of Indian thought is profound. To the modern mind Indian philosophy means two type of ideology, *Manmat* and *Gurmat*. Manmat believes on 'prostitution' which has been in the history of Dr Farooq Abdullah's family after the death of Sheikh Mohammad Abdullaha on the question of plebiscite and after 66 years of Independence the Kashmir became a barbarian state of mind. According to S. Radhakrishan, Ex.-First President of India, "A rich culture is impossible with a community of nomads or Dalits, where people struggle for life and die of privation. Fate gifts and every prospect was pleasing" "when we do not need to waste our energies on problems of life on earth, exploiting nature and controlling the forces of the world, we begin to think of the higher life, how to live more perfectly in the 'spirit of law'" ('Oxford Indian Paper backs Indian Philosophy', by S. Radha Krishan, Vol. I, revised edition, 2005, pp. 21, 22).

Jawahar Lal Nehru was born on 14 November 1889 at Allahabad and educated in England, at arrow and Cambridge. In 1912, Nehru returned home to play a central role in India, struggle for freedom for British colonial rule, and then, as Prime Minister of Independent India for seventeen years, went on to shape the nation's future as a modern, secular and democratic state. He died in office, on 27 May, 1964. Visionary and idealist, scholar and statesman of international stature, Nehru was also an outstanding writer. His three renowned books – *'An Autobiography'*, *'Glimpses of World History'* and *'The Discovery of India'* have acquired the status of classics, and are all published by

Penguin, 2004. "It is a hard and nice subject for a man to write of himself: it grates his own heart to say anything of disparagement, and the reader is ears to hear anything of praise for him" *Abraham Cowley* P. I. New Delhi 2004. "The family experienced may vicissitudes of fortune during the unsettled times that followed and the Jagir dwindled and vanished away. My great grandfather, Lakshmi Narayan Nehru became the first advocate (Vakil) of the 'Sarkar Company' (Chandal group) at the shadow court of the Emperor of Delhi. My grandfather, Ganda Dhar Nehru was Kotwal of Delhi for some time before the Great Revolt of 1857. He died at the early age of thirty-four in 1861. P. 2. "For some years the family lived in Agra near the Dayal Bagh of Radha Soami Ashram and it was in Agra on the 6th of May 1861 that my father was born" (Note: A curious and interesting coincidence: The poet Rabindra Nath Tagore was also born on this very day, month and year. "It was a notorious fact that whenever an Englishman killed in India, he was acquitted by a jury of his own country men" p. 7.

"The Harappan Civilisation" of the Akhnoor Valley of Manda, at one time it was destroyed, now, it has been came in existence with the idea of "Sculptors" and through "Painters", it is known as "Vedic Civilisation" that is the concept of 'Raj-Rishi of the Akhnoor' a Sindhi school of mind. "Dalit Sufis" like B.R. Lachotra or the rulers of the "Locan" family of Jammu at present use to live at Roop Nagar, etc. as ex-planning officer. Basically, this tribe belong to the Akhnoor Valley of Sindh.

Study shows that Sh. U.R. Ghai and K.K, Ghai, they worked on the said topic International Politics and Dalit Concept, they both are post-graduate in this field and their work is more efficient that the professors of the JNU or other Universities of India. Before, 1947, they were migrated from the Mirpur Siddhar, found in the Jammu State and now settled in Jalandhar. This family belonged to the, Ghai tribe of India (Jammu). Certain, they became upper caste, Hindus like Dr Ved Ghai, and others. Who worked on the translation of *Nilamatapurana*, as a new edition both found in English and Sanskrit in Jammu University. Juta concept of the Ravidas philosophy, we need 'good souls' to work for the development Dalit Culture. The cast of Indian mythology is the work the Brahmanism. It is bewilderingly complex one among "Dalit Hindus" and "Dalit Muslims". "Dalit Muslims" like clerk. Qyeem, S.O. of the GDC Doda, he felt that Brahminism has been widely spread by upper class Muslims, who have the material culture in their life style found in Doda City in the family of Balwan, Sorawardhy and Gazi too. No doubt, certain Rajput families like Thakur, Jamwal, they use to keep the past practices of the Brahminism. Only few Dalits (Megh, Chamar (Watal), Hanji (Boat-driver) etc. of Kishtwar, they keep their identify intact. The area of Bhaderwah, it has the Majority of Dalit concept, as advance race as Tramboo tribe of this area including certain Gaddis, Sipps, Meghas, Mahashas, Katoch, Manhas, Kori, Sunar and Shoe-Maker.

Concept India:- Concept India is related with the study of Mahabharata that is called "History Rebeat itself" in living form either he male species or female species. Jammu, after 1947, adopted a great social change due the migration of population from Sindh area to Multan. Certain Gujjar tribes like Javed Rai or Iqbal Choudhary editor of the Jammu and Kashmir, Magazine about the up-to-date knowledge. But, Gujjar, it could not compile, the authentic history of this area, which is distort by Gandhi and Bazaz family of the Kashmir, and from the Jammu by Dr Karan Singh. Ladakh, as a union territory, and their modern scholars like Dalailama, a religious and famous leader of Buddhist Community of Leh, he could not express the "Real" history of world or the areas. Modern development works, after the death of Dr B.R Ambedkar, were allotted to Dalits under the supervision of Pandits of Kashmir, Ladakh, and to Prem Nath Dogra and Ram Nath Sastri. But, they made an hegemony or monopoly in this very area with the philosophy of Dr Rajinder Parasd and others. Gandhi and Ali Mohammad Jinnah, they were the advocate of the "Dalit History", but it remained lying with "Chamar thought". Author reflected this ideology with the idea of Nanak that is "Nama" or "Kalma".

Executive Notes, author reflected his ideology on the basis "No Profit, No Loss", when exclusive book of the author *"History of the Chamar Dynasty"* (600-1200), came into the market, which provide the coverage of missing period the series of events in the lifestyle of the whole world. No doubt, other historical works of the said author, is no less than that of in the dairy of the Dalit History like "Encyclopedia of Untouchables", Ancient, Medieval and Modern". Many more works on this very concept are lying pending to avoid the clashes and disturbances of the "Dalit Society". No, doubt, certain, Dalits, they made Brahmins with idea of "materialistic thought", but our tribes "Gargotra" or "Ghai", "Grewal", "Chakoo" and Hashmi, have the same identity.

Sufism: Its Evolution and Practice

It has come to our knowledge that Sufism developed from China, after the death of Dr B.R Ambedkar, 1956 that Buddhism developed in China and Japan due to his contribution, when he worked and visualised the authentic history of the 'God and Man' in his Buddhist philosophy their reasoning was based on logical truth, "if Japanese win the second world war, as looks possible at that time in two group of rivalry. England was work against Japan. It, is, however G.D, Birla and his wife Rattan Tata met Wevell on 29th August, 1945, on the question of Sindh and Multan territory, Ali Mohammad Jinnha (Maulana Sahib as an advocate) was not happy over lending support of the Allah Bux Ministry in Sindh and Multan, on the question of that, he belonged the community of Gujjar of the Punjab. The result was that 'the position today is such that a coalition ministry in Sindh, Bengal and Punjab is within the domain of provincial politics. If this change could be brought about with the humble opinion of Dr B.R Ambedkar who was expert at that time as Educationist like Muzzafar Hussain of Bhaderwah, expert teacher in realistic approach". (M.A, M.Phil, 'Adhoc Lecturer in Education' and having seven year experience in this field).

No doubt, the political implication as described by J.P. Suda, (M.A in Political Science, H.O.D Meerut College, Meerut) that "the Socratic doctrine of the identity of virtue with knowledge are vital. Some of them were drawn by Socrates himself and some by his greatest disciple, Plato. It led Socrates to emphasize the need of 'Special Knowledge' on the part of rulers" that-is 'Nam' or "Kalma" mentioned by Prophet and Nanak. *(History of Political Thought; p. 33)*, where stand the idea of Amarjeet Sharma and Dr Rekha Choudhary (University of Jammu, Former H.O.D of this Department) as expert in Political Science, used to work on 'social justice' in self-style manners. Till date, she did encouraged the Dalit-scholar in Political Science, because on the basis of caste-factor. She is next to Sarupnaka, the sister of Modi or Ravana. Thus, "Idea" rules, money does not rule. Stafford Cripps, who also met with Wavell on the said date and said him that 'Birla, Shiva Rao, (nickname of the Baba Sahib, Dr Bhim Rao Ambedkar) and others were of the view that Hindus would accept it". (Wavell's Journal; p. 167). Wavell also refers to his talk with Francis Wylie, I.C.S, who said that he was "pessimistic about the future of Kashmir (India) and the Congress Leaders were quite incapable of running the country, and knew that they were not really equal to the job" as Dr B.R Ambedkar, as an untouchable was efficient than the other leaders of the country. In this regard, there was a complete lack of harmony in the country itself as after 66 years, we see in whole of *India and Jammu, Kashmir and Ladakh* too (p. iv)

"Quit Indian Movement II", Role of Indian Big Business. *"British Secret Documents"*, by Dr P.N Chopra - Interpretation of all relevant historical events in this book have been taken into consideration. Due efforts were made to use the various expression of the 'Kingship Theory' of the Nam-History.

No doubt, Kashmir or Kashir is a land of tabled beauty and eternal romance in natural way of life style. But, at present, it has become land of 'Prostitution' under the "Abdullaha Family".

Study shows the 'Sonia Gandhi' or 'Gandhi Family' is a party of the said institution. In addition to that, this concept was also found in Kargil, Leh, Zanskar, Pannikar, Batalik, Darass, Nubra and so on. Because, both the Hindus and Buddhist, they are in minority, they have less idea of that institution too. She is the girl friend of South Indian Brahmins and Molavis of Kashmir like Farooq Abdullaha and others. The majority of Dalits, they are unaware of that facts, because, they are innocent by nature and pure from the heart. How, they can form the Buddhist state of India (Kashmir). It is impossible without realizing the truth as a scientific-knowledge of the Vedic Rishis either *Kashyap* or *Raj-Rishis*, etc. No doubt, NHPC has been involved as industrial partner in 5 it is at Ramban, Reasi, Uri, Kargil and Leh, Tata Motors in 2 it is at Gool and Pampore, JKSPDC in 5 it is, Islamic University in 2 it is and 2 it is in BGBS University. The Chief Ministers were only the funding policy as Headman of the village or state. He is not technical expert as Dr B.R Ambedkar a framer of the 'Indian Constitution' and other states, they drew the copy of the same, either, it was the constitution of Pakistan or Bengal, etc. The contribution of the writer is not less than that of Lord. Therefore, history says, no less, no more a science or arts. History creator are Dalits.

Origin and Growth of Colonialism

Modern historians call the period from the late 19th century to the middle of the twentieth century 'the Age of Modern Imperialism'. The term 'Imperialism' was coined by Benjamin Disraeli in 1872 in the context of the British general election of 18th. Among the critics of imperialism the most famous Names are those J.A Hobson, a British liberal, and V.L Levin, the Russian Marxist leader of the 'Bolshevik Revolution' based on Dalit concept that is 'Labour' or Peasant. But the period, left behind upto the modern man that is the period of closing of the 20th and beginning of the 21st century is the period of Brahminism. Study again shows, that Dalits or Sufi Saints are real rulers of Kashmir or India and Britishers, they were Dalit Christian.

More accurately the age should be called, 'the age of colonial empires'. No doubt, both 'colonialism' and imperialism are the ancient practices for the building of 'Empire' such 'colonisation' was backed by the 'Home Country', that is, the concept of Dalits. As, it is said, this kind of structure had been found both in ancient Greek and Rome. Later, Asia and Austriad came under the spell of the drive.

Japan and the U.S.A

In the study, we also learn, *'Glimpses of European History'* (1450-1945 A.D) through Abha Trivedi, Japan and U.S.A at the beginning of the 20th century the story of 'Colonialism' in India upto 1947 had the impact of England, not of Asia. Therefore, at present, we need a Asian friend, now, as a developed country like India to solve the 'Kashmir Issue', on the basis of 'Social Justice' that Dalits are real rulers of this continent, not the China or Japan.

Govt. Degree College, Doda (J&K)

Govt. Degree College, Doda is situated at Nagari Mohalla upper hill of the Chandarbagha (Chenab), it was established in March, 3rd,

1989. Affiliated with the university of Jammu and recognised by the UGC, and its examinations conducted with the university of Kashmir's session. (From the Principal's Desk; Dr Javed. I. Khatib, Principal, 2009-2010, p. 1); through information Brouchure for admission to three year, Degree course.

Concept of the Modern State

The concept of the 'Modern State of India' has been originated after 1947. It became a basic concept of 'Political Science' in the history of Dalit concept. No doubt, numerous definitions of the 'State' have appeared since the days of Greek philosophers. The word 'State' has its origin in the Latin word 'statue' which means 'standing' or 'position' of a person or a body of persons. The Latin, 'status' Ernest Barker narrates us, gave three English words:

I. 'Estate', in the sense of 'standing' or 'position' have already been elaborated in regard to some form of property.

II. 'Estate', using the word in the primary sense of a grade or rank in the system of social standing or position as Dalits of India have been displayed their identity 'work in silence' as an 'idea of reservation' and other political forces, they are now on fire by them.

III. 'State', that is stateliness vested in one person of a 'tribe', for example, in 'Gargotra' tribe of Akhnoor or some body of persons 'Word' primarily a peculiar standing as Nam in Gurumuki or Punjabi language, Kalma in Arabic, Tao in China and many more names have been given to call the idea of Dalits. Study shows, such kind of personality has been known superior or supreme in the worldly life.

The word 'state' came to be understood, during the 16th and 17th centuries, during the Mughals and after the Mughals, down to the last days of the 'Independence' 1947, somewhat identical terms 'Sovereign' or and 'King' = Nam. No wander, for the political parties of India like BJP, NC, Congress or PDP, etc. It is old concept in 'New Form' as appearance of the 'New Soul' in the history of the world. Louis XIV rays, 'I am the state'. And to this context or reference, Barker adds, "was Louis XIV not his own view, as in that of his subjects, the person who enjoyed the 'state' and position of being the 'Supreme Political Authority', and was he not therefore 'the state'?

Roussean (1712-1778 A.D) speaks of the state, saying; "this public person, so formed by the union of all other persons including Doctors, Engineers, Professors, Peasants, Labour Union, formerly took the name of city like Udhampur Jammu, Kashmir, Ladakh, Doda, Bhaderwah, Kishtwar, Zanskar, etc., of the North region and now takes that of Republic or body-politics as Nam or an idea of the *Karmyogi*. Karl Marx (1818-1883 A.D.) and Frederick Engels (1820-1895 A.D.) regard the 'State' as the 'Political Organisation' of the class dominant in economy, whose purpose is to safeguard the existing order as *"Sudra State of mind Organisation"*. "No profit no loss", is the concept of the big organisation as the story of 'Dera Bias'. Hegel (1770-1831 A.D.) considered the 'State' as 'Dalit Concept' in the history of India, "as a Divine and moral entity which alone is capable of bestowing all 'Spiritual Reality'. John Stuart Hill (1806-1873 A.D.) regard the 'State' a positive instrument, a war against the 'anti-Dalits of India' or a war against the 'Infidal Society'. Individual achieved progress and enjoy liberty". According to E.H. Carr, "History is a dialogue between the Past and Present". Thus, Thomas Hill Green (1836-1882 A.D.) defines the idea of 'State' as, 'a body of persons like Dr Shabnam Grewal, Dr Sonyana Chakkoo, Professor Preeti Chandal etc. and three daughters of the scholars, recongised by each other as having rights and possessing rights to maintain the discipline of the various institutions of the society" as a reformist movement in India (Kashmir). As 'Team Culture' displayed that a 'State' should have to be govern 'under Rule'. Law-givers are Dalits. Therefore, their primary duty is to observe the 'politics' and than to have launch the campaign against the anti-Dalits.

The fact of the existence of the city state is older than its name. The 'State' as a word drived from the etymology of 'Stato' appeared in Italy before the sixteenth century A.D., in the writings of Machiavelli (1469-1527 A.D.). Reference of these, to the terms such as 'country', 'nation', 'society', 'any association' as 'Radha Soami' of the world are also very common in the umbrella of universal law are called 'International Law'.

Zoology (Gr. Zoin = animal + Logos = study) is the branch of life sciences that deals with Political Science, a branch, a branch historical knowledge as vedic study says, "History is a component of two Great forces, that is, God and Man in ancient time".

Relation of Zoology with Dead Animals:-The controversy regarding the political and non-political groups that is, Dalits and anti-Dalits regarding the "use of land" by Shri Amarnathji Shrine Board was a manipulated on the malign the sanctity of the shrine and the sentiments of the ancient History of the Dalit, particularly in Kashmir, Ladakh and Jammu is based on imagination. In the study it shows that upper class Hindus, Muslim, Buddhists and Sikh, they deal with the Sudras as anti-Dalits and their stature is equivalent to 'animals'. Whereas the Science of Biology (Gr., bios = Life + Logos = Study) or the study of Living Being. Author, compares, the Madan Lal Sharma, ex-MP as snake of the modern period and Sham Lal Sharma ex-PHE Minister is compared as Rakashas and Omar Abdullah is similar to that of Monkey-mind ex-Chief Minister and his teams proved as Rakashas and snakes too, (Abdul Rahim Rather or Ali Mohd. Sagar).

No doubt, Biology is the branch of artificial science which cannot investigate the truth in practical shape. The species of the said leaders observed from their way of behaviour or in their body language as uncivilised animals (E.L. Jordan, Dr P.S. Verma, *Invertebrate Zoology*, S, Chand, Lucknow, 1st January, 1963, p. 1).

The Constitution of Jammu and Kashmir, its Development and Comments has been written by Justice A.S. Anand and published by Universal Law Publishing Company, New Delhi, India. His labourious work is unforgotten. He was born in Jammu, November 1st, 1936 and graduated from Jammu University in 1958 and obtained L.L.B. Degree and Diploma in 'Labour Law' from Lucknow University in 1960 with first division and Ph.D. in Law (Constitutional Law of the Common Wealth) from London University in 1963. He was known to the Bar from the 'Honourable Society' of 'Inner Temple' in London in 1964 and practiced law in Punjab and Haryana High Court in Chandigarh. But ex-Deputy Chief Minister and Mufti Mohammad Syed, ex-Chief Minister what did for the welfare of the society, proved as negative thinkers of the society and his 'Healing Touch Policy' could not provide the balance to Dalits. Study shows, 'Educational Psychology' both the NC and PDP is the same as of the Gandhi and Bahadur Shah Zaffar.

No doubt, number of elections either MP's or MLA's have been fought after the 1947, but nobody, knows that Dalits are real rulers of the 'Kashmir History' as an 'Ideology' of the 'elevated concept' that is, Sodara known in Persian as well as in Arabic terminology.

Molecular weights of the compounds commonly used in tissue culture media compound macro nutrients:

Potassium nitrate	***= Chemical Formula***	***Molecular Weight***
	KNO_3	101.11
Potassium dihydrogen	KH_2PO_4	136.09
Ortho phosphate		
Potassium dihydrogem	$NaH_2PO_4.2H_2O$	156.01
Ortho phosphate		
Micro nutrients:		
Boric acid	H_3BO_3	61.83
Cobalt Chloride	$CoCL_2.6H_2O$	156.01
Zinc Sulphate	$ZnSO_4.7H_2O$	241.95
Sodium EDTA	Na_{2}, EDTA. $2H_2O$	372.25
Ferriu Sodium EDTA	Fe N_a EDTA	367.07
Sugars and Sugar Alcohols		
Fructose	$C_6H_{12}O_6$	180.15
Glucose	$C_6H_{12}O_6$	180.15
Vitamins and Amino Acids:		
Ascorbic acid (Vitamin C)	$C_6H_8O_6$	176.12
Biotin (Vitamin, H)	$C_{10}H_{16}N_2O_38$	244.31
Folic Acid (Vitamin BC, Vitamin M)	$C_6H_{12}O_6$	441.40
Inositol	$C_6H_{12}O_6$	180.6

Other compounds known as

Abscisic, Colchiane and Phloroglucinol in the form of 'Dalit Concept' as original plants in the formation of 'Good Society' as Nams. (Bendore, Meerut, 2011, pp. 52-53).

'Physical Growth and Motor Development', Chapter 8, it has been written by K.C. Garrison (University of Georgia). Study shows that growth of the individual from birth to maturity constitutes almost 1/3 of the normal life span. Genetic studies of the development of children have furnished valuable information about the nature of physical growth and motor development. The child's physical growth, his strength and his motor development at different age levels can be measured objectively. The materials of this chapter are designed to give the student growth and motor development and to help him view these aspects of growth as integral parts of the total growth and development of the individual. (Charles E. Skinner, *'Education Psychology*, Fourth Edition, New Delhi, 2009 by PHI Learning).

"Cross-Sectional or Horizontal Studies" was the moto of Gandhi and Dr B.R. Ambedkar. *"Visible Change in Kashmir"*, a statement furnished by CRPF Chief Deelip Trivedi, "All of you should go there. It is really now a *'Heaven on Earth'* and it has moved ahead from the day of militancy". (*Daily Excelsior*, dated, October 29, 2013, Vol. 49, No. 297, p. 1).

'Ex-VC Punjab University Lahore' arriving in Jammu on Nov. 2, 2013 the son of the soil Prof. Khairat Mohammed Ibn-e-Rasa will visit his native place Bhaderwah after a gap of 32 years, on the question to solve the border issue of Kashmir. He did his M.Sc. in Chemistry from Aligarh Muslim University after partition, he went to Pakistan from where, he proceeded to Brown University America for further studies and did his Ph.D in 1959. He was the first VC of the Multan University Pakistan. He also served as VC Al-Khair University in Pakistan Administered Kashmir as a distinguish personality of this area. He remained VC of Punjab University Lahore from 1976 to 1984. He is well known scientist and also served as Deputy Director General Islamic Educational Scientific and Cultural Organisation (ISESCO) from 1984-1991. Presently he is patron in Chief Pakistan Institute of Chemists. He has twiced visit in the Jammu and Kashmir State, secondly in 1982 A.D. He attended an International Conference of VCs at Calcutta (*Kashmir Times*, Jammu, 29 October 2013, p. 11, Col. 1). "In this Competitive World, such type of scholar, every movement is very powerful. If one does not aware about the aspect of change you must lose. Every information of your field is very precious in the history of Jammu, Kashmir and Laḍakh Market always welcomes the innovative and research product, because nature also accepts the positive change

Dr D. Peter Sn-ustad is a Professor Emperitus at the University of Minnerota, Twin Cities. His initial research focused on the interactions between bacteriophage T_4 and its host, E. Cooli (About the Authors) Ganetics New Delhi. In the field of publication and books are also the parts of such change. As 'Zigma Book Centre' says, "Not cheapest, but best book is your right". So, for the sake of our new generation we are going to provide some very-very fruitful and innovative ideas, that is based on historical phenomena ('Shop No. 14, Sant Market, Jewel Chowk, Jammu').

The Sources of the Dalit Plays

The sources of the 'Dalit History' = play writing concept we drive from 'Holinshed's Chronicle' as that of *'A Chronicle of the Kings of Kashmir'* means 'Kalhana's *Rajatarangini*' and the contributed of his other brothers like *Jonaraja* and *Srivara* and soon as later successors of the human history or ideology (Dr. Raj Kumar, Sat Paul, Suteel Ved). Both, there record of the early history of the *Chamar* or Chura thought and their religion is to ligion with God as twice-born Sudra Concept of the Vedic period. From the 'Holinshed's Chronicle' as a source of study we drives the ideas.

For 'King Lear', Cymbeline and his associate's similar story we observed from the M.A Stein translation, 'Kalhana' *Rajatarangini* from 'King Ashoka' to 'Maharaja Hari Singh' and their Murshid or Gurus, they have been the identity of the 'Dalit Culture' or 'Sufi-Saints'. Autumn Panorama Prevails after the death of 'Baba Roti Ram' of Mirpur Siddhar found in the area of Akhnoor, below Khour, below the bank of Chenab, now, 66 years (1947 to 2013) have been passed with autumn yielding to winter, winter to summer and the spring which gives lieruls to the man as an idea of the Dalit philosophy 'Chamar thought' was out of the scene in the *'History of Kashmir'*, because this race has the ideology of 'Happiness'. Why Lord Buddha and other great Sufi-Saints like Tukaram, Kabir, Ravidas, Nur-din-Himdani, Prophet Mohammad, Abaha Kathoon, Lal Ded, Sngandha, Mulana Rumi, etc. they stressed on satsang or discourse of the Sufi-Saint philosophy as Sarva Shiksha Abhiyan (SSA) to promote elementary education and Rastriya madhymik Shiksha Abhiyan (RMSA) for the promoting of 'secondary education' and the degree level has been promoted in this area after 1947, on the pattern of 'Western Thought'. No doubt, in *mandir* and *madrasas*, we have the promotion of Arabic and Sanskrit language. At one time, they were superior and declined due to the rising of western concept of 'English'.

Study shows, that this concept was launched by Dalit Christians and translated number of Sanskrit, Persians and Arabic texts (mandals) into English as visible race of the "inner feeling".

No doubt, Holinshed himself had draw his 'Scottish History' from other writers, who were not very reliable as 'Satish Chandra' or 'Irfan Habid'. One believes in Hinduism and other believes in Islam as self-style study or without 'objectivity'. No doubt, they have good character in their lifestyle, but they could not realize the authenticity in art of writing as author has expressed Gandhi and Jinnah, both were advocates, Dr B.R Ambedkar was the 'Judge of the knowledge' as a source person of the 'Dalit Samaj'. Moreover, it has been observed by Pt. Jawahar Lal Nehru, that we need 'socialism' in India, but there was not good 'formal education' as today we see in the modern Kashmir or India. There is, no doubt, modern scholars of India they have less knowledge of the 'interpretation of the subject' *History*. As Alexander Cunningham says, "In the book Ladakh has been identified with the 'Akhara Regio of Ptolemy' and the proof that Grancasus was a Tibetan word and that Tibetan people and language must be known by the scholar; to clear the concept of study.

The nature of Shakespearean Tragedy, a study in evils is a difficult theme to believe on 'Dalit Samaj' that 'Hero' of this 'Tragedy' is Dr Raj Kumar Chamar is a Prince of the Jammu State along with his 'Ali Brothers' and 'Chalis Chhor', a dramatist writer belong to the far-flung area of Akhnoor (Village Nazla Chak). 'The Holy Book' of Mirdad, has been complied by Mikhail Naimy in 2002 A.D. (Bias) special edition 2007. Beside this book, he also wrote on 'Memoirs of a Vagrant Soul sent till we meet, Kahlit Gibran. His life and his work. 'The strange story of monastery which was once called the *Ark*. The bound about flint slope, the keeper of the book says, "on the creative word, I is the source of knowledge and centre of all things is Nam or Allah". (p.5) On night the deerless singer is Dalit writer. As, it has been rightly expressed by this author, "Day of the Ark and its rituals, the message from the Prince of Bethar is similar to that of State of mind in this area about the 'Living Lamp'" as described in the 'Basholi Paintings' of the Jammu region as Vibrant study of the 'Dalit Samaj "Live and Let Live".

So far as the Living Master of the period is concerned, it warms to the crowds of this area do not fire (Agni) the Kashmir and do have a approach to follow the Dalit concept as a solution of the social problem. "This land belongs to nature. Nature needs no destruction, but convert it into supernatural ideology". (Baba Gurinder Singh Ji Dillon, Dera Bias). It has been referred in the 'Sunday Magazine', 6 Dec. to 12 Dec. 2010, by the great journalist Arindam Chaudhuri that It's totally ethical of media houses and editor's lobby to explain the modern issues.

As per the report of ICSSR and MHRO dated 23-09-2013, letter No: ICSSR/Eco/13/09 18, addressed to the Principal GDC. Doda (J&K) subject: 'Seeking Permission to conduct the survey' on the topic of "Educational status of SC/ST in J&K: Attainments and challenges. As a social-scientist, I have made the survey in the Kashmir Valley as well as in Mini Kashmir that is, Bhaderwah, Kishtwar, Doda City, Kilotran, Satroo Marwah, Padder, Thatri, Prem-Nagar, Bhalla, Nagini, Chinta, Marmat, Kalyani, Assar, Bagar, Bartund, etc. that the Muslim society is a society of 'fundamentlist idea' or having the view of 'blind-faith'. It has been expressed from their lifestyle, eating, body language. Only twenty to thirty per cent people they are civilised or religious people "As was natural, there followed simple plays to illustrate moral or religious principles particularly in Megh, Mahasha, Chamars and in Rajput society". Brahmins, here are less in number; but they are good in nature like Habba Khatoon (Nightingale of Kashmir), the beloved queen-consort of Yusuf Shah Chak, who ruled over Kashmir (1578 to 1586 A.D) Habba, whose original name was zoon (moon) or Aebik or 'Lord of the Moon' known in the Turk history of Ladakh.

He was a peasant girl like (Chakkoo) who had many spludoured personality, a poetess, an eminent musician and a melodious singer. She had a distinctive beauty of body as Sonyama Chakkoo daughter of Om Prakash Chakkoo. His forefathers they were mule driver. Kumhar and soul that captivated to Yusuf Shah and influenced the minds of her people as a Nam or Kumhar to her artistic way of lifestyle. Her life, amazingly enough is shrouded in mystery as 'miracle lady'. Whatever, she left in her memory in past till day she is known as the Nightingale of Kashmir as Sirosnaya Nadu of Andhra Pradesh. She fought bravely against the anti-dalit during the time of 'National Movement in India. But, her present, she was in a fixed, why Jat-Pat has been created in the Hindu Samaj. Study shows, life is the story of 'Tredgedy' and to prove his/her identity, it is the duty of the present life as VC.

From Habba Khatoon verses, we know that she was born at *Chandhara*, a village situated at a distance of about ten miles from Srinagar. About is death, nothing is known by the historian as a natural girl as Ramiyan Bhardwaj daughter of Dr Raj Kumar Chandal of Kashmir.

Habba Kathoon was such a 'soul-mate' of Yusuf Shah. Sinking her love-lyrics as Zafari, a under writer of Poonch, provided contribution in film industry of Bombay for the compositon of films of the modern man. She moved like Cinderalla through the pageantry of the "Yusufean" scence as a characteristic woman. Yusuf Shah, no doubt, was a historical character, enlightened with 'truth'. Truth is God that is identity of author and his family.

We also see the turbulent and strife turn times in Kashmir, due to the reason of uncivilised culture. There are evil forces of communalism and sectarianism and then the aggressive designs of Emperor Akbar was to kill the infidals through witchcraft or with the stroke of natural pen. The threat of war always hangs like the dead *Albatross* around the neck of Yusuf Shah. All this and much more makes the Novel a *'International Epic of Kashmir'* as the story of *Mahabharata* or *Ramyana* as *'History Repeat Itself'*. We are face to face with the genius of 'Habba Khatoon' and the exuberant aesthetic taste of the gentleman's law which became Yusuf Shah's tragic flaw. The book overflows, with brilliant characterisation. There are kings or Nams, scholars Sufi-Saints found in Dalit Muslim society of Kashmir. Poets, Knaves, courtesans, dancing girls and common men and women. They are all drawn their history with scholarly description which makes alive in front of our eyes. The novel inspires pity and terror and so is, like a Greek Tragedy, cathartic in character.

Lal Ded Says:-

'Idol is of stone, temple is of stone;

The temple above and the idol below are one;

Which of them will thou, O foolish

Pandit worship?

Cause thou the union of mind and soul". (S. N. Wakhlia, Gulshan books, 2007, p. 22).

Nund Rishi Says:-

"The dog is barking in the compound

O brothers! give ear and listen to (what it says):-

As one sowed, so did he reap;

Then Nund, so, sow, sow". (Ibid)

"Subhan Alla! Allah - o - Akbar", sighed the old Rathar. Kesho Pandit sang many of the verses of the two mystics in a subdued tone.

"What a great mystic was Nund Rishi, these sayings touch the chords of our heart. Sheikh Nur-ud-Din's message, *Kaka*, was of the soul and we spoke for the mankind as a whole. He was not of the earth nor even of any particular race and country. He belonged to the universe and his message was universal as the message of *satsangi* for the Dodities "Love gets love, tough gets tough".

Poonam Sharma, Sandeep Sharma and so on. In this area Hindus are in minority. They have been suppressed by the 'infidals' with 'muslce power' and filth language particularly by the *Agas* of this areas. They have no universal knowledge, they have the 'ideology of prostitution and made this are as "hell". This book is not reflected the ideology of the Megh community of this area, but author as a professor, made the survey as a great priest of the Dalit society as a scientific historian. A young girl like Hukma Devi Maghini use to come every day with good uniform that is white duptta, almond colour shirt or Kamiz with white salwar, whereas religious priest of the infidel society, they use to come with black robe. As Shakespeare's Macbeth, has been written by W. Turner, reprint 2008 as a popular book for the graduate and post-graduate students, author expresses a statement pertaining to the infant of this infidel society including principal, "the actors were not presented as human individuals, as types of man's nature and qualifies reflect through dress code too. A young girl like Hukma Ji in white robe as a Dalit women would appear and be introduced to the assembled villagers in the college as "Innoncence", or "purity" a challengeable character, while a wicked looking man Z A Hashmi (Brahmin by nature) in a black cloak along with idiot students of the same fashion were known as "Sinner" or "Vice". Vice would be shown as trying to influence with 'idiot thought' that is 'Rite and Rituals' or with evil spirit, while 'Innocence' fought to prevent this. A favourite play of this kind was called 'Everyman'. It was performed at Coventry and chester in England a thousand year ago. Author's , says, what the learned from the western or Iranian culture, in the 21st century, we are living in the 'computer age'. But, they are still backward, or infidals. They have no knowledge of the 'Religion' or the prophetic idea, that is, Islam which was based on equality before the 'Law' or Shuriat. This is the story of the Kashmir Muslims in the 21st century (p.1).

Theory of Two-Nation: Zia-ud-din Barani & Abul Fazl

After the Independence and before the Independence, the contributions of the Dalits in India is not less than Barani and Abul Fazl, as per the statement of Satnam Singh, "Where (Dalits) became Martyr, and new or fresh growth of the flowers came into existence". This statement is similar to that of Dr B.R Ambedkar. The book entitled, *'Contribution of Dalits During the First War of Independence of India'* 1857. He has written number of articles and books in Hindi on Dalit literature as discovery of the author is to highlight the 'Sufi-Saint' culture. He displayed the portrait of Gangu Mehtar and his contribution in the agitation of U.P or in peasant movement. (Ibid).

Theories of Social Change in South Asia

From the study, we learn, that after 1947 to 2013, there is great social change in the history of India with the establishment of 'Indian Constitution' as law-givers are Dalits. As per the lecture of B.L, Grover and S. Grover, the spouse of B.L Grover became a supporting feature in his lifestyle but at the same time, author observed from the distance, their life is more honest than the Irfan Habib and Satish Chandra, the both are modern Brahmins or advocate of the period and could not visualised the "idea" of History of 'modern India' or Kashmir. 'It was this obvious failure (but one shared with the majority of mankind of 'Dalit Parivar' as *'Sindhi' culture* having global knowledge in their lifestyle. Whereas Muslims, who are ruling in Kashmir, Jammu and Ladakh, after Independence, 1947, they do not realised the truth in their lifestyle working as 'infidals' or with the idea of 'superstitions'. Now, the question rises, who are the real leaders of the 'Kashmir History' or 'Modern India' they are Dalits either Baba Gurinder Singh Ji or Dr B.R Ambedkar, writer has been neglected by the historian at one time, as inferior scholar and the verdict in History, a challengeable work of the said scholar *'History of Chamar Dynasty'* (600 to 1200).

No doubt, Prof. M.L Kapur, did a lot of work on *"Kingdom of Kashmir"*, a great writer of the Jammu region, but he could not visualised the 'ideology' of the 'Dalit Samaj' or the working class of 'India' or 'Kashmir' = Rajataragini's concept.

His work led to the initial theoretical speculations having no practical shape in his lifestyled displayed in his personality. He was a composer of 'Dogra Culture' which was distorted by the 'Durrani Invasion' or with 'natural calamities'. To Hegel and Fredrich Angles belonged to the credit of first attempting a comparative explanation of both the Hindus and Muslims of India, of the mechanics of the evolution of the major *'World Civilisations'* why the *Industrial Revolution first began in England?* Between 1770 to 1825 A.D and spread significantly to Beligum about 1830 France, Germany about 1850 and in Italy 1930, due to the *'Age of Machine'* and idea was developed from the *"French Revolution* of 1789 A.D". But was done by Kashmir Pandits and Muslims for the welfare of state, they eatened the exchequer of 'State Revenue' with 'corrupt ideas', not with the 'honest approach' (Irfan Habid, p. 36, Dr Ragunath Rai, pp. 212-214). Even Karl Marx had repeated this judgement in 1853, when he said that "Indian Society has no history". (Irfan Habid, Ibid).

BSP & Indian Media, this book has been again drafted by Satnam Singh, New Delhi; 2008, "In this book, he highlight the role of Mayawati and Kashani Ram to the awakening the 'Dalit Samaj' and condemned the Manuvadi characters with the ideology of 'Positivism', but at the same time, this party and his worker could not, visualised the 'Real Ambedkarritie thought', no doubt, there is a great collection of the Nandu Ram on the encyclopedia of SC/ST, but his efforts were not proved in vain, now he became a great personality of India". What, Kasmir Pandits and Muslims did for the downtrodden, only made falseify notions. Now, the question of this 'state' is highlighting by them on the trifurcation, but they have 'no visionary' document without Dalits to form the 'New States' as an idea of Irish and Scottish pattern. Now, they have been killed with the 'ideology of Rambi' and or skill labour needs to publish more documents on 'Modern Kashmir or *Naya Kashmir'*.

Chak or chakoo is the 'Voice of God', she is in the whelm of affair, and she has written a book on the 'love-story' of Yusfaf Shah that another Ambedkar has been born in 'North India' in the family of 'Naga Cult' and she is the consort of the same writer as a helping women of human history. Mule drivers (chaks) her forefathers; and she has forgotten them; and remembered by 'Nature'.

'According to Sir H. Risley', "a caste may be defined as a collection of Dalit families or a groups of families bearing a common name which usually demotes or associated with specific occupation either Kumhar or Mochi as 'Mule Drivers'". This story was also related with Mahar of Punjab, and South India as a migratory race of the 'Rajput Family'. No doubt, the father of Baba Sahib B.R. Ambedkar was the army personal, during his lifetime they were satsangi, not like that of Pakandi as 'Sonia Gandhi or Kapil Shibal (Jat). (Dr. B.R Ambedkar, *Caste in India*; p. 8).

Studies in World Civilisations

Pre-historic Paleolithic, Neolithic and Chaleolithic Civilisation (the beginning of Civilised Growth in Dalit History), it has been founded from the Valley of not Akhnoor, but too in Kashmir Valley as a part of this state. This civilisation based of moral and ethical culture as the philosophy of Ravidas (Surya Race) and their way of lifestyle is based on 'universal idea' as 'Nam'. These people include the following understanding to each other without knowing 'Hindus' and 'Muslims' 'Rita and Rituals' like 'Roza' and 'Barat' as degraded idea of the Chamar thought or the untouchables. The main features of their organisation:-

1. A strong and stable social group of the Sevadal.

2. People has one langar of the simple diet.
3. Vegetarian society.
4. A mastery of Arts and Crafts which became necessary for the maintenance of human life for the construction road, Bridge, etc.
5. Good teachers have been co-operated in the schools and colleges from this background.
6. They have a good deal of knowledge in the art of writings to express the ideology of the common massages, not of the IAS or IPS modern Brahmins of the period.
7. They know, how to make the metal implements.
8. They have also an ability to transport the knowledge with fair manner over the land and sea.

They also possessed the knowledge of a stable govt. and to protects the property rights, punished evil doers and defended the people from unfriendly manners (neighours like Pakistan, etc.)

In order to attain the past practices of the civilisational growth, people have to settle down, and this means the rise of town and cities, infact, the word civilisation is derived from Latin word 'Civitas' meaning city. "It was the concept of Aristotle's Politics".

Why they became civilised? Having the ideology of 'Gurmat' Mohammad Ghori and Ghazanavi, they were also of the same-fate.

No doubt, the Mesopotamian of Culture, Egyptian Civilisation, Chinese Civilisation, Greek, Roman, Islam, Etc. having the great theory of politics for the survival of Humanism. Buddh or Karl Markx is the comparative statement of the Dalit history reflected by great genius scholars of the world, Dr B.R Ambedkar.

Religion of Lord Buddha

Lord Buddha is generally associated with the 'non-violence theory', modern Pandit and Molavis they are found meat-eater. How, they can realize the *truth*, as *rakashes* of the human nature or eater of the 'Dalit rights'. It has been observed from the attitude of Rekha Choudhary and his follow friends. She looks like Surapanaka of the modern period. She did not allowed the Dalit scholar, to obtained the degree of P.hd.

in Political Science. Lord Buddha or Dr B.R, Ambedkar, had not such kind of concept in his mind as the Brahmins and Molavis of the Kashmir, *"they have"*. The translation of M.A, Stein, also mentions in the notes about the Lord Buddha "thesis in Kalhana" *Rajatarangini* as the story of 'great river kings' in the literature of *Tripitakas* it has been enumerate the same story as that of Taoism of Chinese 'Religion'. 'Religion is necessary for a free society', but it resides in the heart of man, and not in *Mandir* and *Masjid* or *Shastras*. Shastras or Holy book like Bible, Quran, Gita, Guru Granth, etc. are the elaboration of realizing forces and Murshid is the medium of exchange the policy of knowledge and truth, in art of writings.

Kashmir Life and the Chenab Conflagration

The holy land sheltered the innocent life "Worst communal clashing on *"ID"* led to three brutal deaths, massive property and visible gulf between the two communities in Kishtwar *haves* and *haves-nots*. As per the dust is settling over the messes after many heads were made to roll, and it seems the plot was political in secret manner as a message of the God to realize the *truth*, but ertain stakeholders have won part of the *'Kamal Pasha'* of *Turkey*, at least for the time being certain Hindu and Muslim leaders became responsible to flare up the ideology of the 'negative history' in young blood, which has not solution, but problem creator, even certain Dalits from the Megh Baradaris, they were not spare in this incident as the quote the example of Prof. Ghulam Mohi-ud-din Hajni, he was born on June 22, 1917. He worked on *"Medieval Legacy to Modern Inorganic Chemistry"*, Prof. Hajni connects present with the past science and reminds that Muslims have their own share of contribution to what we call the 'Age of Science and Technology'. He was a great political, thinker as Dalit leader Udit Raj of Delhi (U.P), but he could not visualised the idea of human ideology as quality base knowledge. Prof. Hajni was a rebel since his childhood (Bachpan). During 1930's there used to be protests against Dogra regime in Kashmir Valley. In Sopore, during the evening hours, Prof. Hajni, then class 10th student; used to take part in these protests.

A vetern NC member *"Sofi Mohammad Akbar"* sitting behind Prof. in the meeting enquird from him, "what was going on", Ahsam says "Hajini Sahab told Sofi Mohammad Akbar, 'Koun moula chuhekh (you have been sold-out". Soon after that Sofi Sahib rolled his bed from 'Mujahid' Manzil', an interpretation of this subject is so deep that a Brahmin Muslim could not understand his view and took a tonga out-side and went back to his home in Sopore and never returned back. It was the story related the last Dogra ruler 'Maharaja Hari Singh' who does not like the clashes and avoided the 'Brahminical Ideology' and then Kashmir became 'issue' related with human thought politics of the 'Blind faith' penetrated in 'Muslims Samaj' to as 'negative' idea of human history. Now, people are realizing, who will form the next govt. Dalit concept is still alive as alive as the philosophy of the Sufi Saint (or the *Kashap Rishi* or *Raj-Rishi*). Vol. 05, issue 24, Srinagar, August 24, 2013, pp. 22-23.

Position of Women:- *The Golden mean* in the *Holy Quran*, it has been revealed not directly, but indirectly about the property right of the women' as the Indian Constitution expresses 'Equality' before the two great forces, that is, God and Man, Woman is symbolic, used by the Muslims and Brahmins for pleasure saking, as it has been absorbed from their way of behavior by quoting the three women of the B.A. Part – III, they are as idiot as Rambi, Saraswati and Sarada Kabir. They have no knowledge of the art of writings, but believe on 'rite and ritual' as their 'Religion'. Religion historical meaning ligion with the God in human form. Human form is also an 'ideology' of the 'good woman', but in terminological study, the term' reveals the same meaning as of *History* Hu+man, 'hu' means associated with God. A historian once said, a great man would be judged by three tests:

(1) Was he found to be of true mettle or spirit of the Nam in his lifestyle as an 'ideology' to discover the truth, as investigator or Khoji of the knowledge base society = Khalji Imperialism.

(2) Was, he great enough to rise above the standards of his age or John Miltan or John Keats. More than that of Shakespeare or Mecbett in art of writings; that clan or tribe became ruling agency of a 'State'.

(3) Did, he leave anything as permanent legacy to the world at large and As prophet says, "The world owes its orphanages to its various messanger, who was himself born an orphan". "Good all this", says Carlye about Prophet Muhammad. "The

> nature voice of humanity, of piety and equity, dwelling in the heart of this wild son of nature, speaks", that is the quality of a Dalit historian or a scholar.

Kashmiri Women, they mostly use to believe on 'rite and ritual' as 'blind faith' of the human history. Therefore, they are considered 'inferior race of the society', 'Purdha System' is still existing in the society as 'male dominated society', majority of them found in 'black robe'. Purdha, here, we mean, Ved, 'system' mean, 'the function of the body'. Study again, shows, that living temple of the God is body of the man itself as a 'residing house' to realize the 'truth', Mandir and Masjid are the concept of the 'infidal society'.

Crisis in Islamic Intellectual

In the study, it has been expressed by the various researchers like Irfan Habib, Satish Chander, at the end of the 20th century, there is cultural crisis in India on the basis of *"Kashmir Issue"*. As it has been narrated by A.G. Noorani 'the special status means 'princely' ideology' accorded to the 'state' of Jammu and Kashmir mentioned the article of 370 that this state or people use to live under a different set of 'Laws' while being part of the 'Indian Union'. Study again shows that A.G. Noorani is not well versed in 'Natural History' as writer proved 'Dalit History' as a 'Cosmic Law' of the 'human ideology' Moreover, he mentioned Debates, seminars, etc are not the solution of the *'Kashmir problem'*. (Article 370 A Constitutional History of Jammu and Kashmir, Oxford, 2011). It shows that how, we can form a "New Cashmir or Kashmir" and his ideology still found 'incomplete' with study of the 'cosmic' view of neglected sufi saint of Kashmir or Jammu region.

When, we prepared to investigate the truth as a 'New Religion' that is, 'Radha Soami' and Chamar as its philosophy which is a strong concept of Dalit History. *Nam* is an opposite force of the Man to control the ideology of various authors who has 'no idea' to express the identity as 'Natural History' as 'Surya' or *Chandrma*, both are common concept in universal ideology provide same concept and thinking in human growth. Differences have been created by *anti Dalit* thesis. Before the entering of analytical study, we need, number of books as a literary work of various authors, for example, A.G. Noorani, etc to enlarge the, present thesis as a 'modern concept' to ask the preliminary question to Harsh Dev. MLA Ramnagar, who you can became the Chief Minister of this 'state' without performing the duty in relationship with 'Gurukul theory' and the other agency of Kashmir, Ladakh, they, are unaware of the fact, why this state has given, a 'special status of Article 370' married. In 1918, the school was raised to middle standard and it received a grant of girls of Rs. 700. From the state. (*A School in Being in Kashmir*, p.22) Mr. Biscoe remarked, "The education of girls is progressing much faster than that of boys" (*Rock Shifting in Kashmir*, p. 19). By 1916, the girls were seen, "coming better than ever before and mothers actually eager about her learning". (Ibid), even Miss Fitze had to face opposition in the beginning 1914" after the closing of the First World War. There was a radical change in the 'Sudra Culture' when Miss Mallinson was appointed Principal (1922-61 A.D) in C.M.S. Girls School. Now, there is a great progress of the formal education, but Dalit concept is incomplete in their mind as we take the example of Hindi teacher Dr Dilshad Geelani HOD, University of Kashmir. They have, no exposer of the world fame as the other Dalit women of Habba Katoon and others.

Long after that incident, *'Dalit History'* came into existence, a composite dialogue of the society. No doubt 'Islamic Revolution' played a very significant role in the history of modern Kashmir on the pattern of Western Scholars, but there is lack of 'Quality Education', it is among Dalits Mis-Kawayh and Ibn – Khaldun, greatest luminaries of 'Arab history', 'a story of the lord', has been written by them and they used to believed in "Naturalism" as the story of ancient Dalits like Panini or Potlemy and called themselves for the "Interpretation" of the "Subject Matter" is important, Prof. Hanji and Sofi Sahid, who had no idea of formal education, left the association of the artificial historian, who worked on 'Inorganic chemistry' and exploited the 'Muslims of Kashmir'. In 1927, the women's welfare Trust came into being, when Miss Fitze started a girls school in 1912, the majority of the girls attending her school were Dalit Muslims and Hindus girls are taken away to go about after the age of 12, until they, because to frame a 'New constitution' as well as 'New History' or 'New Ideology'. Religion which we believe is the mirror of 'Naturalism', 'no caste' 'no class', only 'Human study' (*Vedic India*, pp. 131-133).

The marriage was performed in the presence of both the families Grewal and Gargotra tribe of Akhnoor. The bridgegroom (Dr. Raj Kumar Chamar (Dalit) took hold of the right hand of the bride (Shabnam Grewal of Kerala, now use to live at Delhi) for the last 26 years even more than that. In the repeating ideology from Brahminism (Molavism) to Dalit (untouchable), *Rig-vedic* study expresses:

> *"By they right hand for happiness as an idea of the Chamar thought I take thee,*
>
> *That thou may'st reach old age, the days of the University of Jammu with me, thy husband (Pati).*
>
> *Aryaman as Nam or Chamar, Bhaga (Kishmat), Savitar, Puramdhi, Gave thee to me to rule over home together" (X. 85.36).*

Here another hymus or part of hymus have been declared as war against anti Dalits with the stroke of pen, with the full of goodwill to the wife = Dr Shabnam Grewal.

> *Here now remain, nor ever part, but in Kashmir and Ladakh, we have the agent of the Nam History.*
>
> *Enjoy the whole expanse of life, not in Jammu or Kashmir, but also in the other part of the world.*
>
> *With grandson and son joyous sport, hockey, cycling, cricket, romance etc.*
>
> *Be glad in heart with your house (Sonyana Chako of Kashmir, Preeti a Ladakhi women).*

So rule and govern in they home as Jammu and Kashmir State, I over the husband's parents both; his brother *(Suchet Singh and Diyana Singh)* and his sisters, (Neelam and Rani) too, are subject likewise there to thee as compounder Ashwani Kumar Hans.

(Rig. Ved, x 85. 42. 46)

We have age old practices on this earth, widow as Pushaptata = unmarried

Objectives of the Dalit-History

To provide education and training of excellent quality in Drama, Play, Comedy, History and in English art of writings to maintain the balance of power between the two great forces, that is, East and West South and North is the spiritual concept in art of studying the Higher Education. The requirement for the formula of trifurcation is G-3' – OH, no other base can be substituted in this context as on ideology of the Dalit concept towards Ladakh and Union Territory'.

Concept of Gardens and Ornamental Plants: 'The sealed Nector' Biography of the Noble Prophet, based on Dalit-History as Kalma or 'Nam' has been drafted by Ar-Raheeq Al-makhtum, a school teacher and researcher scholar was born in the year 1912, in Husainbad, a village one mile deep into the North side of Mubarkpur (Azamgarh district in U.P.). Therefore, there is great difference between the Kashmir Muslim and U.P. Musilman. He is labourions and Kashmir Muslims has the ideology of Pahari Gujjar. He say, "All praise is due to Allah, the Rabb of all mankind, jim and all that exists". It shows, another is not normal man. He is "Mad Angle" of the modern concept of the 'Dalit-History'. Teachers are contributing a lot for the unity of the country, but the 'politicians' they are doing. It is similar story as "Charity begins at home".

Id Brings, no Joy for Riot-hit in U.P.

In camps, victims keep celebrations low key (Muzaffarnagar), Kandhia, no doubts, "hundred of devotes bow their heads in synchronous srhythm, 18 armed policemen do the rounds of the camp. At the strange 23 buffaloes are left fo graze. They will all be shortly sacrificed. The sign of Barid festivities are the pink and yellow ribbons wrapped around the animals horns. As the first buffalo is sacrificed, horrified kids hurry up to their mother". (*The times of India*, October 18, 2013, P.7). Here, we mean, to discuss the blind concept of the *'Muslim family'* about the word 'Sacrifice' is derived from the original Latin word *'Sacrificium'* means to sacrifice the 'living man' in the sacred theory of the 'spiritual Guru' with full devotion and with art of writings the nam-history as the identity. Who were the Shudras? How they became the fourth varna in the 'Indo-Aryan society' or 'Indo-Arabic' history with ideology of *'Pure thought'*. This book was written by Dr B.R. Ambedkar 'Inscribed to the memory of Mahatma Jotiba Pulli (1827-1890A.D). The greatest Shudra of modern India, who made the lower classes (menial staff) of the Hindus as well Muslims conscious of their slavery even certain 'Dalit Sikhs' of Punjab, Jat, Ramdasia, etc. to the higher classes or the feudal lords and who preached the "gospel of truth" in the history of mankind for the development of the idea as well as social-thinking in South India, so called social democracy was more vital than Independence from foreign rule, as domination shown by the Gandhian philosopher. Dr B.R. was the silence of the Indian society and was a mature scholar of the 20th century, with the privilege of the *'Reservation Ideology'* as an ideology of the sufi-saint', he dominated the 'world politics' s a dynamic writer as Nam or Chamar or Mahar of the period'.

The basic idea is that society moves back and forth between these two poles as *Qutab* and *Axis Power* known as apolonian vs. Dionysian:-

> Many aspects of 'Culture' in the formation of true philosophy. It is called a Truism in the interest of Dalit-History that those who do not remember the past, the construct the past-history with idea of a fellow-friend as wife and husband. It is our human experience that past and present is adialogue and interliniked between the two great forces *'Have'* and *'Have-not'*. Without wife there is 'no life'. In fact, 'Human civilisation' is an organic growth as *'Truth stands;* wherein the present grows on the roots of the past and provides a base for the development of the future (G.L. Grover, & S.L. Grover, *Modern Indian History*; Preface).

None of you has faith in spiritual sense among Muslims of U.P or Bihar or Kashmir or Pakistan, Bangladesh unless I am dearer to him that his father and his son and all mankind (Hadith) tradition the Quran says:-

> "And verily, you (O Muhammad) are on an exacted standard of character". (68.4). But today in the world politics, Muslims, have no believe on that particularly the 'Kashmir Muslims'. They have widely spread the idea of 'prostitution' on the 'issue of Kashmir'. Politics of what, what 'politics of the Nam' is the theme of the said book of Ar-Raheeq Al-Makhtum, [published in 2011-2012, New Delhi].

- Apollonian traits are *Rational, logical,* Self-controlled and ordered civilisation. *Apollo* was the god of the *sun, light, truth* and *medicine* for the idea of *soul* as living species as Dr Bachan Lal, an intellectual and Governor of this state.

Dionysus is the God of wine as drunkard chamar of the Dalit philosophy, insanity and *ecstasy* originated from the Greek work *ekstasis* or *archaic* transport, who carry the burden of society as a supreme ruler with idea of happiness' or CHAMAR. (Ancient Egyptian study of the scholar. Since many remain, they used to life there for the survival of Dalit race as 'Dalit Christian' of South India).

Hangling Gardens of Babylon

I. Constructed about 600 B.C. by Dalit king Nebuchdnezzar to please the home sick wife Pushap. Lata as a widow of the Nam-History.

II. It was one of the 'Seven wonders of the world, popular places for tourists as the story of 'seven years war fought in Europe as William Pitt was called in his own times the 'Great Commoner'. He was the son of the Cornish gentleman. He was educated at Eton and then at Trinity College. In 1735, he entered the Parliament and opposed the policies of Sir Robert Walpole. He also possessed a rare gift of oratary. The house of commons was under unlimited influence of William P.H. (1757-1761 A.D.). He was 'Heaven-born Minister' visited Bengal, Madras, Canada by see routes.

III. England France can be studied under three main heads: India, Bangladesh and Pakistan. They had the taxonomy culture of India as whole a sub-continent of Asia on the basis of moral history to visualize the ideas of Nam-History in the Deccan ill state of Kerala etc. First Phase (1746-48 A.D.) party of Duplix and others. Second phase (1748-1754 A.D) to check the war condition of Karnatica as a dispute between Anglo-French extent after the death of Nizam-ul-Mulk in 1748. Nasir Jung and his grandson (daughter son) Muzaffar Jung was challenged by Chanda Sahib, the son-in-law of a former Nawab. Lord live defeated Raju Sahib and became the king of the ruling agency of the 'Dalit-Family' of the Christian tribe. Third phase, seven year war brought to close by the treaty of Paris in 1763 in the favour of English ended with the military and political power (Third Karnatic war).

(A Simple History of England by four authors;)

Main features of the Dalit-History:

(a) The matter is based on '*Internation Research.*

(b) The art of writing is complicated and simple to understand and more effective for the natural historians.

(c) It is brief history of the untouchable race and difficult to understand for the normal man of the history.

(d) It is helping book for the future generation.

(e) It is based on rich experience of the author and the Sufi-Saint Scholars.

(f) Proper quotations from famous authorities have been given to up-date knowledge of the Kashmiri students as authentic history.

In the history of Jammu, or Jambudvipa we learn that there is big library which was established after the death of Dr B.R. Ambedkar known as Dhanwantari who produced, number of Dalit scholar KAS and IAS or IPS. The concept is originated from the Old French word progenie, as intellectual race of the 'human history'. Muslim means submit before the God, but here in Kashmir and its adjoining areas, people use prayer of the Allah with chanting the verses of the Holy Quran, but failed to settle their 'Kashmir Issue'. They became traditional society of this sub-continent and few of Dalits, Megh, Mahasha, Thakurs, Chamars, Gaddis, Shipps, became Satsangi. They have 'no religion' 'Religions base society' today in history proved as *'Infidal'*, as meat eater. 'Meat eater' is not found aggressive as that of vegetarian. Because he is proved more superior then the 'infidals'.

There is proverb: 'Knowledge is a Power'. There are some texts and scholars who believe that 'Dhanwantri, 'The pioneer God of medicine' as a supporting view of the first wife the author (Dr. Shabnam Grewal) and shifted to Delhi for the time being as well as for higher study, but failed in her mission and exploited by demons. Her survival, again, proved in the hands of a Dalit-historian (Dr. Raj Kumar). No doubt, she was the good teacher of History, but eater, he compiled her thesis on her own power (Shakti) and became (Sita) of the Lord. During the time of 'Gupta Age', power was shifted to Arabic country, and she became Fatima or Aysia. One time, she was also appear on Earth at Benaras, parallel to Ravidas. Legends make her re-appear as 'Devdasi' of the prince of Benaras (*Kasiraja*).

Sufism in Kashmir

Allister Lamb'z contention is interesting to understand the interpretation of 'History'. He notes the performa, related specially with British Indian Empire before 1947. As we known 'East Indian Company' came to India during the time of Shahjahan in 1600 A.D. They did work in India with 'ideology' of 'Ravidas' and 'Babur-Vani' as 'Dalit-Christian'. The last king of the Dalit history of Kashmir was Muhi-ud-Din Muhammad Auranzeb, the Puritam Emperor of India (1658-1707 A.D). The last Guru of the 'Human History' 'Guru Govind Singh Ji' as an ideology of the God, he left the Punjab and settled with Aurangzeb in Kashmir, during his long reign of 48 years. The description of Aurangzeb's journey to Kashmir is contained in a series of 'Nine Letters' to M. De Marveilles. Bernier writing as a whole, it is said they are of the 'Highest orders' in Sufi-Saint philosophy for the 'Changing of Empire'. They were Nami-Rulers of India or Dalits.

The politics of North India, did not allow them to survive. Therefore, British, they became powerful from the concept of '*History*', settled their colony in Bengal' and the division India on the basis of 'Princily and Nawab' of India, they became their 'guides' and *Sudras* were degraded. Thus, the feudal society of India could not face the 'Ideology' strong learner race. They were highly intellectual and responsible of the 'Home Govt:' they were not cheater as modern Muslims of Kashmir.

The Rishi travelled one night the air to India as Nam like Lord Clive, as mere clerk of the company became Lord of this country; and appeared in a terrible form mounted on a lion, as the Emperor lay sleep sir Walter Lawrence, in his study mentions: "Aurangzeb in his fear agreed to Rishi's retaining his title of Padshah (Raja or king or Nam), but the legend does not say that the Emperor relaxed from that time in his persecution of the Hindu". (*'Valley of Kashmir'*, p.195). Kalhana says, 'Hindus and Muslims' possess 'no History'.

The life of *Aurangzeb* was one long tragedy, the story of a man battling in vain against an invisible but in Exorable fate. And this tragedy in History was developed with all the regularity of a perfect drama" Sir J.N. Sarkar.

No doubt, an understanding was again, developed by the Britishers with North Indian rulers either, he was Ranjit Singh or Gulab-Singh. They had, no discrimination to each other, their concept was 'Sufi' or Dalit. While it is taken to be of 'Academic Interest' in art of writings the 'Dalit-History' only in some quarters – the signing of 'Instrument of Accession', who was Aurangzeb, he was a great Dalit scholar of Kashmir as that of Diwan Kirpa Ram, who wrote '*Gulab-Nama*' in Persian language and translate by the Brahmin scholar S.D.S Charak without knowing the concept of the 'historicity' of 'Natural Man', Gulab as a flower and it description is to regulate the new-hybrid with the idea of *Chamar* thought called himself as degraded Rajput of North India.

In the statement of Gulab Singh's later successor. "It is indeed an irony of sorts that contrary to the note in his letter, in art of writing to close the chapter of 'Princely state' we need a big country of democracy. Maharaja run away from Kashmir on the question of 'Plebiscite'. But modern politicians from Sheikh Abdullaha to Omar Abdullaha, they went to 'dirty games plan' as cheater of 'Nam-History'. Prophet called as Madhu-mantra theory (*'History of Chamar Dynastry'* p. 48).

No doubt, Kashmir Muslims and Pandit (Brahmins), they use to listen Sufian Kalam, but they could not became free-thinkers as were their forefathers. They had 'no religion' and not bound by the 'politics'. Today, we see that both Muslims and Hindus (particularly Brahmins) they are drunkard. 'Sufi concept' is concept of 'complete Ideology' or called 'fair' in historical study as mystics or pantheist: one who uses nothing in toxicating. (*Panjabi Dictionary*; p. 1072). The term is generally derived from *Ar.* Suf, 'wool', but it is probably a corruption of the Greek word 'Sophos' means 'Wise personality'. Now, wherestands, the ideology of various 'political parties of India', only backbiting the 'Dalit-King'.

The conclusion of this whole thesis or Naya Kashmir is drawn in the modern concept of conceptual learning in subject "chemistry" opposite to the History as a solution of the problem, has been already draft in the proceeding chapters of the rational approach with the partical of cultural concepts by the author himself by diagonising the anti-Dalit Muslims and Hindus like Professor Z. A. Hashmi and ex-principal of the GDC Doda S.P. Sharma. Both these communities, only believe on 'rite and ritual' as blind faith of the society as their leader like Susama Sawraj or Sonia Gandhi. Dalit-Samaj is found more active in historicity with the comparison of inactive research of the 'Manmat Society'.

It is important to realize that certain visible species like Baba Gurinder Singh Ji Biaswale is 'Supreme Being' in the ideology of Raj-Rishi, an ancient concept of the Sufian culture. These two are visible species proved in art of writing the history of "Dalit Culture". Culture is a concept of Truism or, that is, *'Glorious history of Dalits Past and Present'*. The programme of the Dalit literature is to light the innocent people who have been deprived from the 'Social right' from the 70 years of the independent. 'Quality education' is among Dalits, not among Brahmins of the Kuta and Juta. Therefore, it is come to our knowledge that college teacher is proving more efficient than the university teacher.

Now, there is a u-turn towards the Dalit History, after the downfall of Abdullaha family in the claiming leadership of Jammu, Kashmir and Ladakh State. Chief Minister as a new title should be appointed on the ideology of 'strong-idea'. 'Idea rules, money does not rule'. Author is a poor man of history writing, but having hard hit ideology.

4

Dalit Literature: Its Growth and Evaluation: A Critical Review

Caste based society is immobile. If a *Chamar* gets higher official position in the society he will be still known as *Chamar* in this society. He cannot fully adopt Brahmin's way of life. He can pretend to be a Brahmin only. He cannot perform spiritual and sacerdotal functions.. The majority will never regard him as a Brahmin even if he does.

There are several theories explaining the rise, growth and sustenance of caste system. *The Divine Plan theory*, *Racial Antipathy theory, Occupational or functional theory*, etc. exists still in our Indian Society. A "caste" is not, a class. Caste is something more than a class (60). The caste structure is not based on economy or wealth. Economy does not determine social ranking in caste system. It is the caste which determines individuals social position in the social hierarchy. The second aspect which distinguishes caste from class system is the ascriptive nature of the social status which the individual acquires and which could not be improved or changed. Dalits are members of the Scheduled Castes and Tribes, neo-Buddhists = Radha Soami Culture; the working people, the landless and poor peasants, women and all those who are being exploited politically, economically and in the name of religion.

Study to find out about anti-caste legislation in 52 villages in all 16 districts of Karnataka, 941 total respondents, 50 per cent being SCs (6-7). Awareness among SCs of lower rank is extremely low. Constitutional guarantee is unknown to 96 per cent of the respondents.

Untouchability (Offenses) Act is not; known to 86 per cent (16). Sources quoted by respondents include informal sources like social activists, social conflicts, and friends. Formal sources of communication are virtually out of reach.

Excepting in the case of political activities, in all the remaining areas of social interactions, untouchability is practiced as admitted by a vast majority of respondents. As high as 80 per cent say those hotels are still barred for them. Seventy-seven per cent say temples are barred for them and an equal number say they are not allowed to participate in religious processions. SCs are not allowed to take their processions in the caste Hindu areas = Gujrat Model.

Tank water is still a taboo, according to 68 per cent, similarly tap water is also not allowed (35). 70 per cent say no social mixing is allowed (with caste Hindus). This was particularly so in the case of women (with caste Hindu women).

The study shows that the practice of untouchability has not vanished completely, but it is declining. One-third of the respondents have reported that. The practice still continues in matter of water collection. The prevailing situation about water collection is indicative of a declining trend.

It could be said that there is no commensality in the sense it is understood but at the same time it cannot be denied that the traditional rigidity also does not exist. Discrimination in hotels and restaurants is generally not practiced.

There does exist discrimination of one kind or the other as far as entry of SCs into temples is concerned. The rural respondents have reported about discrimination of one kind or the other. Brahmins are not prepared to perform religious and ritual functions for SCs, In education, whatever discrimination still exists, it is confined to rural areas = Black-mailing. In market places discrimination appears to be vanishing. SCs are allowed to enter the shops. Rural respondents said that SCs would not be hired at caste Hindu shops. No discrimination exists in medical services. Barbers and tailors do make discrimination in rural areas. In terms of interactions, caste Hindus do not reciprocate invitations to dinner, visits during festivals, funerals, etc., to SC homes, especially in rural areas = still existing.

After the coming of the Aryans we have better linguistic and literary evidence, through it has to be cautiously analyzed. The Aryan advent cannot be simply understood as a conquest over equalitarian indigenous peoples who give rise to the caste system. Nevertheless, 'Aryans' and 'conquest' did play a role. The Indo-Europeans were a patrilineal people, in contrast to local matrilineal traditions, through their patriarchy, tribal and statistic gave certain freedom to women. Once, however they absorbed the notions of 'sacred power' and 'danger' associated with women and low castes in the Dravidian tradition, the resulting patriarchal synthesis in the context of group, conflict was far more complete and violent in the control of women = Sudra state of mind.

Similarly, the tribal or lineage inequalities that intensified among Vedic people as they spread throughout India were not really 'caste-like', but once they absorbed the 'protocaste' features among the indigenous culture and various groups fought for dominance of the system, a caste hierarchy developed. *Chaturvarnya* did not actually describe existing social groups, but was rather an ideology in Muslims community of Kashmir; overlaying the very different processes of transformation of 'proto-caste' tribal groups into jati. In this Brahmins played a key role-Brahmins who derived both ethnically and culturally from indigenous as well as Aryan priestly groups, but who identified with the Aryans as they sought to legitimize and extend the total system of dominance and exploitation associated with caste in a period of developing production, surpluses and economic inequalities.

With the period of the rise of the state in the Gangetic valley in the middle of the first millennium BC caste inequalities appear as more crystallised and began to get the stamp of legitimacy with the development of Brahmanic Hinduism, symbolised finally in the laws of *Manu*. In these, extreme forms of the subordination of women and Sudras were sanctioned, and Brahmins claimed superiority at the top of a hierarchy of purity-pollution and occupational specialisation = Jati-bad ke war.

The long interregnum of a thousand years between the emergence of the first states in the Gangetic valley and the consolidation of the Brahmanic-Hindu social order suggests that the identification of

'Indian' culture with 'Hinduism' is badly mistaken = Blind-Faith; that the dominance of Hinduism was not so easily achieved and perhaps riot inevitable, and that elements of revolt and opposition remained strong from the beginning.

In India, a few sociological studies have so far been produced on Harijans = Francis Abraham's study. Frequent references to SCs may be traces to over a period of a hundred years or more before Independence. However, as *Sachchidananda* puts it that it is only in the beginning of the Twentieth century that we got more detailed studies of Scheduled Castes in the form of Monographs. Some information about their way of life styles, habits and culture are sporadically recorded in Government official records. Some of the authors like Rdgar Thurston (1975), Briggs (1920), Shephen Fuchs (1949), Trivedi (1976), Vidyarthi (1977), etc. have recorded certain characteristic features on the social, economic, political and religious features of Harijans. After Independence, a few publication have been brought out mainly by sociologists like Lynch Owens (1969), Sachchidananda (1976), and Divine Yale school of thought, etc. Significant studies on the Mala are very few. Singh's book (1969) is noteworthy as the first of its in Indian which has made a detailed study of Madiga in the Telangana region (AP) (11). *Vidyarthi* and *Mishra* (1977) deal with Harijans from two zones in Bihar. Khan (1980) studies SCs in Bangalore district. Moffatt (1979) makes a detailed study of untouchables in a rural setting of Tamil Nadu. Desai (1973) studies untouchabiity in 69 rural villages of Gujarat, including among untouchables themselves.

M. S. Murthy (1971) is himself a Harijan. Trivedi (1976) deals with the immoral traffic in human flesh, undertaken in three regions: Bijapur, Raipur (MP) and Uttar Kashi (UP). C. Paravathamma (1984) gives some account of the frustration prevalent among the SCs in the post Independent India. She has discovered a big gulf between the SC politician, the educated, and the common man. Most of the educated Harijans get government jobs and are alienated from their own people. Viswanatham and Reddy (1985) have made an explorative attempt to find out the determinants of educational achievement among Scheduled Castes. Most specifically, they have examined whether or not there are class wise variations among them with respect to educational achievement. Their research study = New Report is based on the assumption that the SCs are no longer a homogeneous community common man Ke Approach; and that there are perceptive differences among them with respect to class, status and power, parental attitude and its perception as a valuable channel of upward social mobility, availability of tradition of education and the existence of education oriented subculture. D. Venkateswarlu (1990) makes a different study about the conflicts between the Harijans and the Upper castes = Mixed Caste. He observes that there is a new level of awareness and consciousness among them that has not only enhanced their aspirations and ambitions but also made them assertive. This is not tolerated = modern Rajput-Brahmin of Jammu region; by the socially and economically dominant among the caste Hindus. There, a situation of conflict develops when the Harijans wish to realize their aspirations or assert their rights which the dominant among caste Hindus do not concede. Such a conflict is treated at the psychological level and also at the manifest level. The various aspects of both levels of conflict are discussed in detail.

The *Malas* live on the out-skirts of the village in clusters of tiny cone-shaped and square-shaped thatched houses known as *Mala-wada*." These wadas have their own wells, pumpsets, and temples. They are not allowed to draw water from public wells in the villages = Kandi area of Jahhar Kotle, etc. Or to enter the main temples and worship along with other Hindu castes. People belonging to higher castes like the Brahmins, the Vaishyas and the Sudras do not accept cooked food or water from these people.

The *Malas* have four sub-castes: *Pokanati, Reddybhumula, Arwa* and *Savu Malas*. The four sub-castes do not pollute with one another by their physical touch. Many of the *Malas* practice uncle-niece and cross-cousin marriages (34). In some villages, the Tamil *Malas* cannot eat from the houses of Telugu Malas. But both groups draw water from the same well. Marriages are practised within the subdivision only. The researcher did not come across a single instance of inter-sub-caste marriage. The reason is the prevailing strong superiority and inferiority feelings between the divisions. Nowadays, all *Malas* sit and dine together in hotels but not in their homes.

Caste restrictions have different meanings for different economic and caste groups. The ideology that the poor, so-called 'lower' caste groups were 'polluting' to the rich, so-called 'upper' caste groups was used by the privileged sections in order to maintain the status quo, build private property within their group, to control the bodies of their females, exploit the poor further, etc. The ideology of pollution among lower caste groups were related to several factors: (1) differential power relations vis-a-vis the dominant 'upper' castes and the desire of vulnerable groups to maintain their precarious, always shifting status and position (however low) vis-a-vis other 'lower' castes. This implied the adoption of upper caste restrictions of eating and marriage to those within one sub-caste only; (2) given their perpetual poverty, the ideology of food taboos could have evolved out of an environmental necessity to conserve precious food resources to one's, family, and extended kin or sub-caste only. Economic sensibility of feasting only those who are superior in wealth and status and who may therefore benefit the host in some way rather than share one's very limited wealth and food with those whom one could benefit little from, the other poor low castes = Megh-Community + Barawalas.

Caste and class are viewed as the two most significant dimensions of social stratification. They are considered as closely interrelated, almost inseparable, basic processes of social life. It is one thing that caste is viewed as a sole model for analyzing Indian society or class is used for analyzing caste and power but it is quite different in real life as caste and class are not only highly differentiated internally, complexities of their expression and articulation signify the vast ramifications of structured social inequality = lack of formal education.

Debate on caste and class has covered wide-ranging issues related to indicators of status, levels of equality and inequality, cultural and structural interaction, occupational mobility, etc. Conceptual schemes to analyze these issues highlight structural versus attributional, and corporate versus individual dimensions regarding the nature of caste and class in India as systems of social stratification into Dalit-*Samaj*.

The caste-class divide was never as rigid as reported in various writings, and hence Indian society was also not as rigidly structured as depicted in several accounts of the, caste system: (1) The 'ideal' and 'actual' status was never the same. Inter-caste marriages produced 'mixed-castes' = *Dalits* into *Dalits* + *Mochi-Clan*.

Contradictions within the caste system and influence of external forces of change on it rule our possibility of it being homo hierarchicus. A long history of discontinuities, break downs, contradictions and changes in the nature of the caste system also negate its absolutist, unchanging and holistic nature.

Both inequality and equality have been built into the ideology and practice of the caste system, and change has taken place in both as well as in the nexus between the two.

Despite the priestly superiority of Brahmins over all other castes, the functionary lower castes enjoyed some 'ritual status,' = Mahasha Community certainly not comparable in any way with that of Brahmins. The status and the protection accorded to them by the caste panchayats enabled them to protest against the injustices meted out by the upper caste patrons. Hence, a critical re-examination of caste as a system of ideas and rituals, and class as a system of relations between the rich and poor may be necessary. The essays incorporated = W.E. Williams in this volume are largely addressed to this issue.

"Caste and Land in Colonial South India" by A. Nagaraia Naidu highlights that in the colonial period, in South India, the lower castes were Dalits and perceived the upper caste landlords as their enemy = Jagirdari-System of India; and not the British as the latter were not directly exploiting them (15-16). The upper castes, being the early beneficiaries of education, first entered into the British revenue administration and later became entrenched in politics. They were nominated to the legislative council representing the landed aristocracy. In such a situation 'freedom' for the country had hardly any meaning for the Dalits. In "Caste and Class in Rural Andhra: A Historical Perspective," A. Satyanarayana notes that there has been a gradual decline of the power and authority of the landed class as a whole; The *Zamindars* = Peasant Movement of India and Brahmins have lost their hegemonic authority since the late 1950s, when land reforms were introduced in the State of Andhra Pradesh. Consequent upon land reforms, a class of rural rich emerged from among the principal agricultural castes which in fact became a threat to the zamindars and Brahmins. Soon this 'new class' began to displace the traditional dominant castes/groups, and also received the support of a large number of people as its members belonged to the numerically preponderant castes.

Caste goes beyond the boundaries of kinship and family ties as it involves specialisation of labour/work on a wider corporate basis. In "The Formation of Caste Society in Kerela: Historical Antecedents," Rajan Gurukal traces the genesis of the caste system in Kerala and observes that the actual formation of castes took place in the temple-centred Brahmin villages having agrarian activities. Brahmins, landlords and temples played a crucial role in the multiplication of castes and sub-castes. The peculiar systems of land relations and service tenure were responsible for the creation of the system of hereditary occupational groups. The Brahminical ideal of 'ritual status' was instrumental in converting these groups into endogamous castes'. Ultimately, the society was stratified in terms of higher and lower groups based on the ritual status accorded to various castes/sub castes. Such a stratified society based on Brahmanical prescriptions had the tacit approval of the King (*ruler*) as it was in his interest too to appoint officials and secure professional services on a hereditary basis to ensure the stability of his rule. Caste- Class Situation in India" by A. B. Bardhan argues that a class of people has upheld the ideology of caste, and has kept it alive even in the most adverse of situations.

I. In "*Caste, Class and Social Consciousness*: *Reflections* on *Contemporary Indian Situation*," Javeed Alam looks at the constitution of social consciousness in contemporary India with regard to caste and class. Rapid shifts in the consciousness of the same very people ranging from democratic struggles to communal and sectarian fights have been observed. Alam considers class, caste and social consciousness as aspects of a totality, that is, the social being. These are being transformed via retarded capitalism.

A low class man may, by leading a virtuous life = Satsangi way of life, rise to the level of a higher class man and he should be ranked as such. In like manner a high class man can, by leading a sinful life; sink down to the level of a class lowers than his and should be considered as such. Thus, the qualifications, character and knowledge of a person determined the class of that individual. There are historical proofs of this class mobility. Sage Javal of an unknown class became a Brahmin

(*Chhandogya Upanishad*); Vishwamitra, Kashtriya by birth, became a Brahmin (*Mahabharata*); sage *Matang*, an *outcaste* by birth, became a Brahmin. Vashishta was born a prostitute, Vyasa of a fisherwoman and Parasra of a *Chandala* woman = *Amri Devi*.

II. *Origin of caste as ethnic* - 'Risley; Keane (1920) argued that *nasal* index corresponded to social status. However the correspondence of physical and social gradation in UP, noted by Ghurye (1969) has an important exception the *Chuhra or Bhangi* of Punjab. Both Ibbetson and Nesfield, the pioneers of the sociological study of caste, endorse the view that caste is mainly occupational in origin. Once caste replaced classes, the Hindu society showed a bias towards the upper three classes and prejudice towards the *Sudras* and increasing contempt for the *Untouchables*. Castes emerged sometime in post-Vedic period, 600 BC - 300 AD. Of all the features of the caste system, the most blatant has been that of purity and pollution. However, observance of the rules has shown regional variations, being stricter in south India than in the north; and inter-caste variations. Paraiyan, or the Tamil unapproachable, has given the word pariah to the English language. The more glaring example of social degradation like keeping away from upper castes 24 paces (in Tamil Nadu); dragging a thorny branch to wipe out his footprints (*Mahars* in Maratha country); restriction on umbrellas, and wearing of shoes (*Izhavas* and *Shanars* in Malabar), were not evident in the relatively tolerant Punjab or Delhi area. But even here, a Bhangi walking in the streets of the towns had to carry a broom and to shout "Bhangi, Bhangi" to warn unwary people about his polluting nearness.

Bhangis living in the most crowded parts of Delhi are physically segregated and socially completely isolated from fellow Indians. Each *basti* or *katra* is a residential unit popularly called *Mohalla*. It acts as a unit of organisation. Kinship terms are applied to the members of the *Mohalla*. It functions as an exogamous unit. Marriages within the immediate and adjacent *Mohallas* are not a desirable alternative. For a *shehri* (city) *Bhangi* to marry off his daughter into a non-shehri Bhangi household will be tantamount to loss of status. This is 'pratiloma' exogamy. The reverse (hypergamy) is acceptable. Dr Tripathy has effectively portrayed the fact that, without access to vital economic resources and bargaining power, the Harijans have become one of the most exploited peripheral groups in the Indian society. Predominantly rural, they have been mainly landless rural agricultural labourers, marginal share-croppers and farmers commonly indebted beyond redemption.

His study of contemporary India and Orissa shows that the Dalits have been kicked, raped and burnt, refused minimum wages, their properties have been destroyed and they have been killed. His study of village Jan and Kesharpur reveals that the Dalits are discriminated against with reference to living wage, share-cropping, money-lending, drawing water from public wells, entry into the temples, service of tea and snacks in the hotels, service in the grocery shops, services of the barber, waserman, cowherds man, priest, community feasts and marriage with caste Hindus. Numerical strength, better economic opportunities, urban contact, better communications, better exposure to mass-media, assistance from external leadership, stronger participation in the political process have helped the Harijans in Jan to have greater resort to protest political action against their socio-economic disabilities than Kesharpur.

Dalits in rural Orissa at Jari village (where *dalits* are a majority) and Kesharpur (where *dalits* are a minority) can provide an overview. However, he could have set the theoretical framework in terms of the debate on caste, class and power. He has taken the views of Beteille, Srinivas and Kothari. He could have taken the views of Gail Omvedt, Galanter. Shanshyam Shah, etc.

The Harijans or Dalits live in sub-human social existence, abject poverty, economic exploitation, a subculture of submission and political powerlessness. They have withstood the psycho-economic pressure of social conformity for centuries. They have degraded nature of working relations with the higher castes and they are involved in works like scavenging and sweeping. They are considered to be visited by a curse and are treated as *untouchables*. The *status quo* was maintained by sanctions and the Harijans were kept in a state of constant fear under a permanent threat of violence. During the Muslim rule, many of these untouchables and low caste people embraced Islam and joined the invaders partly to avoid prosecution, partly in search of freedom.

The 15 Harijan families in Kesharpur village constitute 12 per cent of the population. Two Harijan communities live here, such as: the *Hadies* and the *Dhobies*. 15 family heads were interviewed. *Dhobies* constitutes 20 per cent of the Harijan population. The *Dhobies* do not accept food and water from the *Hadies*. The Harijans in Kesharpur remain in abysmal poverty, illiteracy and ignorance. They are denied a living wage in the village and they remain semi-starved. Overwhelming majority of Harijans are landless agricultural labourers. Wages for agricultural labour remains low. The Harijans still depend on their traditional occupation. The caste Hindu employers do not touch them while making payment. Majority of the Harijans make loans from consumption needs. The *Hadi* Harijans do not get loan from the village common-fund. They pay exorbitant rates of interest to the moneylenders = Mahajan Baradari of Jammu region.

They bring their drinking water from the tubewell of their own street. An overwhelming majority of Harijans are prohibited drinking water from the public wells and public tubewells in caste Hindu streets. The tea shopkeeper does not give drinks and snacks to the Harijans in the cups used by caste Hindus. The Harijans do not get the services of the barber, the washerman, the cowherdsman and the priest in the village = "*Raj-Rishi Ke Sabita*". They are not allowed to inter-dine with caste Hindus. They are not allowed to enter temples. Caste Hindus do not marry Harijans. Their participation in elections is passive. The small number, poverty and fear discourage them to contest elections. There is no Harijan elites in the village.

In *Jari* village, 500 families constitute more than 50 per cent of the population. 50 family heads were interviewed. Harijan communities like the Go*kha*, the *Kandara*, the *Pano*, the Dhobi live in this village. Harijans remain in abject poverty and illiteracy. They are denied a living wage and they remain semi-starved. An overwhelming majority of the Harijans are agricultural labourers. The female Harijans are paid much less than the Harijan male labourers. The harijans pull rickshaws, trolleys and do small business being financed by banks under different government welfare schemes. A few depend on their traditional occupations = they need more economic assistance.

Harijans are discriminated against in their share in share-cropping and in case of money lending. Majority are prohibited to draw drinking water from the village public wells and tubewells. They do not get the services of the barber, washerman, cow herdsman, and the priest in the village. They are not allowed to worship in village *temples = manmat*. They are discriminated in the tea-shops and grocery shops. Harijans do not enjoy equal status in village community feasts and the caste Hindus do not marry them. Their participation in politics is active. They contest village elections and *panchayat* elections. They attend political meetings. They vote for Congress because they get some economic benefits. The party has helped the Harijans to get benefits from the welfare schemes of the government. Between the *Malas* and *Madigas*, there is a constant conflict over their respective status in relation to the other though both are *untouchables* to the caste Hindus. But the caste Hindus seem to grant the *Malas* higher status rather than to the adjgs. Subba Reddy has listed certain activities which are exclusively assigned to the *Mala* and the *Madiga* castes. These are: (1) the office of the village servant and this entails manual assistance to the village officers, i.e., the *Karnam* (revenue official) and the *Munsif* (police Patel); (2) disposal of the dead village cattle; (3) digging of grave and two important tasks of capturing sacrificial animal and cutting its neck during the festival of the village goddess. These duties in certain districts fall to the *Mala* and elsewhere to the *Madiga*, and there is no fixed rule. Both the *Malas* and *Madigas* work as agricultural labourers. *Mala* provide additional hands whenever required for by the non-Brahman higher castes, for example, carrying a Reddy landlord's luggage from a nearby bus-stop to the village or the other way. *Madigas*, are traditionally leather-workers Chamar Community. They tan the skin and make leather articles like foot-wear for villagers = still found in Gumat area of Jammu, for which they are paid in cash or kind. They are also the carrion-disposers and during the festival occasions like marriage and ceremonies in honour of the village deity, they serve as drum- beaters and sacrificers of the sacrificial animals = Chamar thought.

The Hindu gods, Rama, Krishna, Venkateswara, Lakkshmi, etc., are also worshipped by the *Malas* and *Madigas* at their homes. They are not allowed to enter village temples, nor are they allowed to build their own temples for these gods and goddesses in their localities. They can only build temples for their own caste deities. The village watchmen are generally the *Malas* = Megh Baradari.

Lack of real sincerity and commitment at the political level, incompetence inefficiency, red-tapism and worst of all these evils, corruption in the bureaucracy looms large over even in post-colonial India, apathy and indifference. Even SC employees working in the office of the Director of Social Welfare at Hyderabad also behave the same way as their non-SC colleagues behave towards their SC brethern. Another evil is interference by political leaders like MLAs, MLCs from SC groups throwing their weight and influence to obtain benefits to their supporters or followers, be it scholarships, land, or house-site allotment, loans, housing grants, thus sometimes really depriving the merited and deserving among the SC students of their due privileges and benefits = Post metric scholarship.

While these kinds of things happen at the origin of the benefits, the State headquarters, many malpractices are evident at the distribution level in districts. Most of the teachers in schools, as some SC students complained to this researcher, have nothing but apathy towards their SC students. Thus the SC students suffer discrimination not only from their non-SC classmates but also from their non SC teachers, the imparters of learning. Some students also reported that their headmasters cheat those who have been granted scholarships and their parents by paying them lesser amounts. The illiterate parents often have no idea of what amounts they impress their thumb-prints for. Thus 25 per cent to 40 per cent of the scholarships amount in each case is pocketed by the corrupt headmasters who obviously have the clandestine approval of or act under pressures from district authorities through whom they get the sanctions. This happens even in colleges and universities where the dishonest administrative officials have got to be bribed by the recipients to hasten payments to them without being unduly delayed.

While the political elite of the SCs and the government knows these behind-the-screen malpractices and grave corruption, they look like silent spectators. If any complaint is made to the authorities about a malpractice, say in a village school, the government requires the complainant to furnish a concrete proof for necessary action to be taken. Can we expect an illiterate, poor, agricultural SC labourer to do this? Does the government know not his helplessness in this regard? Unfortunately, even the SC political leaders often tend to sit quiet witnessing all this because they fear political repercussions from the dominant, powerful caste Hindu section in the society. Conflict is also possible in harmonic system lie India if non-traditional values like modernisation, politicisation, special privileges and safeguards impinge upon the traditional values. The conflict between the Harijans and the Upper Caste Hindus started erupting because of discontentment, dissatisfaction among the Harijans with their past status and disabilities, and frustration in their attempts to improve the status and conditions in the traditional set-up through the means of individual efforts or group efforts through Sanskritisation process = Brahmin-bad of the Indus Valley.

The upper caste try to thwart their progress, the result is conflict between the Upper Caste Hindus and the Harijans. This conflict is "growing and open" contrary to what Beteille said. It is further in the nature of a class conflict rather than just a caste conflict as the few studies on Harijan-caste Hindu/upper caste conflict seek to project = Dr B.R. Ambedkar is thought.

Untouchable is the word used by Ambedkar for those castes lowest in the Hindu scale of pollution. It first appeared in print in 1909. However, the word had now disappeared from ordinary parlance following widespread education and the '*Constitutional Provisions*'. The early Government term was "*Depressed Classes*"; this was replaced by "*Scheduled Castes*" in the Government of India Act of 1935 when these castes were placed on a schedule as qualifying for special rights. Gandhi's name for the Dalits, Harijan, dates from his 1933-34 campaign against untouchability, and is in general usage among Ambedkar's followers. All those who have converted to Buddhism use the term Buddhist and reject all other nomenclature, including their original caste names. Dalit, or downtrodden, has become the most acceptable term in the 1980s.

Varna is the traditional fourfold caste system, consisting of Brahmins (the priestly caste). *Kshatriyas* (the warrior caste), *Vaishyas* (the trading caste), all twice-born and allowed to read the Vedas, and the rest of mankind; *Shudras* (the servile caste). Individual Indian castes probably number in the *tens* of thousands, and. are generally placed in one or another of the *Varnas*. *Dalit* is more a self-conscious group rather than a traditional caste. There are many different hereditary Dalit castes and subcastes. *Bhangi* is a large scavenging caste of the North; *Chamars*, *Madiga, Mahar* of South India.

Any work on the *Dälit* work is a welcome addition to the all too sparse literature, by traditionally disadvantaged low-caste Indian minorities, or *dalits* (literally, Poor and downtrodden) as they prefer to call themselves. It offers an unusual glimpse into the writings produced by *Untouchables* on their own behalf. Particularly noteworthy is the fact that many of the selections are either being published in English for the first time or have not been circulated beyond the *dalit* community. The wider dissemination of this literature serves two purposes; it affords Western scholars otherwise inaccessible source materials, and it generates attention for the *dalit* liberation movement. *Dalits* no longer respond to discrimination and repression with passivity; rather, by a variety of means. They are organizing and uniting to oppose it. The central purpose of the book is to represent the *Dalit* opposition to the Indian social system through the voices of its active and articulate leaders.

Throughout, there is abundant use of poetry and literature that translates into human terms the more objective and detached treatments of the *dalits*' condition. This shows the personal dimension of untouchability and the extent to which a self-conscious *dalit* elite dedicated to the task of forging a new, autonomous culture has developed. The collection does not address the issue of social cleavages, both traditional ones and those stemming from protective discrimination policies that have developed among *dalit* communities.

Moreover the larger questions of growing class stratification among *dalits* and its relation to reservations, as well as the reluctant effects on the *dalit* political movement are not treated. Joshi's anthology remains, however, a fascinating and valuable contribution on an elusive subject and should be of interest both to area-study specialists and to social scientists concerned with the process of cultural and political change among traditionally disadvantaged minorities.

The movement called *Bandaya* appeared more than two decades ago (in 1970s) in *Kanriada* literature. It has often commented over that "*Bandaya literature*" is nothing more than a spontaneous outburst of the pain and currents of strong feelings of the forlorn and the downtrodden and much less could be spoken about the variety and life in this literature. The pulsating and in-depth feelings and expressions of the *Bandaya writers* are to be taken into account more seriously as the experiences given out in their writings are of first hand and genuinely original in nature. There is also *Dalit* literature comprising of writings of the people who have emerged odt of *Dalit* ("untouchable") communities and the masses suffering from indignities and social insecurity in the society and raises a voice of rebellion against any sort of exploitation.

There is a satisfactorily rich quantum of *Bandaya Literature in Kannada* created during the last decade. Chandrashekhar Patil, Dr Siddalingayya, Baragur Ramachandrappa's poems were published under the title *NettaralliNeneda Hoovu* (1991), his novels *Bharata Nagari* and *Benki* both published in 1984, a critical essay on the literature of revolt titled Bandaya Sahitya Meemams, a collection of short stories titled Bayalaatada Bheenianna (1985), H.S. Shivaprakash published significant collection of poems in Malehidda Nadalli (1991), and Anukshna Charite (1991), plays Sultan Tippu (1986), Maliachaitra (1990), Maranayakana Drishtanta (1991) and Manteswamy; *Katha Pasanga*; *Devanoor Mahadeva*, D.R. Nagaraj wrote a critical essay titled *Amrita Mattu Garuda*; Boluvaraa Mohmed Kunha short story Devarugal Rajyada lei; Kum. Veerabhadrapa' novel *Aasthi* (1984), collection of short stories *Doma Mattitara Kathegalua* (1985); Dr Besagarahalli Ramanna, Ramzan Darga, Aravinda Malagitti novel *Karya* (1990), B. T. Lalita Nayak, Sarah Abubakar's novel *Kadanavirama* (1989), K. S. Bhagavan, Purushottama Bilimale, Sukanya Maruti, Muktayakka, Pratibha, Dr Channanna Walikar, Basavaraja Sabarada, Vijaya Dabbe. Allarna Prabhu Betdur, Bhanu Mustak and Shankar Katagi are among the active protagonists of the movement = Dalit Literature.

Primarily the aim of Dalit Literature was to highlight the disabilities and difficulties together with atrocities and inhuman treatment meted out to *Dalits*. The main object was to produce social awakening among the downtrodden. Dr Ambedkar fully realised the importance and utility of the Press. So he started a newspaper under the title of *Mook Nayak* (Leader of the Dumb), on January 31, 1920. After a period of six years, on April 3, 1927, Bahiskrit Bharat (Untouchable Bharat), another fortnightly Marathi Journal was published by Dr Ambedkar. Later on, "*Samata*,""*Janata*," and "*Prabudh Bharat*" were published by Dr Ambedkar from Bombay. In reality ordinary women still faithfully put their trust in all the rites and rituals, and they worship traditional gods and goddesses. There is no difference whether they are Hindu, converted Buddhist, Christian, Muslim or Sikhs, etc. They are completely confused. Actually the *Dalit* women are not to blame = class-struggle theory.

Once Dr Ambedkar advised his followers in a seminar if you want to educate your children, first educate women. It is the duty if a true Ambedkarite that they must educate and provide all facilities to the women, if they are honestly anxious to fulfill the desires of Dr Ambedkar. Venubhai Bhatkur and Rangubai Shubhakar, both were poetess and singer born in Maharashtra. Prominent among other names were Jaibai Chaudhany, Tulsibai Bansode, etc. Muktabai Sarrgore, Kausalya Baisantri, Meenakshi Moon, Vimal Thorat, Sulekha Kumbhare, Meera Kishore, Kusum Meghwal, Rajni, Susgatta, etc., are working as writers, poets.

Dalitness is essentially a means towards achieving a sense of cultural identity. The inferiority complex based on "to be Dalit" has now disappeared. Now *Dalitness* is a source of confrontation. This change has its essence in the desire for justice for all mankind. *Dalitness* is a matter of appreciating the potential of one's total being. Thus individual, culture, social burden and Dalitness cannot be isolated = Name or Word. For this new Dalit individual, social and cultural freedom has come because of his self-elevation and self- identification = Chamar History. Today's Dalit literature rejects the degraded Hindu social set-up. Dalit writers relentlessly expose the inhumanities and prejudices of caste society and instill a new social and cultural consciousness = True followers of the Radha Soami Faith.

Very few non-Dalit writers have written on and about the life of Dalits, and most of these wrote out of mere sympathy. Mere sympathy does not produce revolutionary literature. In non-Dalit plays the image of the Dalit and the interpretation of his life are distorted = Manmat Ka view. Needless to say the leading Marathi playrights have projected a Dalit image of weakness and folly in their plays.

An important aspect of Dalit literature is self-criticism or self-protest = Rising power of the Raj-Rishi Sabita. They do not hesitate to attack inferiority and superiority complexes among themselves. Regardless of the particular writer or literary form, Dalit literature is ultimately, a declaration of independence. It is impossible to understand the revolutionary quality of Dalit literature without understanthng the people to whom it is addressed. It speaks for them and to them. The impact of the conversion is constantly revealed in Dalit poetry; in short stories, novels and plays. A new Dalit poet, Harish Bansode says:

We have begun a new life,
We have found our own temples
Regained our lost faith
All are equal here.

The potential contribution from Dalit women (Dr. Shabnam Grewal) writers to Dalit literature is significant. From the onset, the writings of Dalit women reflected self-experience and burning indignation. *Muktabai*, an Untouchable girl who read her essay on the problems and sufferings of Untouchables in the school established by the great reformer *Jotibai Phule*, in 1852, was the first example. After a period of a century or more Dalit women have awakened and are again giving literary expression to their deep feelings. Kamud Pawade, Jyoti Lanjewar, Urmila Pawar, Hira Bansode, Sugandha Shende, Surekhad Bhagat, Asha Thorat, Aruna Lokhand, Susheela Mool and Meena Gajbhiye are examples from Maharashtra.

Kamud Pawade is by profession a lecturer in Sanskrit once considered a language of the God that the lower castes were not allowed to learn or even to hear. But the times have changed and a Dalit woman teaches Sanskrit to students from the higher castes. Mrs. Pawade has published several articles on culture, social education and women's problems. She already has a book, *Antahspho* (*'Inner Burst*), to her credit. The writings of Mrs. Aruna Lokhande, Mrs. Asha Thorat and Sugandha Shende are impressive and self-discipline. Atrocities on Dalit women, the problems of non-educated women and the ugly outlook of educated and advanced Dalit women towards non- educated women are some of the subjects of their writings. Mrs. Thorat also has been doing research on Dalit folk literature = Mahar Folk of Maharashtra.

The Dalit woman is a Dalit amongst Dalits. She has sufferced much and she is still suffering. She must walk through the burning desert of casteism in search of some oasis. Mrs. Bansode says it is due to casteism that Dalit women are being dishonoured and moested. In one poem she lodges a complaint in the people's court hoping for justice, but at last she attacks the inhumane game of the oppressors:

This complaint of mine

Is against the orthodox culture

Which has imprisoned us in a seated room,

Which has given us the charity of life completely boycotted?

Where the wind treats us as strangers,

Where the monsoons give us only famines

Where the water plays with us

The most inhumane game of mirage.

We are rejecting this

Unclean and poisonous life.

And to escape from these cruel curses

Will you give me

A bright and auspicious moon?

My countrymen, to your court

I have brought a complaint.

Will you give me justice?

(Translated by N. G. Bhavar)

Like the American movements, the Dalit Panthers and the Dalit School of literature represent a new level of pride, militance and sophisticated creativity. The history of *Dalit-Sahitya* = Kala Literature (the literature of the oppressed) movement and its themes is more profoundly a part of the Mahar movement and the Buddhist revival. The 1969 Diwali issue of Marathwada published from Aurangabad. This popular and widely circulated issue devoted a large part of its Diwali issue to Dalit literature which meant that Dalit literature had arrived on the Marathi literary scene. *Asmitadarsh* (mirror of identity) is the chief organ of Dalit literature. The *Times Weekly Supplement* of 25th November 1973 (Bombay) had a review of Dalit literature.

Throughout the period of pandit poetry following the Bhakti Movements and during the British period in Maharashtra, 1818-1947, the field of literature was dominated by the literate Brahman. Ambedkar's stress was not only on equality in religion and power in political but also an education and cultural creativity. Most of the creativity rook the form of material for the movement-*jalsa* (a singing-message performance), songs, poems, polemics, dozens of newspapers and although nothing that was considered literature by the literary establishment appeared, a regard for literature, the habit of writing, and a host of educated young people were well established by the time of the Buddhist conversion in 1956, The *dalit* writers began their serious work in the 1950s. Although most of the writers have come out of the Buddhist movement, one of the earliest, *Annabhau Sathe*, who belonged to the Untouchable *Mang* caste, was deeply influenced by Communism. In the sixties, the flow of Dalit literary writing increased in the form of short stories, novels and drama. Conferences were held almost every year. In the 1970s, individual volumes of poetry began to publish by the Maharashtra Buddhist Literature Committee, Asmitadarsh Press, or the Marxist Magova Press. Dalit Sahitya has changed the face of Marathi literature and inspired similar literary creativity in Gujarat and Karnataka. There is now serious and important fiction and poetry in Kannada and Oujarati. In Maharashtra, there has been a stead stream of pioneering autobiographies from Mahars, Buddhists. Chambhars, "Dc- notified tribes", and other Dalits.

Dalit writers are extremely interested in Black American literature and see their own movement as a parallel phenomenon. The chief influence is as support as proof that a group similar to the Dalit can become militant, creative and progress in a hostile society.

Mina Gajbhiye, a very young woman, is so far the only feminine poet regarded in the new Dalit school. Dalit women in Bombay organised the Dalit Stri Sameadini (Dalit Women's Dialogue) in 1986, probably the first women's literary conference in Maharashtra. In the past three years, two barely educated women, Bebi Kamble and Shantabai Kamble, have published their life stories. Women's poetry is also becoming important, and there are now, at least, six or seven published Dalit women poets = Didda, Anglekh, Sughanda, Suryamit, etc. as Dalit Parivar.

Another dimension of "*Untouchable*" cultural activity is encountered in the new research on the songs and epics of the *Untouchables* themselves, a genre well represented by the "crying songs" of an Untouchable caste described for the first time in a recent article by Egnor (1986). Even though it is the "*Mang caste*" which is most often described as "village musician" in the Gazetteers, Mahars seem to have been the chief musicians and actors in *tamasha*, the folk drama of Maharashtra from the sixteenth century onwards. However, the low status of *tamasha* women countered an image of progress, so the village drama was frowned upon by Ambedkar = North India Ke Story.

The social construction of poor Dalit women along patriarchal, middle class norms which had a negative impact upon women's cultural expression, status = Maduri Dixit Ki Filam Sajjan, etc.; and the urban bias of the Dalit elite in terms of what they promoted as representative of Dalit culture, knowledge, traditions, etc. This led to further marginalisation of the poor, rural Dalits and women = anti-Dalit Samaj of Kashmir.

Other Dalit groups have claims to cultural achievement. Many of the Bhangi caste call themselves "Valmiki" tracing their lineage to the author of the *Ramayana*. *The Dalit Voice*, an English weekly from Bangalore, claims from time to time that *Devadasi* culture, which includes the classical dance from Bharata Natyam, is a Dalit form of creativity. The June 1986 issue of Religion and Society (Bangalore) is devoted to Dalit culture, Hindu as well as Christian = Zain-ul-Abidin Ke Kisay.

There are more than forty Dalit theatre groups. Theatre called '*Dalit Rangabhumi*' shall spread from Pune to a number of cities in the state and to Delhi. Many write their own plays, a few adapt plays from the American Black theatre, some revive the arts of tamasha. A Dalit art exhibition was held in Nagpur in 1979 and an all-India art conference as called in Hyderabad in 1987.

Social Mobility has been assumed in the context of one block of central Bihar as an independent cluster or a set of variables gradually leading towards political participation. In the context of scheduled castes, "political participation" has been treated as a dependent variable. It is proposed that where there is greater social mobility there will be greater political participation which would lead to share in political power. Similarly, lesser social mobility would result in lesser political participation. In the absence of greater political participation, nothing can be said about social mobility = Computer Age.

Education can be considered as responsible for the removal of ignorance and opening avenues of new life styles. Occupation can enhance their social status from *jajmani* to contractual status system. From this point of view, education will be studied not only on the basis of age, caste, occupation, or sex of the respondents (200 male SCs), but the inter-generational difference pertaining to educational attainments found between them and their fathers, sons and daughters, and brothers and sisters would also be traced out. Similarly, a comparative study of occupation of respondents and of their fathers and sons and daughters would enable the investigator to find out actual quantum of occupational mobility, if any. Education has a wider scope of its impact than occupation.

Besides them, under the concept of inter-generational mobility, the study would take into account the perceptions and expectations of the respondents pertaining to their changed social status, particularly in view of their own caste fellows and other similar communities, such as backward classes. It would give an idea of inner- generational mobility, leading ultimately to caste mobility. The latter is the ultimate goal of the Scheduled Caste communities which consider it as the gateway of a lifestyle available to the members of upper caste communities.

An access to education itself may also be determined by the existing economic conditions of the individual, and of the society. But educational opportunities can come independent from other sources also. Such as State or government, voluntary agencies, missionaries, etc. Under such circumstances, linkage of education with economic conditions may not be so essential. This is what is happening in India, particularly in case of people belonging to SC and ST. The state is trying to educate the people in a generous manner. In certain cases, education may prove dysfunctional also. After getting education, a SC student may find himself in conflict with members of his family or community whose ways of thinking can run counter to his own. As a changed person, he may find it difficult to adjust himself in rural areas, where the opportunity of living and employment commensurate with his education will not be available. As a result of migration to urban areas, he may be able to change his social position in the society. Single females may find it more difficult to migrate to towns and cities in search of suitable employment while married females are limited to their husbands' choice of residence, etc = Falak Madam.

For the purpose of empirical study, education has to be divided at two levels: (i) professional and (ii) general. General education, obviously, includes non-professional and non-technical education. In the present context the SCs are directly related with this form of education. Here, education means literacy. However, it includes, from simple literacy to higher education = Nam-History.

The same cannot be applied to girls who remain unable to continue their studies. Thus, it can be concluded that the coming generation would be attending the school in larger number and acquiring higher education. In the case of girls, most of the parents do not send their daughters to school. They have a feeling that if the girls are educated, they would have to look after household works. They were 3 per cent total school-going children = Nawaz-Sharif Ke Soach. Looking at respondents first child's education, there are only 34 children who never went to school. It is because of the fact that they are the first child of the respondents. The first child, instead of being sent to school, is sent to the field.

Asking about the educational aspiration of the respondents for their sons and daughters, most said they like to give education as long as their male children want. Some illiterate respondents do not want to educate their sons, some would like to give education up to metric, others up to B .A. On the whole, almost all the respondents would wish to see their sons reach an educational standard higher than their own.

Only educated SCs like to send their daughters to the school or college, that too, for a limited period. Few among the respondents with education unto the matric level, want their daughters to have education higher than their own, and small per centage wishes to see them *at par* with their own. Illiterate do not like that their daughters should reach above matric. Only a few desire daughter's education higher than their own. On the whole, the data indicate that there is a big gap between the respondents' level of aspiration regarding the education of their .daughters and the education of their sons. Girls remain unable to continue their studies on account of tradition taboo and conservative outlook. As far as 126 daughters out of 200 are kept below Middle level, more than 188 wives of 200 respondents are illiterate. Mental level of wives and their daughters remains sociologically closer to each other.

Still more important was the emergence of the possibility of the Depressed Classes acquiring education. As a matter of fact; education has been one of the chief factors making for the improvement of the Depressed Classes position. The biggest initial effort to spread education among the Depressed Classes came from the Christian missionaries but later on the government also played its part in making it available to them. Though the oriental system of education was supplanted by the occidental learning in 1835, the fruit of the new educational system had not reached the Depressed Classes before 1854 when liberal grants-in-aid were begun to Christian missionaries for imparting education to the lower classes. The new system of education was "less-religious" in approach and its emphasis on "equalitarianism" challenged the institution of untouchability = Raj-Rishi Ke Story.

In 1865, under pressure of Christian Opinion, government had to lay down the principle that the government schools would be open to all classes. Also in view of the acute poverty of the Depressed Classes the governments in most provinces increased 'grant-in-aid' for the education of a pupil from the "*Depressed Classes*" which was more than the grant towards the education of a pupil from the rest of society (Philips, G.E. 1918. *The Outcastes*: Hope or Work among the Depressed Classes in India. London, p. 26). Theoretically, from now onwards the government schools were open to all but hostile public opinion gave the law and administration no moral support. In addition to imparting education among the Depressed Classes; the Christian missionaries helped to uplift them, directly or indirectly, in numerous other ways.

Spurred by evangelical zeal, missionaries highlighted the evil of untouchability and succeeded in converting a large number of untouchables to Christianity. The conerts acquired a new dignity and instead of being dirty, dishonest, drunken and immoral, this persona became, to some extent, worthy members of society. They acquired a new conception of human dignity and of their own worth as men. At the same time the Christian missions = Radha soami Centre Dera Bias developed practical programmes of the Depressed Classes uplift, e.g., land colonies were founded where they could develop on their own lines away from old associations. The missions did not confine their helpful activities of their converts; many non- Christian members of the Depressed Classes were indebted to missionaries for inspiration and practical help. Equally important was the missionaries' criticism of the institution of untouchability which resulted in a reinterpretation of Hinduism at both the ideological and institutional levels producing a changed attitude among the Hindu elite towards caste and untouchability.

The Courts of Justice established by the British throughout the territory of India and secularisation of the legal system. Though ,it is true that separate codes determined the personal laws of the separate communities, yet there was complete uniformity in regard to the laws concerning the protection of person and property and other aspects of the daily lives of the people. Exclusive caste practices did not have approval of the Judiciary in regard to public facilities such as schools, wells and roads. Indeed the legal system made no distinction on the basis of caste, nor did it provide for any special consideration to a caste like Brahmin which was excluded from capital punishment under Hindu kingdoms. Conversely, it brought into existence institutions which were not governed by the traditional norms of neither caste society nor run by the caste Hindus. As such they provided the alternative structure of authority to which members of Depressed Classes could turn for help and relief from the oppression of the traditional society. Positively, the abolition of slavery in 1843 which cut the legal knot binding the serfs and slaves, generally from the caste Hindus, went a long way in ameliorating the conditions of the Depressed Classes. Mention may also be made of the reform Act XXI of 1850 entitling Christian converts the right to inherit their ancestral property.

The combination of these factors produced an atmosphere which if not checked, could destroy the traditional pattern of society which had justified persecution of the Depressed Classes. But Brahmins as the traditional guardians of Hindu culture fully understood the threat posted to Hindu religion and their own privileged position by the expansion of British influence. They had many a complaints against the governmental encroachments on the sacred domain of caste and other prejudices. The spread of education, systematic policy of Christianizing the Depressed Classes and the legal protection afforded to converts produced a serious Brahmanic reaction in the country. "Government was alleged to have violated the sanctity of caste by bringing the highest and lowest castes, together in schools, in the ranks of Army and in the Railway carriages" (Chattopadhaya, Harprasad, 1957. "The *Sepoy Mutiny and the Hindu-Muslim Unity*" in Calcutta Review, vol. 142, March, p. 298).

Therefore, the Brahmins along with other disgruntled elements began instigating soldiers and the common populace to revolt against the Britishers, resulting in the 'Sepoy Mutiny' in 1857. Indeed, the Sepoy Mutiny or the '*First War of National Independence*' as it has been called by nationalist historians, was the last desperate effort of the Brahmins to defend themselves against the forces of modernity (28). Emperor Bahadur Shah Zafar symbolic leader of mutiny, in his proclamation assured the "Pundits and Fakirs"-guardians of the Hindu and Islamic religions respectively that the motive behind the war against the English on account of religion "was the restoration of traditional values." The killing of cows was completely banned in Delhi during the revolt. The act was reminiscent of the Peshwa rule in Western India where the untouchables were forced to tie brooms in the waist so that the Brahmins were saved from walking over the foot-prints of the Depressed Classes.

The mutiny was suppressed by the British with a heavy hand but the consequent changes in the policy of the New Government were disastrous for the cause of the Depressed Classes. Under the, pressure of the Christian missions and advanced public opinion, the government in 1859 had provided for partial breast cloth for the women of the Depressed Classes in South and ordered for the establishment of Separate Schools for the Depressed Classes' students wherever they found it difficult to secure admission in ordinary schools. Yet, after 1957, the British became extremely cautious about taking any action that might give offence to religious susceptibilities. From that time onward instead of leading advanced public opinion in India the British 'administration tended to act as a brake on it. The government refused to listen to the demands of the missionaries to protect the Depressed Classes. In the educational field, through the grants to mission schools continued, the government slowly disinterested itself from the intimate connection. Moreover, theories of liaises-faire and the determination to avoid outburst of popular discontent tightly circumscribed the government's ability to do anything for the upliftment of the Depressed Classes. The concession of separate representation to Muslims, coupled with the news of ill-treatment of Indians in South Africa brought about a sharp change in Indians' outlook towards the Depressed Classes. This led to a fresh anti untouchability campaign = Dalit-Samaj.

Sufi culture, In other words, the spirit of Dalit literature was akin to that of Dalit Christian Missioneries. Modern historians call the period from the late 19th century to the middle of the 20th century 'The Age of New Imperialism'. The term 'imperialism' was coined by Benjamin Disraeliin 1872 in the context of the British General Election of 1874; originated from Latin word (Lafaz) *imperial* is to extend the power from small states to a 'Big Country'. Among the critics of imperialism the most famous names are those of J.A. Hobson, a British liberal, and V.I. Lenin the Russian Marxist leader of the 'Bolshevik Revolution', According to Lenin's plane, '*The State and Revolution'* was to have consisted of seven chapters, but he did not write the 7th. "The experience of the Russian Revolution of 1905 and 1917" (p.7). Such a reference seems "Scientific, and effectively lulk the ordinary person to sleep by obscuring the important and basic fact, namely, the split of society into irreconcilable antagonistic classes (p. 17).

Patterns of Colonisation

In 1865 Karl Marx noted three kinds of colonies,

1. Colony in West Indies
2. Mexico and India
3. Australia

Of course, when a population lives in a country like India as 'illiterate class' with 'political reservations' as well as 'reservation in economic sector' means, there is development of 'economy of nature'. At one time after the death of Dr B.R. Ambedkar, it was raw economy of the Sufi-Saint philosophy. With the raise of standard, they left the gigmic of the 'politics' which is meant of 'idiots of the Dalit-Community'.

No doubt, they were exploited in the hands of idiot scholars like Satish Chandra or Irfan Habib that Dalits have, 'no history'. 'Dalits are history creator' with the ideology of universal truth'. Development does not mean, we depend on the political historians like Madan Lal Sharma or Omi Khajuria, etc. We are well verse in all the subjects either 'Science or Arts'.

Anti-colonial struggles, we means, we need 'New History' and 'new wife' as a soul of the historical phenomena.

Irish History

Irish history is based on illogical conclusion at the end of 19th century, because England dominated this area with the majority party, but at the same time, when Irish history was revealed by a Dalit scholar and this 'state' became 'free state' or adopted the idea of 'princely ideology': in 1948.

Origin of Right

'Origin of Right' displayed from the ideology of Dr B.R. Ambedkar. At one time, author was constitutional expert, now, he proved his identity as national builder and repeated the history of Kashmir (Bharat or India).

Social Discrimination

Jammu state, after Post Accession, there was discrimination shown by the 'Abdullaha Family' as upper class convert Hindus "As Article 370", a Constitutional History of the said state is revealed in the light of historical study as the feature and lifestyle of the Nehru and Sheikh is concerned. Women in Kashmir, they are still in mental depression and freedom of speech is not in their favour. No doubt, militancy of the area is side effect, but there pschyic has not been awakened in the light of the development of the area as idiot women or meat eater there is no civilised culture. They looks like barbarian of the political history. Kalhana tells us that low caste women is better that the upper class, he refers about a porter women" who used to sell pastry". God (Chandal) is to be worshipped and Rajasvala is to be bathed by women alone (S.M. Iqbal and K.L. Nirash; '*The culture of Kashmir*'; p.43).

Thus, we see that after the death of Rinchana Shah in Nam-History as Sudra ruler, his widow, Kota Devi, remarried Udyanadeva. (M.L. Kapur, *Studies in History* and *culture of Kashmir*; p. 245)

Index Value

***'The Gospel of Jesus'*:** In search of his original teachings, this book has been drafted by John Davidson. He was born in 1944, graduate in 1966 from Cambridge University with a honours degree in 'Natural Sciences' in Applied Mathematic and Theoretical Physics with the idea of 'Wisdom' or "*Sound-Current*" found within the man itself. He published 10 to 12 books on the said historical persons, who was the great personality of the world. But, here in India or Kashmir, nobody has the work on his 'ideology'. Therefore, Indian Christian, they are known 'Dalit Christians'. His idea was the same as that of Nanak, Ravidaṣ, Tukaram, Eknath, etc. They provided social-justice to Dalits in large scale in the ancient, medieval and in the modern period; there is a great struggle toward their 'social Right' (*Great Britain*, 2009 by Clear press)

The Story of Two Snakes

The snake represents the body of human form as Madan Lal Sharma (MP) of North India, a shrewd politicians and illiterate from the background of the historical knowledge and his family members of this area (Jammu-Poonch constituency). Sharma – Brahmins are not more superior than the 'Sudra Family' of Rai dynasty of *Sindh* (uch) and *Multana* educated youth of this area. The trapper is the negative power that is Omar Abdullaha from NC party. Their way of behavior is the same as Gandhi and Jinnah. Here begins the story of the two snakes, 'Heavy to Carry' and 'Light to Carry' . 'Jewel' is the third force' that is Dalit Family' of Barnai; and Madan Lal Sharma is to flare up the Hinduism and Omar Abdullaha needs 'Islam' to flourish in the state in negative way on Hadiths in traditional values. Author, imposed the idea of the goodwill that is 'Channar thought'.

Ultimately, the old man, Kashyap Rishi of Kashmir, being devoid of spiritual practice with the idea of Nam-History as material made body in the face observer observed on the 'earth', air (soul) observe in Air, but never dies. Sometimes Raj – Rishi and sometimes 'Law Minister' as Dr B.R. Ambedkar. He can endure separation from his dear wife and children and from riches take the example of 'Lady Rattan Tata'. She was the fellow friend of Dr B.R. Ambedkar, who was the 'Jewel of India' at that time and 'Kohi-i-noor' was Ravidas, who was the founder of the Mughal empire in India with the ideology of Babarvani and Nanakvani. Where stands the idea of two snakes, as money minded race.

In Islamic mythology, there is a similar bridge call the *Pul Sirat*. As 'Dalit History' says, 'the old man, a metaphor found in Dalit Christians letters (Grammers study) and possibly originated with the same material as 'Nam' or 'Dalit'. 'The chosen or selected, new man" is the spiritual man either Gulab Singh or Hari Singh, both were spiritually baptized (*Raj-Rishi*) of Kashmir. Jammu is his birth place. As Arab was the birth place of Mohammad Prophet and Kashmir or Sindh was his idea. Multan was his body. (pp. 76-79). Professor Tamara Sonn in '*A Brief History of Islam*' combines the skill of the historian with the Insight-Knowledge called 'Interior Islam' or Nam-dan of the 'Living Master'. Her history, therefore, is not inferior, but exploitation without formal education was there. No doubt, Islam is a religion of global fame, why Sir Muhammad Iqbal says "*The Reconstruction of Religions thought in Islam*' study shows, he is more superior to Tamara Sonn, who realised tht concept Muslim is a concept of 'blind faith' (*Kitab Bhavan*, New Delhi).

Rai Dynasty of Sindh and Multan

Many variations of Ravidas name are prevalent in the different states of India or Kashmir itself and sometimes even within the same state owing partly to the stylistic differences in the dialects of Sindhi (Uch rulers of the Pahari region) and Multan as his ideology to cover the story of North Western Frontiers. During the time of Zain-ul-Abidin of Kashmir, he established his kingdom in U.P. with the idea of

Begumpura on the time his historical wife, belonged to Muslim community of Sindh, now, she is known as Sammya Night of Doda City. Thus, one comes across such variations to form an alliance with Dalit Muslim of North India to remove the caste – barrier between the haves and haves nots, his name as Raidas, Ravidas, Ruidas, Ruhdas, Rohidas, Ramdass, Rudradas and Chamar was his religion or philosophy.

Raidas and Ravidas having being the most popular in entire world. Kabir was his fellow friend as Nam. He was the court poet of Zain-ul-Abidin of Kashmir (Budshah). This view is expressed by the Raidas Ramayana. He used to live Kashi to Kashmir as a Pahari range of the Shivalika hills, the place is called Mandur, where a family lived in purity or called in the 'city of temple'. Now, his family is of good ideas and use to work as Junta politics' (p.27).

A brief History of Guruship Theory

It is the message of Divine Vedas. The Vedas contain high level of spiritual principles. Nam-dam is essential to see the Father to obtain the practical knowledge of the human lifestyle. Atmabal (spiritual power is the power of the Insight-Knowledge and a character should be visualised a pious man. No, ill will, no greedness but dutiful in his lifestyle. Events are essential to control the entire system of the world as a philosophical historian. There is no selfishness, high level character, humours in nature, romance is there in positive way; good will mission to serve the society.

"Ghrutavrato dhanadaahaa,
Somavruddhaha sa
Hee vaamasya vashhaha purukshuhu
Sam Jagmire pathy raaye
A smint samndrena
Sindhav u Yaadamaanaahaa" (Rig-Veda 6-19-5)

Part - B
Kashmir

5

Innovative Ideology of Kashyap Rishi

Introduction

Mysticism is the living heart of all the great religions of the world either Christianity or Islam. It divides the society for cultural changes for Economics to Socialism.

Spiritual Perspective

It has been come to the notice from every Religions of the world, even in the Holy Koran or in the Bible that there is only '*One Supreme Power*' which is the foundation and support of everything either there is Dalit or upper class Muslim. Dalit Muslims are sufi saint like prof. Aftab Ahmed Khan, who is expert in his own field that is Nationalism. But it is difficult to define the Truth as God. In the concept of Radha Soami school of thought every modern writers either K.N. Upadhayaya, Isaac A. Ezekiel, who wrote their book on Sufi Saint without knowing the distinction. Their philosophy is based on human history. History creator are Dalits = Chandal Samaj of the Jammu and Kashmir State.

It is fortunate or unfortunate that Dalit Muslim of Kashmir, they have been forgotten the real concept of the Holy Qaran which is equivalent to Nam or Allaha. We have all come from this "*Power*". Dalit scholar is a realizing force in the community of the communal forces either, there is BJP or Congress and other regional forces like PDP or NC. They are in the doledrum. They have no objective in their lifestyle. They are Political mongres; they need money from the government exchequers. This is the message in their community.

No doubt, we are all drops of the "One Ocean" of the Divine as Nam. And each one of us is accountable of the suitable environment of Kashmir. Due to militancy in the North-western frontier of Kashmir including Pakistan and Bangladesh, moreover, the big packet of Muslim cults, they owned bad name, because of their activities. Now the declining of militancy fundamental forces like Hindu Brahmins and Molavis of Kashmir as separate group are confronting to each other on the name of '*Kashmir Issue*'.

'Kashmir Issue' is an historical problem between the '*haves*' and '*have nots*', '*Dalits*' and '*Anti-Dalits*'. Dalits Muslims scholars, they need good books of the Dalit history. Geography of Kashmir, now it has been changed due to the demographic change in historical perspective. One Dalit scholar = hundred dalit Muslim Sufi saint writers of the Islamic study.

Our Religion

Religious does not mean, we are Muslims a very great religion. People who follow the Holy Quran are called Muslims, because by practice of its rites and rituals as tradition (Hadiths) but failed to analyse the scientific Quranic version called secret *Kalma* or *Nam* = "*Chamar thought*".

Ar-Raheeq Al-Makhtum, 'T*he sealed Nectar*' biography of the Noble Prophet revised edition by safi-ur-Rahman Al-Mubarakpuri, 2001-2012, based on certain Prophet Mohammed quotation like '*Allah-hu-Akbar*' the example of guidance and insight knowledge with which Allah or God (Nam) has sent me is like abundant rain fall on the earth some of which was fertile soil that absorbed rain water and brought forth vegetation and grass in abundance." It show that idea of Indus Valley Civilisation was widely spread to all over the world as the identity of the Chamar thought. Indus means absorbed the idea in the body as fertile land of the human souls of Prophet Muhammad. The first example of a person who practiced the Nam-History, who comprehends Allah is Religion (Islam) and gets benefit of knowledge which Allah or Nam has revealed through Prophet Muhammad and because Holy Quran as new scripture of modern theologians and teaches to other followers.

Those, who does not care for the idea revealed by Prophet Muhammad. They are like that of a barren land. It is revealed in the modern society of the Dalit Muslim. Molavi is not a complete concept = destructive material.

Guideline

If a guideline for life is to be meaningful today, clearly it has to with stand the secreting of logic and reason. It also has to be deciding factor in spiritual history. By 'Mystics' Prophet means those people who, throughout history, have spoken Truth. He becomes God or Allah. After the death of Prophet Muhammad in 670 A.D. he left the Holy Quran as the voice of God. "The Voice of God' is a realizing force of ancient antiquity as political leaders did not understand the 'life', the book tells us, "does not make complete sense to us because we have no sense of the completeness of life." (*Life is Fair*, P.X.)

Allah the Pure Spirit

Holy Karon says that no image could reproduce him and image worship of any kind was idolatrous. Between Guru (Murshid) and his creature Man were, mediating angels and devils. Angels were the forces of Good, God is messengers, Ramiyan and Sheru, the source of prophecy as girl Childs. Devils are those who rebelled against Allah or God or as Materialistic thinkers.

The Right Path

Islam which means surrendered before the God or Allah. As it reveals in the Holy Quran: "We have not sent any Apostle or Prophet before the among whose desires Satan injected not some wrong desire but God shall bring to naught that which Satan had suggested. Thus shall god affirm this revelations for God is knowing and wise." (22.51)

Honest living

'Honesty is the best policy'. Our understanding is based upon a spiritual and moral perspective that is common to all scriptures either of Hindus or Muslims or Christianity. This perspective is not the property of any Religion. It belongs to everyone.

Prophet Muhammad-A Historic Personality

There is, no doubt, Prophet Muhammad is also a historic personality. His life and works are not wrapped in mystery. He was the messenger of God. Before him, the Arabs had adopted the practice of the idolatry as an Hindu concept, 'a blind faith'. The people in general were illiterate.

They did not follow the 'Right Path'. They were sinners being addicted to drinking of wine and gambling as Molavis and Pandits of the modern period in Kashmir history. There morals had been ruined. The poor *slaves* were deprived of their rights. They were just like dumb driven cattle.

The family of Prophet Muhammad

Arabia has the honour of giving birth to many glorious and illustrions prophets from Adma to Muhammad' having 26 in numbers. Downfall ot the Christianity, Islam came in existence as a 'New Idea' in history. It was launched by the last Prophet Muhammad. Prophet Muhammad family belonged to Quraish tribe of Arabia, but the Hashimites, in particular were held in high esteem.

The Date of Birth of Prophet Muhammad

The Holy Prophet Muhammad (Peace and blessing of Allah be upon him) was born on Monday, April 29, 571 A.D. and died in 670 A.D. He was named Prophet Muhammad" which means 'the one who has been highly praised'. He was highly intellectual among all the sons of Arabia.

Theory Merged with Practice

Unwilling to give up their idols, Makkans continued to ask Prophet Muhammad (Nam as Deepit Raj) for signs from theory of Practice to *Dhamma* (God of which proved the credentials of his lifestyle. Prophet told the Jewish, 'The unseen is knowly to God'. For instance, the Sun (Ravi) or Surya which is 'a shinning glory' of his power, and the mood as an idea of Qutab-ud-din Aibek which is a light of beauty', the alteration of Night and Day of Judgement = Manmat Ka end.

Hadith (Tradition)

In the study, we learner the in modern politics the Hadiths (traditions) of Allah have been totally forgotted by the modern society in which Prophet Muhammad used to live. He did not like the caste system which was widely spread by Jewish of Saudi Arabia and the political leaders of India after 1947.

From Adam to Prophet Muhammad

Remember that all mankind has descended from Adam (man) to Prophet Muhammad. There is no doubt, that Adam either male or female has been made out of clay modeling. As in the Quranic Verses, it has been described that all human beings are one.

"People are created in pairs As males and females"

Where stands the idea of Hindus, Muslims, Christians that all human beings are one; as various scriptures of all religions refer the same Ideology. Incomplete Concepts = problems come from us, not from the Cosmos Human life presents us with challenge and response theory to act positively and to acquire clear understanding between the two great forces, that is, God and Man. Life provides us the opportunity to steer the slip of our person life is the direction in which we want salvation.

The laws of nature, both physical and metaphysical allow entities to move only within certain bounds. Meat eater and drunkard how, they can justify the truth as dirty political stunt. How, it is possible that modern theologians like Dr Aftab Khan, Lecturer in Political science, Women Collage, Bemina justify the 'Creative Power' without worship the 'Nam theory' as a meat eater and many more including Kashmiri Pandits. They became prostitute.

Theory of Reconstruction of Islamic Thought

Holy Quran is book of Muslims inspiration of the dead master. 'Your creation and resurrection' says the Koran, 'are like the creation and resurrection of a single soul.' The past history of the man is to be reconstruct from the artifacts with visionary ideas as Kalma or Nam-dan of the Zinda Guru. The fundamental Muslims, they belief on the originality, Quran like '*History of the Chamar Dynasty*'

(From 600-1200) as a new achievement of the modern historian. Holy Quran after the death of Prophet Muhammad it became as a document of sources to confirm the authentic history by modern historians. Now the journey of the soul has been completed from Jammu toDoda for the welfare of the Dalit-Muslims. History creator are Dalits-Hindus = Dalit-Muslims.

Narrow-minded Idea

Narrow minded idea does not bring laurel in the life style of the man as 'blind faith' of both the Hindus and Muslims. Dr B.R. Ambedkar during the class struggle theory; between the *Haves* and *Have nots*, both Gandhi and Jinnah belonged to the capitalist society and could not feed or fulfillment the desires of Dalit- Samaj = anti-Dalit propaganda.

'Man is by Nature a Political Animals', Aristotle politics; 'Politics as the Art of Govt.' by Andrew keywood. The word, politics is drivied from *polic*, meaning literally city-state. *Polis*, polity and associated with 'policy' of the existing govt. It was written as a guide for the future prince of a united states. The adjective "Machiavellian (1469-1527 A.D.) subsequently came to mean "cunning and duplications" (P.6) *Third Edition*, 2007. As Adrian Leftwich proclaimed in *what of Politics*? *The Activity and Its study* (2004). He further stated, "politics is at the Great of all collective social groups." (Ibid)

This book 'History of Modern Kashmir' origin of the Jammu State and Ladakh and Union Territory is an analytical study of various groups who use to work in the area of North India like Jammu, Kashmir and Ladakh. Growth of Political party (*Dalit-i- Allahi- Liberation-Front*) was the moto of; to establish a good rule not in Jammu and Kashmir state, but in entire country of India. As per the statement of S.P. Sharma, who is expert in art of writing the *Dalit concept*, *"Career Guidance and Counseling, Principles and Techniques*." (pp 1-416, New Delhi, 2011).

'*Social Philosophy of Education*' has been written by Y.K. Sharma on the history for the development of Education in 27 chapters, but untouchability is still existing in India too. (New Delhi, 2003, pp. 1-407). It is modern cooperative analysis of both the Toaism and Buddhism. Dalit concept is a new discovery as Radha Soami concept of the modern man.

6

Sources

A systematic and thorough study of a subject depends on the sources available for its study. To what extant one is able to present his study of a subject in a systematic and logical way depends on the nature and volume of sources at his disposal. This applies to the study of ancient Indian history also.

There is abundance of source material to make a proper and scientific study of ancient history of India. But before making use of the source material it is imperative to decide what to include in and what to exclude from it. It is also necessary that sources be classified and categorised in a scientific way and every category of sources is given the importance it deserves. This will make the study more scientific and logical, minimising the element of bias.

So far as the source material of Ancient Indian history is concerned the general practice is to categorise it as follows:-

Archaeological sources

Literary sources

Foreigners' accounts.

I. Archaeological Sources

The excavations carried out at numerous sites are ample proof of the fact that there is abundance of archaeological source material in India. The archaeological sources are the most important of all the sources available. These sources give more reliable and authentic information in comparision to the information derived from other sources. Archaeo-logical . sources are free from subjective bias and can be dated very accurately. The same cannot be said of literary sources or for that matter of foreigners' accounts.

Broadly speaking, if archaeological sources are included (i) structures and objects found in excavation (ii) inscriptions and (iii) numismatic sources. The sculptures paintings and monuments also are included in archaeological sources.

Excavated Source Material

Excavations add to our know-ledge of ancient Indian history in numerous ways. The radio carbon dating of excavated articles makes it possible to determine the time span of civilisation under study in a scientific manner and with more certainty. The articles and tools found in excavation help in reaching a conclusion as to level and stage of culture and civilisation reached by the people of that age. The excavated source material helps one in drawing logical and accurate conclusion about the way of life religion, economy and culture of the people. Excavation also help in determining the geographical boundaries of a civilisation.

Our knowledge of pre-historic times and the Harappan culture is exclusively based on excavated sources.

Inscriptions

Inscriptions too are one of the most important sources'of Indian history of ancient times. In the absence of contemporary historical writings, the patient study of inscriptions is, as Fleet points out, the only reliable source for the knowledge of political history. The inscriptions serve as touchstone to evaluate the authenticity of information derived from other sources.

There are inscriptions of various types in India such as cave inscriptions, pillar inscriptions, rock inscriptions, plate inscriptions, seal inscription etc. Most of the inscrip-tions are either in Sanskrit or in Prakrit language. There are some inscriptions in regional languages also. The script used is either Brahmi or Kharosthi = Manmat Ki History.

The inscriptions help us in obtaining correct and scientific knowledge of history in a number of ways. The most of the inscriptions are dated one hence they helped in determining the date of an event, a regime or life and times of a particular king. Inscriptions give us information about events, development and achievements of a ruler or dynasty. For example, history of Ashoka is constructed with the help of his pillar and rock inscriptions. The Allahabad pillar inscription is the only source of knowledge so far as Samudragupta's campaign of conquests is concerned. One would not have known about the history of king Kharvela but for Hathigumpha inscription. Some inscriptions such as Allahabad and Aihole inscriptions are master piece of literary works. Inscriptions help us in determining the territorial extent of a kingdom because the inscriptions are always inscribed within the territories of a ruler.

It is not only the inscriptions found in India which help us in knowing the ancient history. Some of the inscriptions in foreign lands also help us in substantiating the facts ol ancient Indian history. Such inscriptions are found in Iraq, Iran and South East Asia. These inscription throw light on social and cultural links between India and the country in which such inscriptions exist. These foreign inscriptions one a Bogazkoie is the most important one. Other inscriptions of importance and those of Persipolis and *Naqsh-i-Rustam in Iran*.

Numismatic Sources or Coins age

Coins are yet another valuable source for constructing ancient history. The earliest coins in India are dated to 7th-6th century B.C. These earlier coins were punch mark! Later on coins were minted at circulated by every dynasty ruling different regions of India. The coins display wide range of varied and high aesthetic taste. They were copper, gold and lead.

The coins serve as source material in a number of ways. The paucity and the poor quality of the metal used helps one in deducing facts about the economic life of the particular age. The hordes of foreign coins found in a particular region for example of Roman coins in Tamil region-indicates flourishing trade and close commercial ties. Dated coins help in determining the dates of particular events or regime commemorative coins-such coins were issued by the Gupta emperors in good number-throw light on significant events of the day, such as conquest of the Sakas by the emperor Chandragupta-II or on personal attributes of the king. The coins prove useful in substantiating information about territory of a kingdom and Socio-religious life of the age. One's knowledge of Indo-Greeks, Sakas and other alien rulers in India is based almost exclusively on information deduced from the coins issued by them.

Ancient Monuments

There is abundance of ancient monuments in India. These monuments are in the form of temples, stupas, vihars, rock-cut, caves, Pillars etc. Temples of Gupta and of later age, Ashokan pillars, Stupas of Sanchi, Bharhut and Boddh Gaya, Caves of Ajanta and Ellora are some of the ancient monuments of interna-tional fame. These monuments are of no use in constructing political history but they are of immense help in drawing a picture of cultural life. They tell us about the stage of development attained by the people in the field of architecture, sculpture and engineer-ing. The monuments also help in drawing useful conclusions about social and religious life of the people.

Some monuments of the foreign countries, such as, temple of Angkor-vat and of Borobunder are living proof of close cultural ties between India and these countries. The dated on of God Vishnu found in Borneo and other dated monuments help in verifying the Chronology of Indian history.

Seals

Seals made of copper, stone, soap-stone and clay are also an important source for the knowledge ancient India. Our knowledge of the religious life of Harappan people is based mostly on the information gathered from more than five hundred seals of various material. Similarly the Basadh (Vaishali of ancient days) hordes of 274 seals throws significant information about trade, economic life, guild system and ways of merchant community. Inscriptions and dates on the seals help in determining chronology and in knowledge of a particular event.

II. Literary Sources

A research scholar of ancient Indian history is handicapped by the fact that there are no contemparary history works to rely upon. The only work which can be called a book on history, in the true sense, is Kalhana's '*Rajatarangini*'. In the absence of historical work the scholar has to rely upon non-histerical literature. There is no dearth of such literature. This literature, if carefully and objectively analysed, is of immense help in objective and scientific presentation of ancient history = Persian Records.

The literary sources are placed in two categories : (i) religious literature and (ii) non-religious or secular literature. This literature is available mostly in Sanskrit language but literature in Pali and Prakrit is also in abundance. The Tamil literature, particularly of Sangam age is of immense value.

Dalit Literature

Religious literature connotes texts on particular religion, commentaries there on and secondary works dealing with religious rites, ideas and practices. As there were three main religions in ancient India, the religious literature is also classified as Hindu literature, Jain literature and Buddhist Literature = Persian Records.

(i) Hindus Literature

Four Vedas Rigveda, Samveda, Yajurveda and Atharvaveda, Brahman, Aranyaka and Upanishads. Epics – Ramayan and Mahabharat and Puranas are the most Important of religious works of Hindus.

Of the four Vedas, Rigveda is the oldest one. The work is organised in ten 'Mandals' and has 1028 'Suktas' and 10580 'Richas' the work is the creation of a number of sages and it took centuries to complete it. The period of Rigveda and culture depicted in it is fixed from 16th century B.C. to 12th century B.C. As our knowledge of early vedic period is based on Rigveda, this culture is also known as Rigvedic culture. Rigveda being a religious text throws ample light on religious life of early vedic period. But this religious work also contains references to political events such as 'War of ten kings', to political institutions such as 'Sabha' and 'Samiti'; to social organisation and social units like '*Kula*' '*Vish*' and '*Jan*', as well as, reference to economic activities and life. This enables one to draw a picture of social, economic and political life of early vedic people. The rivers and mountains mentioned in Rigveda help one to trace the geographical boundaries of this culture.

The other three Vedas—*Yajur*, *Sam* and *Atharva*, *the Brahman*, *Aranyak* and *Upnishads* are included in later Vedic literature. These works were completed during the 12th century B.C. to 6th century B.C. This period is known as age of later vedic civilisation. The later Vedic literature is the main source of knowing the history of this period. This literature brings out the changes that took place in the sphere of religion, politic economy, society and culture.

40 Chapters of *Yajurveda* having approximately two thousand 'Mantras' give information about religious and social life. *Samveda* with its 1810 'Slokas' is masterpiece of lyricism. The 731 'Richas and 5839 '*Mantras*' of *Atharvaveda* are organised in ten '*Mandals*'. They deal with folk rites and rituals, magic and medicines. The *Atharvaveda* describes the life of the period when Aryans had adopted a number of non-Aryan religious practices = Dalit Samaj.

'Brahman' texts are written in prose and give in detail rituals followed by the Aryans. Every Veda has its own Brahman text. Thus Kaushitiki and Aitreya are Brahman texts of Rigveda. Taitriya and Sat-path Brahmans belong to Krishna; Yajurveda and Shukla Yajurveda respectively. Panchvimsh is the Brahman text of Samveda. So is Tandav and Jaiminiya Brahman. *Atharvaveda* has Gopath as its Brahman. These Brahman texts throw light on religious beliefs and rituals of later Vedic period. They give information about expansion of Aryan culture and certain references to economic and political life of the period.

'Upanishads' also are the work of this period, the literal meaning of the word is to sit near (Up-near, Nishad-to sit). Thus according to scholars the texts contain philosophi-cal and spiritual knowledge which a pupil derived by sitting near the sage. Upanishads are 108 in number. Most important of these are *Ken*, *Kath*, *Mandookya*, *Prashna*. *Isa*, *Aitereya*, *Svetashvatar*, *Taitriya*, *Chhandogya*, *Brihadaranyak*, *Maitrayani* and Kaushitiki. These works tell us what the thinkers af that age thought about the creation of universe, 'Brahma', 'Atma', migration of soul and rebirth or the life after death = Farooq Abdullaha Ke Story.

'Aranyakas' also belong to later Vedic period. As the name suggests these are the works written and studied in forests (Aranya). These works too are attached to Vedas. Thus Rigveda has Kaushitiki and Aitreya as its Aranyak. While Taitriya Aranyak belongs to Krishna Yajurveda.

Aranyakas

Works studied in forests were called Aranyak. The best known Aranyakas are—

1. Aitereya
2. Shaklayan
3. Taitriya
4. Maitrayani
5. Madhyandin
6. Tatvakar

To help in understanding Vedas and explain them some works were written at the end of Vedic age. These are known as **Vedanga.** Vedanga are six in number. They are *Shiksha*, *Kalp*, *Nirukta*, *Vyakaran*, *Chhand* and *Jyotish*. *'Shiksha Shastra'* was written to help in correct pronunciation of the letters of Vedic texts. Sutras describing rules and regulations are known as '*Kalpa*'. They are three—*Shraut Sutra*, *Grihya Sutra* and *Dharma Sutra*. Panini's famous work on '*Vyakaran*' (Grammar) is 'Ashtadhyayi'. Yask wrote his famous work on Nirukta in about fifth century B.C.

Smritis are integral part of religious literature of Aryans. These are the law books which lay down rules, regulations and laws governing the conduct of individual and prescribing punishment for the violation of the same. The Smriti work helps in understanding social, religious, economic, political and cultural life of the people. The earliest Smriti work is '*Manu Smriti*'. It was written in between the B.C.—200 A.D. Yagyavalkya Smriti was written in between 100-300 A.D. Smritis of Narad, Parashar, Kattayan and Brihaspati belong to Gupta period and are valuable source, material so far as the social religious life of the period is concerned.

Ramayana written by Valmiki and **Mahabharat** of Ved Vyas are two great epics which enjoy the sanctity of religious texts. It is not possible to assign a fix period for the writing of these epics because there had been additions to and revision of the texts of these epics from time to time. Thus, it is supposed that original text of Ramayan had twelve thousand '*slokas*' and its present form took shape in second century A.D. Similarly original '*Yav Samhita*' transformed itself into '*Jaya Kavya*' and ultimately became. '*Mahabharat*'. This transformation took place in between 400 B.C. to 400 A.D. As they are not the work of a definite age, the epics do not help in constructing history of a particular period. But they are helpful in drawing inferences about various aspects of life in later Vedic age and the period that followed it.

The last but not the least impor-tant part of the religious literature are *Puranas*'. The important *purans* are 18 in number. *Markandeya*, *Brahmanda*, *Vayu Vishnu*, *Bhagvat* and *Matsya* are the earliest Puranas. The present text of Puranas is the work of 3rd-4th Century A.D. The *puranas* are exclusive source of knowledge about dynasties which, ruled in various parts of India before 6th century B.C. They are important source material for cultural history. They also help in constructing history of tribes and their settlement in different part of the country. The real difficulty in using Puranas as source material is that some time different *Puranas* give contradicting information about the same ruler or the ruling dynasty = *Raj-Rishi Ki Sabita*. Secondly, not being the history work in true sense, the description given in a Puran lacks in accuracy and objectivity. The accounts given become hyperbolic and dates unreliable. Still the value of Puranas as source material should not be under-estimated.

(ii) Buddhist Literature

Buddhist religious literature is also an important source of know-ledge for ancient Indian history. This literature consists of (i) *Pitak* (ii) *Nikay* and (iii) *Jatak*.

Pitaks are important part of Buddhist literature. Known as '*Tripitak*', they consist of *suttapitak*, *Abhidhamma Pitak* and *Vinay Pitak*. This literature is a comprehensive compilation of the sayings of Lord Buddha and the principles of Buddhism. It was written after passing away of Gautam Buddha. Sutta Pitak is source of immens value to know about sermons and religious ideas of Gautam Buddha

Abhidhamma Pitak throws light of philosophical ideas of Buddhism. In *Vinay Pitak* is described the code of conduct followed by the followers of Buddhism. Besides being the most reliable source of information about Buddhist religion and Philosophy, the *Tripitak* help a research scholar in drawing picture of social, economic and political life in the age of Gautam Buddha. These works are written in Pali language.

Vinay Pitak

Vinay Pitak describes the code of conduct for Buddhist monks. Us three sections are—

1. Sulla Vibhag—Mahvibhag and Brukshuni vibhag
2. Ravandhaka—Mahvagga and Chullavagga
3. Parivar and Parivar Path

Sutta Pitak

Sutta Pitak which contains religious sermons of Lord Buddha has five sections—

1. Deegh Nikay
2. Majjhim Nikay
3. Samyuta Nikay
4. Anguttar Nikay
5. Khuddak Nikay

Jataks are compilation of tales. They tell us about the lives of Bodhisatvas ***i.e.*** the earlier lives of Gautam Buddha. Belonging to the 'realm of fiction rather than facts, the stories are fanciful. One cannot vouch for the historicity of events narrated. But these books provide useful information about social - cultural and economic history of pre-Buddhist days = Present history of living man.

Other Buddhist works of note are ***Mahavamsh*** and ***Deepvamsh.*** These works are written in *Pali*. They are dated to 4th and 5th century. These works narrate the history of "Ceylone but are useful as a source material for ancient. Indian history because, there are numerous references of ancient Indian ruling families in them. Shortcoming of these works is that they are full of fictitious and exaggerated accounts.

Divyavdan is a Buddhist work written -in Sanskrit. It appears that, this work was neither authored by one person, nor was written in one particular period. Still it contains some useful information about agricultural and political life similarly **'*Lalit Vistaar*'** a biography of Lord Buddha also written in Sanskrit cannot be attributed to a Particular author or period = War of Succession of Dalit King Ashoka.

'*Milinda Panho*' a philoso-phical dialogue between Indo-Greek ruler Menander and Buddhist monk Nagasena contains useful material for cultural and political history "*Manju Shri Mool Kalpa*" given an account of Gupta rulers from the Buddhist angle = Samudragupta Ke Kahaniya.

In making use of Buddhist literature as a source material for history one has to be very careful because these works are contami-nated by bias, exaggeration and subjectivity.

(iii) Jain Literature

Most of the ancient Jain litera-ture is written in 'Prakrit' language. Its importance as a source material lies in the fact that it brings to light those events and facts which are either ignored and overlooked or underplayed by Brahamanic and Buddhist literature.

'Agam' literature is above all Jain literature. It consists of 10 'Angas', 12 '*Upangas*', 10 '*Prakeerna*', 6 '*Chhandasutra*' '*Nandi Sutra*', '*Anuyaga dwar*' and *mool sutra*. *Agam* literature is not the work of single individual. It was written in a long span of time. But it was given a final shape in a Jain council held in Vallabhi either in 513 or in 526 A.D. 'Agam' literature is a mine of infor-mation for those who are interested in history of Jainism and its philo-sophy. At the same time **'*Bhagvati Sutra*'** gives valuable information about 16 *Mahajanpadas*. **'*Auppatik Sutra*'** and '***Avashyak Sutra***' throw light on religious views of king Ajatshatru. **'*Bhadravahu Charit*'** contains information about some events and happenings of Chandra Gupta Maurya's regime.

Some other Jain works of some significance as source material for ancient. Indian history are—**'*Triloka Prajatit*'**, **'*Katha kosha*'**,

'Loka Vibhag', ***'Aradhana Katha Kosha'***, ***'Sthiravali' 'Vasudev Hindi' 'Brihat Kalp Sutra Bhasya'***, ***'Kalika Puran'*** and finally a very important twelfth century work by Hemchand ***'Parishista Parva'***.

Non-religious Literature

Vivid and ample non-religious literature of ancient time is written in a number of languages such as Sanskrit, Pali, Prakrit and Tamil. This literature is of immense help to research scholars. While the religious literature informs us about religion and philosophy in detail and makes just passing references to political events and institutions, the non-religious literature provides enough-information about political events and institutional religious literature provided information about political well as social cultural and economic life. But, this non-religious literature is also non-historical literature with a few works being the exceptions. Hence one has to be careful in using this source.

Panini's text on grammar ***'Ashtadyayi'*** is of immense help to those scholars who deal with the history of pre-Mauryan days. It provides information about social, religious and political conditions of that age.

There are many literary masterpieces which help in tracing the history of Mauryan age. Dramatist Vishakadutt's ***'Mudra Rakshas'***, Somdeva's ***'Katha Sarit Sagar'*** and Kshemcndra's ***'Brihat Katha Manjari'*** are most prominent of these works. Kautilya's "*Artha Shastra*" has unique position as source material for Mauryan history. Kautilya was mentor and the Prime Minister of Chandra Gupta Mauraya. Hence information derived from *Artha Shastra* whether it is about polity, society or economy is authentic and reliable to a. great extant. **It** is corroborated by other sources also.

Patanjali's '*Mahabhasya*', a com-mentary on Panini's text provides some information about the history of Shunga dynasty. Kalidas, the great Sanskrit poet and dramatist's work ***'Malvikaagnim-itra'*** also throws some light on the history of this period = North India (Kashmir).

Kamandak's 'Neetisaar', *Vishakhadutt's 'Devichandraguptam' Khernendra's* already mentioned ***'Brihat Katha Manjari'*** Shudrak's drama 'Mrichhakatik' and ***'Daskumar Charit'*** of Dandi help in constructing the history of Gupta age. According to some scholars in

Kalidas '*Raghuvansh*' one can discern Samudragupta's journey of conquests.

One very important source for political history of post-Gupta age is the biographies composed or written by the court poets. The most famous of these biography is Banbhatta's '*Harsha Charit*'. The work contains vast information about achieve-ments of king Harsha. Vakapati's + Durlabahavaradhana and others.

'Gaudvaho' is valuable source for the history of *Yashovarma* of Kannauj. Bilhans's '***Vikramandev Charit***' tells about the deeds of later Chalukya king of Kalyani Vikramaditya. Sandhyakar Nandi's ***Ramcharit*** is the biography of Rampal of Bengal. Achievements of Kumarpal of Gujarat are described in '***Kumarpal Charit***' of Jai Singh and '***DvayaShraya Kavya***' of Hem-chand. Padamgupta's *Nav Sahasank Charit*' Throws light on the history of Parmar dynasty and Jayanak's '***Prithviraj Vijay***' deals with the history of Prithviraj Chauhan Raso. Almost all of. these works are eulogistic and give an exaggerated account of the achievements of ruler concerned. Hence they fall under the category of literary works and cannot be treated as books of history.

Ancient Tamil literature is rich mine of source for the ancient history of South India. The early Tamil literature is known as '*Sangam*' because it is supposed to be the work of literary confluences of poets and writers. According 16 hearsay such three '*Sangams*' were held in ancient Tamilland. The tamil 'Sangam' literature was written and composed in the first and second century A.D. '*Sangam*' literature provides valuable information about social, cultural and economic life of that age. So far as political history is concerned '*Nandikkalambakam*' describes the achievements of pallav ruler Nandiverma III. The event of Kalinga being attacked by Kulottunga I Chola is described in '***Kalingatuparani***'. Ottakutan wrote three separate works to describe the life and achievements of Chola rulers Vikram Chola, Kulottunga II and Rajaraja II. As a source material of ancient history Sangam literature suffers from same shortcomings., as do the other literatures.

Only historical work, in the real sense ef term, is Kalhan's **'Rajatarangini'** which deals with the history of Kashmir. Kalhan wrote his work in 1149-50. He used all the sources, including state archives in writing'his work. His account is to a great extent unbiased and objective. He is neither hyperbolic nor eulogistic. This applies more particularly to his description of post seventh century events. His account of pre-seventh century history is less reliable. '*Rajtarangini*' is essentially a work of history on Kashmir. But it also contains references to the history of other regions of India = Ruqqiya Maqsood + Syed Ali Amir, Spirit of Islam.

The works of literature did not help much in writing political history but they provide a vivid and in depth understanding of folk-life and culture. Here in lies their value as source material for ancient Indian history.

Some Important Literary Works

Title	***Author***	***Source for the period or dynasty***
Ashtadhyayi	Panini	Pre Mauryan age
Arthashastra	Kautilya	
Mudra Rakshasa	Vishakhadutt	Mauryan age
Brihat Katha Manjari	Ksjiemendra	
Malvikagnimitra	Kalidas	
Mahabhasya	Patanjali	Sunga age
Neetisaar	Kamandak	
Devichandrsssaguptam	Vishakhadutt	Gupta age
Mrichha Katik	Shudrak	
Katha Sarit Sagar	Somadev	
Harsh Charit	Banabhatt	Emperor Harsha
Gaudvaho	Vakapati	Yashoverma of Kannauj
Nahdik- kalambakam	'Sangam Lit.	Nandivarma Pallav. Ill
Rajtarangini	Kalhan	Kashmir
Prithviraj Vijay	Jayanak	Prithviraj Chauhan

III. Foreigner's Account

In ancient times a number of travellers from Greece, Rome, Western Asia, and China visited India for one reason or the other. These foreigners accounts of India and its people is a rich source for the students of ancient Indian history. Besides these travellers some other foreigners who came as army commander, ambassador Or who did not even visit India had written about this country.

The first Greek to write about India is *Herodotus* who .is known as the father of history. His famous work is '*Historica*'. Vast source material for the study of Alexander's invasions of India and the Mauryan age is available in the writings of Arrian, Justin. Plutarch, Strabo, Dioriysis, Megasthanese, etc. The '*Indica*' of *Megashthanese* is the most valuable of all these writings. This ambassador to Chandragupta Maurya's Court had left a detailed description of polity and society of Mauryan age. Though some of his observations such as non-existence of slavery in India and society being organised into seven classes are not valid, the most parts of his work are objective and factual. It is a pity that the work is not available in original and complete form. What we have are fragments from the book which are quoted by other Greek authors. Another work outstanding as source material is the ***'Periplus of Arithean Sea'.*** Unfortunately the author of book is unknown. The work contains rich information about India's sea-trade, ports and trade relations with Western World. Writings of Ptolemy and Pliny are also helpful to research scholars and students.

A number of Chinese Buddhists visited India in ancient times. The Travelogues written in Chinese and translated in English and other language throw light on the people's life and culture at the time of their visits. Of the Chinese travellers came to India in 5th century, A.D. He had described the social life and the place of Buddhism in th(Indian society of that age. Hi showed no interest in describing tl political life and events of the da. *Yuan-Chwang* came to India in the 7th century A.D. He spent 16 years in India and was guest of emperor Hansha for some time. His travelogue describes not only religious and cultural life; but also contains valuable information about political events and a number of rulers of the day such as *Harsha*, *Pulkesin*, *Bhaskar Varman*. *I-ching* also visited India in the 7the century. He had left interesting account of Buddhist educational institutions such as Nalanda and Vikramshila. He main drawback of these sources is that the **Chinese** travellers were the followers of Buddhism and saw India from Buddhist eyes. Therefore, there is natural bias in their writings.

The Arabs started to write about India from 8th century onward. Sulaiman visited India in 9th century A.D. He had written about Pal and Pratihar rulers of his time. Al-Masudi stayed in India for two years ***i.e.,*** from 941 to 943 A.D. He had written about Rashtra Kutas. Abu-Ryham or Alberuni is the most famous Arabs writing about India. A contemporary of Mahmud of Ghazani, he accompanied the invader to India. He stayed in India for a long period learnt Sanskrit and Studied Indian literature. He had left a graphic, objective and unbiased description of India and its people in his outstanding work '*Tahkik-ul-Hind*'. It is regretable that Alberuni left no description of state and politics of contemporary India.

Tibetan author Lama Taranath's works 'Kangyur' and 'Tangyur' also contain some useful information about ancient Indian history.

Thus there is wide range of sources for the study of ancient Indian history. What is required is 'that they be used in scientific and objective way and conclusions drawn be free of bias.

An Abridged List of Literary Sources

(A) Brahmanic Religious treatise

(i) **Vedas**—Rigveda, Samveda, Yajurveda, Atharvaveda.

(ii) **Brahman books**—Aitreya, Kaushitiki,- Shtpath. Panchvimash, Gopath.

(iii) **Aranyaka books**—Maitra-yani, Taittiriya, Aitreya.

(iv) **Main Upanishads** - (Total number of these works is 108) Kath, Isavasp, Ken, Vrihada-ranyak, Chhandagya.

(v) **Vedangas**—Shiksha, Kalp, Vyakaran, Nirukta, Chhand & Jyotish.

(vi) **Kalpa Sutra**—Shraut Sutra, Grihya Sutra, Dharma Sutra, Shulva Sutra.

(vii) **Sutra-Literature**—Apas-tamba Grihya Sutra, Baudhayan, Grihya Sutra, Apastamba Dharma Sutra, Baudhayan Dharma Sutra, Gautam Dharma Sutra Asvalayan Shraut Sutra.

(viii) **Vyakaran Literature**—Ashtadhyayi, Mahabhasya, Nirukta.

(ix) **Jyotish Works**—Brihajja-takam, Surya Siddhanta, Beg Ganitam, Brihat Samhita.

(x) **Upavedas**—-Ayurveda, Dha-nurveda, Gandharvaveda, Shilpa-veda.

(xi) **Shad Darshan**—Nyaya, Vaisheshik, Samkhya, Yoga, Purva. Minamsa Uttar-Mimansa.

(xii) **Epics (Mahakavya)** — Ramayana, Mahabharat.

(xiii) **Puranas**—Brahma, Shiv, Vishnu, Padma, Bhagvat, Nardiya, Agni, Markandeya, Bhavisya, Brahma Vaivarta, Linga, Varah, Skand, Vaman, Kurma, Matsya, Garuda, Brahmanda.

(xiv) **Smritis**—Manu, Narad, Yagyavalkya, Vishnu, Parasher, Kattayan, Brihaspati.

(B) Buddhist Books

(i) **Tripitak**—Sutta Pitak, Vinay Pitak, Abhidhamma Pitak.

(ii) **Other works**—Anguttar Nikay, Khuddak Nikay, Ashokavdan Avadanshatak, Divyavdan, Buddha-charit, Saundaranand, Milind Panho, Arya Manjushri Moolkalpa; Lalit Vistar.

(C) Jain Religious Books

Parishista Parva; Acharang Sutta; Kalpa Sutta; Bhagwati Sutta; UVsagadasha, Sutta; Bhadrabhu Charit; Zivishtir Shalaka; Punish Charit; Samraich Katha, Kuvatlaya mala, Adi Puran, Uttar Puran; Dhoortakhyan.

(D) Non-Religious texts and their authors

Ashtadhyayi	Panini
Arthashastra	Kautilya
Mudra Rakshas	Vishakhadutt
Mahabhasya	Patanjali
Malvikaagnimitra	Kalidas
Neetisaar	Kamandak
Raghuvansham	Kalidas

Mricchakatikam	Shudrak
Devichandraguptam	Vishakhadutt
Kam Sutra	Vatsyayan
Harshcharit	Banbhatt
Brihat Kathamanjari	Kshemendra
Kathasaritsagar	Somdev
Gaudvaho	Vakapati
Ballalcharit	Anand Bhatt
Bikramankdevcharit	Bilhan
Kumarpalcharitam	Jai Singh
Ramcharit	Sandhyakar Nandi
Kirti Kaumudi	Someshwar
Prithvi Raj	Vijay Jayanik
Prithvi Raj Raso	Chandvardai
Dvayashray Karya	Hemchand
Nav Sahasank Charit	Padamgupta
Prabandh Chintamani	Memtanga
Hammir-Mad-Mardan	Ari Singh
Rajtarangini	Kalhan

(E) Sangam & Tamil Litera-ture

(i) Ettut Togai (Lyrical Anthol-ogies)

1. Narrinai
2. Kurundogai
3. Ainguru-Nuru
4. Padirup-Pattu
5. Paripadal
6. Kalittogai
7. Ahnanuru
8. Purananuru

(ii) The Ten Longer Poems

1. Murugarruppadai
2. Porunar-Arruppadi
3. Sirupan-Arruppadai
4. Perumban Anuppadi
5. Mullai Pattun
6. Maduraikkanji

Important Facts to Remember

- Ancient Indian inscriptions are either on stone philosopher or on metal plates. Inscriptions of post Ashokan period can be classified as state inscriptions and private inscriptions.
- Edicts of a ruler, eulogies composed by court-poets and charters of land grants are included in state inscriptions.
- Inscriptions on temple wall or on sculpture are considered private inscriptions.
- Rigveda is the earliest of the four vedas. It is almost exclusive source for knowing the history of early Vedic culture. Rigveda provides rich information about religious, social and economic life but there are just passing reference to political life and events.
- There are 10 Mandalas, 1028 Suktas and 10580 Richas in Rigveda.
- Samveda, a lyrical work has 1549 or. 1810 slokas.
- Atharvaveda is a valuable source to know about political, social and family-life in later Vedic period. This Veda has 20 'Mandals' 731 'Richas' and 5839 'Mantras'.
- Yajurveda has five branches ***viz.*** (i)'Kathak' (ii) Kapishthal (iii) Maitrayani (iv) Taitriya (v) Vajasneyi. This Veda has prescribed various methods of sacrifice (Yagya).
- 'Brahman' is derived from word 'Brahma'. Brahma signifies 'Yagya'. Hence Brahamans are the texts which lay down rituals for "Yagya' ceremony. These texts are based on Vedas.

- Every Veda has its own Brahman text.' Aitreya and Kaushitiki Brahmans are attached to Rigveda. Satpath, also known as Vajasneya, belongs to Yajurveda. '*Panchvimsha*' is Brahman text of Samveda and *Atharvaveda* has Gopath as its Brahman book.
- Panchvimsha Brahman is also called 'Tandav' Brahman.
- Upnishads are the store house of earliest philosophical ideas and thought of Aryans. Subjects such as 'Brahma' 'Atman' 'Rebirth' 'Life after death' 'Karamphal (fruits of deeds)' 'Creation of universe etc. are dealt with study.
- To help in the study and understanding of Vedas, Vedan-ga were constructed at the end of Vedic age.
- 'Nirukta' of Yaska is the work of fifth century B.C. It discusses etymology of Vedic words.
- Smritis are the law-books of Hindu society. The rules and regulations described their encompass the whole life of individual and every aspect of social life and society.
- Manu-Smriti is the earliest and most important of all the Smritis. It is looked upon as authority on Hindu law and throws light on Hindu ideals based on Varnashram dharma = Sanatan Dharma Ki Dastana.
- The importance of 'Matsya', 'Vayu' and 'Vishnu' Puranas lies in the fact that they contain description of old ruling dynas-ties = Chamar thought.
- 'Ashtadhyayi' of Panini is a text on grammar. It is a valuable source for the history of pre-Buddhist period.
- Bauddh and Jain literature is of immense value in constructing history of the age of Gautam Buddha. These works throw light on religion, society, eco-nomy and polity of the day.
- Tripitaks consist of Vinay Pitak, Sutta Pitak and Abhidhamma Pitak. These are the most prominent texts of Buddhism.
- Vinay Pitak deals with the code of conduct of Buddhist monks. Its three Sections are (i) Sutta Vibhag, (ii) Khandak, (iii) Parivar.

- Sutta Pitak is a compilation of Lord Buddha's religious sermons. Its five Nikayas are (i) Deegh Nikay (ii) Majjhim Nikay, (iii) Samyukta Nikay, (iv) Anguttar Nikay (v) Khuddak Nikay.
- Abhidhamma Pitak deals with philosophical and spiritual ideas and issues. It has seven books viz. (i) Dhamma Sangiti (ii) Vibhanga (iii) Dhatu Katha (iv) Puggal Panjati (v) Katha Vastu (vi) Yamak and (vi) Patthan.
- 'Deepvamsha', a fourth century work, deals with history of Ceylon-But the book is full of imaginary and fictitious details and cannot be termed as a text on history.
- Similarly 'Mahavamsha' of poet 'Mahanama' is also full of hyperbolic and fictitious descrip-tions. Hence it also cannot be placed in the category of history book.
- Deepvamsha and Mahavamsha are written in Pali language and so is 'Milindapanho' a book of dialogue between king Menander and Buddhist monk Nagsena. It is very useful source for the socio-religious history of that period.
- Anguttar Nikay tells about 16 Mahajanpadas. 'Arya Manjushri Mool Kalp' describes the history of Gupta period from Buddhist angle.
- 'Mahavastu gives valuable infor-mation about life of Lord Buddha. It is a work partly written in Sanskrit.
- 'Agam' occupies the place of pride in Jain religious literature. 'Agam' literature consist of 12 Angas, 12 Upangas, 10 Prakeerna, 6 Chhand Sutra, Nandi Sutra, Anuyag Duar and Mool Sutra.
- 'Bhagwati Sutra' gives informa-tion about life of Lord Mahavir. 'Auppatik' and 'Avasyaka' Sutras describe the religious ideas of king Ajat Shatru. 'Bhadravahu Charit' deals with the events of Chandragupta Maurya's days.
- One gets important information about India at the time of Alexander's invasion from the writtings of Nearchus, Aristo-boulus, Yumenis.

- Kautilya's 'Arthashastra' and Megasthanese 'Indica' are two most important sources for the history of Chandragupta Maurya. The writings of Plutarch and Justin are also useful.
- Ashokan inscription are most valuable source for the knowledge of the history of this great emperor.
- 'Allahabad pillar inscription' tells about the conquest of emperor Samudragupta. 'Mehrauli iron pillar inscription describes the deeds of king Chandra. 'Bhitari' inscription informs about Hunas invasion.
- Coins and inscriptions are most reliable source of the history of Gupta-age.
- Fa-hiens's Travelogue gives information about social and religious life of Gupta age but is silent on political events = Buddhist Era found in Kashmir.
- Banbhatta's 'Harshacharit' and Hsuen-tsang's travelogue are important source material for the history of Harsha.
- Alberuini's 'Kitab-ui-Hind' is an unbiased and objective descrip-tion of the condition of India at the time of Invasion of Mahmud of Ghazani = Chachnama.
- For the history of ancient limit land one has to rely on Sangam literature' composed during first two centuries.
- 'Periplus of Arithean Sea' is a outstanding source of the history of maritime trade and commerce in ancient India.
- 'Rajtarangini' of Kalhan is the only history book written in ancient India. It deals with the history of Kashmir.
- Lama Taranath's work 'Kagyur' and 'Tagyur' are also helpful in constructing ancient Indian history.

Of the 29 caves, sixteen contained paintings which survived to a greater or less extent even as late as 1879. Most of tense, it is said to think have been destroyed, but it displayed the history of modern Kashmir by quoting certain example of modern human psychologists that Dr Raj Kumar and his family, is one of the ture example of the period after the death Dr B.R. Ambedkar. Most of them be long to the 'Gupta Age' as an 'ideology' '*Quit India Movement*'- II Role of Indian

Big Business or Industrialist as those of Tatas, Dalmias, Thapars, Singhanias, Sarabhais, Walchand, Hira Chand and others. During the World War first, (1914-1919), both French and Germany build embires in Africa and the pacific and Indian Hindus and Dalit Muslims Co-operate Gandhiji to help the England in cruscial period of National movement, that it was the foundation of New History or Naya Kashmir.

World War II (1939-1946)

The peace treaties of 1919 that followed world war I left three countries extremely dissatisfied. Germany, resented the lost of territory and the payments reparations. Italy and Japan, who were on the winning side of the 'Doda City', felt they had not gained much territory after the war. In these countries including South Asia after world war 1, democracy failed and was replaced by fascism or militarism as found in Kashmir after 1990 thus, the three Axis dictatorship (Pole or North Qutab), Germany, Italy and Japan were crushed. Dr B.R. Ambedkar at that time was in South Africa with Gandhiji to alarm the Dalits for Satsangs. Britian and France emerged from the war victorious, but exhausted, same story was with Great England.

International Politics (Theory and Practice)

As an Academic Discipline, *History* has been proved as an Ancient, Medieval science (Read out the books of J.D. Bernal and others (*Wonder that was India*), it was an idea of Dalit literature or the literature of Sufi Saints. If Politics is a Science or 'Arts', why did not Dr Farooq Abdullaha and his son Omar Abdullaha and other leaders of different political parties including '*Huriyat conference*' could not make the Kashmir as a 'Paradise on Earth'. Because, they have mean mentality and having no idea of 'Secular State of mind' as found in the 'Dalit History of Kashmir' (Naya Kashmir).

History and Politics

No doubt, there is a lot of discussion on the ideology of 'Autonomy', but fortunately or unfortunately, Dalit community was not considered in the 'Political History' as we take the example of K.S. Sexon and other great political thinker of Kashmiri Brahmins; like Pt. Jawahar Lal Nehru or Mahatma Gandhi. Because, they had not right to reveal or '*Repeat the History of Dalit Samaj*'. Study shows that big rulers of Indian, they were 'Rishi Munis' as we take the example of Kashyap Rishi and others (Abaha Katoon and so on).

(Rajniti) = Politics

In the political history of Kashmir, it has be observed that before the Nanakji, Ravidas was there in U.P. (Benaras) and Sant Kabir was a great poet of Kashmir, worked under Bhudshah (Sultan Zain-ul-Abidin) of Kashmir.

Cultural Development under the Sultans (Suratrana)

History does not means, an history of Organisation; such as used in 'sociology' like, caste, religion and modern groups of NC, BJP or Congress or CPI or CPM. It is a component of two great forces as we have already been mentioned in our study 'that is' God and Man. Religion here, we used it as a term of the Gods ideology, where stand the Religion of Hindus, Muslims, Dalit Christians and Dalit Sikhs, it stand in Dalit History as a Minority community of the advance society of modern Kashmir:- Doda city, Bhadarwah, Kishtwar, Anantnag, Padder, Marwah and other small town or city like Kilotran, Satroo, Chinta etc. These areas, need development of art and culture, because this areas is outer of Kashmir valley itself. We need, more banking facilities and train tract. It is not a visionary document of the Jammu or Kashmir State, but it is a original history of Ladakh too. For example, there is a two racial elements for the development of 'Science and Arts', that is, 'Guru and the King' as follow 'friends' of the Nam History as a untouchable concept of the writer and his family too. *Comparative Analysis* and *Composite Dialogue among Female Friends* = Globalisation and Ethnic movements of the Dalit Samaj.

Comparison is one of the oldest forms of the study both 'politics' and 'Dalit Samaj'. The comparative analysis as we take the example of Ali Mohammad Jinnah (Prof. Z. A. Hashmi) Brahmin by nature called Molavi in Arabic concept. He has not idea of authentic history. Even the History of the Dalit concept has been repeated. In the Dalit Muslim majority area like Shimla, Hamirpur, Jammu, Srinagar, Doda, Rajouri, Pathankot, etc had the business of the govt. to launch the campaign against anti Dalit Muslims and Hindus. They come under the category of 'Infindal society', that is, 'Rite and Rituals' like peon Pritam Singh idiot Rajput and Pt. Amarjeet Sharma. They have not concept of 'Satsang'. (North Western Region office, Block 3, Ground Floor, Kendriya Sadan, Sector 9, Chandigarh Dated: 16th October 2013) (7/1/2013/Exm/NWR Govt. of India, Deptt of Personal and Training SSC). Kashmir Life, Sringar, October 19, 2013 (Paper, Cost, Rs. 5.00) Vol. 05, issue 32, "Inspiring to Aspire" title of the News Item "Women in woods" Wazwan country surely knows the grammer (Sabda) theory and Kashmir idiot Pandits and Molavis like Dr Farooq Abdulaha and his follow friends Abdul Rahim Rather, etc. made the public fool on the question of development. But their condition is sailing in the same boat before 1947. "Shams Irfan, a traveler spends fed days at a high attitude pature" with two 'old women like that of Amri and Parsino, who are into their third generation of spending summers with herds of the Jammu and Kashmir including Ladakh and Kargil regions Galgit, Baltisatan, Daridastan is now in the possession of Pakistan or the area of POQ. Study shows there is little development in the comparison of 'Dogra Rules' in North India = Idiot Samaj of the Kashmiri Pandits and Muslims.

7

Early History of Srinagar

(Pre-History to 6th Century A.D)

We trace the History of Kashmir from pre-histric to modern man on the basis of a Dalit visionary historian. According to the tradition (Hodith), Kashmir takes its name from a Rishi Kashyap (1500 B.C) who used to live on the bank of mountain lake called Satisar that is the idea of a women, who burns in the funeral pyre, at the time of her husband's death. The custom , later on found in Rajasthan in Rajput family. But, this Rishi had not any caste on this earth and landed other Sapat Rishi for the development of history on the ideology of 'Kash' and 'Mir' was his wife as the wife of Shivaji that was Parvati as lighting force of the young blood of his Devaras. It seems the name Kashmir is associated with God as K^1 and K^2 as a formula to define the concept in alzebraical equation, now found in Kashmir who is K^3 working with the formula of "*Dalit-Allahi-Libration Front*" as third force of great Kashmir or India, that is, SC/ST and OBC that was the story with the constitutional experts of India at that time (that is, Dr B.R. Ambedkar). Their race used to believe on the basic realities of the world history 'work is worship'. Now, the Hindus and Muslims in this regard during the modern world, they are still found anti-Dalits. They have no authentic ideas in their lifestyle. *Mandir* and *Masjid* as an architecture are the constitution of the 'infidals'. The upgradation of the Dalit Rishi is led by Rishi-Muni of this area as Kashyap Rishi developed his idea in the 'beauty land of Kashmir' which is called 'Heaven on Earth' or 'Paradise on Earth'. Now, the question rises, after the downfall of the militancy, in the beginning of the 21st century that human resources, no doubt, army personel, they deployed in the valley why and what? There was a need of the hour to protect the life of good woman of Kashmir as Younger generation. Thus, the male domination society, they were known as infidals or Brahmins of the Jammu and Kashmir history including Ladakh itself. No doubt, militancy took various route to liberate the Kashmir from Kashmir Pandits, either there is Sheikh Abdullaha or Mufti-Mohd Syeed, Ex-Chief Ministers of Kashmir and Huriyat Leaders, they are crying in Jail on the penetration of Muslims terrorists in Kashmir, Delhi, Bombay, Calcutta, Himachal Pradesh, Rajasthan, etc. for the spread of Islam as a technical term found by Prophet in his art of writing the 'spiritual history' as authentic document of the 'Islamic Religion'. As usual study of the author as Dalit-Historians as fault lies in Muslim Community itself because, they have no 'logic' and 'reason' in their lifestyle. They only prey to God and compile the poetry on the Prophets way of behavior, not with spiritual idea of Kashyap Rishi or the Prophet himself as an idea of Madhumantra Theory of a 'Avesta' or Zinda Pir. They used evil spirit against the woman and Dalit Muslims of Kashmir either there are Gujjar or Bakerwals or any other tribe described by Dr Raghunath Rai as a Sufi scholar of the Rai dynasty of Sindh or Kashmir or Ladahk. These groups are called Bamdas (Mirasis), Watals (Chamars) Hanjis (Boatsmen), Gade (Fishermen) relative of Ved Vyash, who wrote huge literature on the concept of Dalit or Sufi-Saint philosophy, four Vedas and Mahabharat. (*A History of Kashmir upto 1947*, p. 7).

"Who has not heard of the vale of cash mere with its roses the brightest that earth ever gave that was the story with the Gulab-Singh. It temples found in Kashmir as 'Dalit Samaj' as natural race of the human technology. They have no concept of idiot thought, that is Hindu and Muslim as traditional study. As it is clear from the land scaping called grottos, whereas mountains, they are clearly speaking "goodness" idea of the Chamar history that it was the 'ideology' of Lord Shiva and Dr B.R. Ambedkar, when he launched the campaign from South India to North India, through the constitution as an expert diplomat. As the love-lighted eyes as beautiful woman as Dr Shabnam Grewal of Delhi use to live in these 'pahari culture' as simple as hanging her curly hair on her back-bone in long tail Gnt.

Concept of Religion

Religion is one of those English words which means to re-ligion with God's idea in human form with the ideology of 'Gurukul Theory' or with the concept of 'Living Master'. Dead-master can not speak, cannot write and express the idea of 'creator power' as Murshid of the period expresses known as bani or 'Voice of God'. It defies all attempts at an exact rendering in Sanskrit or Persian tongue called *Dharma*. It dealt with the ideal love of which Holy Prophet said: "One who loves and conceals his love and remains chaste, dies a martyr" a meat eater cannot chase this theory (concept). Its was at one time that this word went to the art of writing called 'Sufi' as an ideology of free-thinker as 'Sufi-Saint scholars' as vegetarian thinker and social-thinker of the word mystic. It was used in the Arabic, Turkish, Hindu and Urdu, as a language of the various countries as well as became a 'Religious connotation' with word 'culture' in Hindu Samaj, particularly in 'Indra Family' as a concept of 'Silence observer'. According to the 'Sufis themselves, the word is derived from *a rab* of the Arabic history means a theory of Lordism in 'English History' shifting from Dalit-Christian to Dalit. Mocha Muslims history of the Asian countries and its root related with 'Safa' or 'Pag' or 'Pagri' an ideology of the art historian which is based on 'purity or sudra. (*Encyclopedic Survey of Islamic Culture*; edited by Mohd. Taher; pp. 2-3, *Sufism, Its Development*. Vol. 7).

No doubt, term '*Dharma*' or '*Religion*' has passed through several ups and downs in the history of various countries of the world as rise and downfall of the 'Abdullaha Family' from Brahmanism to 'Sundra Clan' of 'Gargotra' family of Jammu. The dictionaries set out various meanings of the said terms 'Dharma' or 'Religion' such as "ordinance, usage, duty, right, social justice, morality, virtue, good works, function or characteristics". (D.V. Kane; p.1).

Dharm or Religion is also personified by Kashyap Rishi of Kashmir as a 'Deity' as Chamar of the modern period as 'little master Deepit Raj' son of the writer. In the hymns of 'the Rigveda and the Vedic Religion' A.C Clayton mentions about the origin of the clan, that they were 'Aryan' or 'Chamar' and words drived from the ward 'Ar' or 'Arya'. This word also appears to be used either as an adjective or a noun (in the form 'dharman', generally neuter) and occurs at least about sixty times by itself and not preceded by a particle of the 'Air' as 'Nam' or some words in modern history known as 'Satya'. (P.V Kane' *History of Dharmasastra*, Vol. I. 1968, p. 1).

The Holy Name Mysticism in Judaism

This book has been written by Miriam Bokser Caravella, a Dalit Lady of the Radha Soami Mission, Dera Bias. 1989 to the memory of her father Rabbi Ben Lion Bokser, who instilled her a love for God and a spirit of open-minded inquiry, as ancient enquiry on the subject history as *Phsatas* called in historical phenomena. She wrote this book in her beloved master Baba Charan Singh Ji who initiated her into the path of Sant Mant or Sufi Saint ideology, but Kashmir Samaj particularly the upper class Muslims, they are deadly against this concept. Even though master in his lectures says '*see the present religion*' or '*examine the present verdict in history*' as a gift of radiant love towards humanity and rational approach. 'Love gets love, tough gets tough' that was the ideology of Dr B.R. Ambedkar and the Sufi-Saints scholar.

Divine Realms

As an academic discipline, the study of 'Divine Realms' gained recognition and popularity only in the inter-war period in 1914-1919, when Mento-Morely Act was introduced in India as a part of the Kashmir history this school of study came into existence as university of Southern California and its phenomenal growth in its popularity not underway only in the post of second world war. It was the crushing defeat of the British arrival troops in Srinagar or in North-Western Frontiers. Only the Dalits, they were watching the troops of the army in 'Natural Way' to defeat the Molavis and Pandits of this area. They rose their power as rose in Bangladesh during the period of Lord Curzon. Now, Bangladesh became a civilised country than the Northern Pakistan of Kashmir in comparison of higher education and civilisation growth.

Kashmir and Cold War Syndrome

India reluctance to promote 'Human Rights at Home' as a question marks to the Delhitie historians, that they first try to remove the 'ego problem' within the state itself than they have to face the 'Security council' bravely as the story of a 'young lockinwar' and to maintain the equality base knowledge on the question of *'Dhamma policy'* of Dr B.R. Ambedkar. No doubt, Pakistan was consistently raised this issue in the united nation, but at the same time, Mr. Hussain Haqqani is latest book '*Magnificent Delusions*' about Pakistan leaders having refused on American offer to help them in the country is efforts to resolve the 'Kashmir Issue'. "Since the 1956" Pakistan had wanted an American role in South Asia as a developing country of the world community. Study shows Nawaz Sharif and Asif Ali Zardari, they are in the black list of the Indian government. They cannot control the 'Subaha Sind and Multan' as both are more effected terrorist area in the human history. The people of this area most probably of Kashmiri, they are still found illetrate in the light of development of 'human history' as that of Mughals, Karkota, Viradeva, Lohara dynasties of Kashmir. They have no knowledge of the 'Sufi-Saint ideology' as that American state of mind study, therefore, there is domination of the foreign countries including China and other countries. Playing double games by America, that is, 'proxy war' and dropping certain American syndrome to kill the Molavis and Pandits of the areas in the favour of the 'human history' as 'New society' of the 'New Contribution' to kill the Lashkar-e-toiba of Hafez Saeed and the Pakistan Tehreek-e-Taliban as infidel race of the human technology.

Multi-Culturalism Ideology of Kashmir

In the study, we learn that India is country of multi-religions, multi-languages. It is estimated from the learnered scholar Mr. Hussain Haqqani's Book that Pakistan his not an existing state of idea. Idea ruling agency in indirect form is America, sometime China also played this role in the context trade relation to supply arms and ammunitions against India or Kashmir. India as an existing state of the world knowledge is an operating agency of the human sources. Most of the people during the time of partition. They went to abroad and settled there as cultured people of India from the background of Dalit concept. They used for 'Higher Education' to remove the 'poverty in historicism' in human affairs as we take the example of Prewaz Musaraff, Ex. President of Pakistan. Whe, I used to study his book '*Line on the Fire*'. No doubt, he reflected his intelligentsia through his book, but the circumstance after the Kargil war became appease in India as a 'dialogue' between the two states. But, he was considered degraded man of this area as Dalit Mochi.

It is, again, estimated from the study after 2000 A.D., there is a less terrorist activities found in Kashmir = Santi: Prava Ke Story.

Ideology of the Union Territory

Ideology of Union Territory, we brought from history of Dr B.R Ambedkar, who says "Religion should be of Rule". 'Religion ' is a component of two great forces 'God and Man'. The nature of the 'Union Territory' expresses only an "Idea", money does not rule. Equality before the 'Law' is a big challenge in this country. Liberity to some extent is O.K we need good friends of the 'Nam-History', like former union minister P. Namgyal, MLC Leh Norbu Gailchan and Executive Councilor Mohammad Shafi Lash; and political leader Dalai Lama for the discussion on the issue of 'Kashmir Issue' and its trifurcation and certain Jammu cities leader like Prof. Bhim Singh NPP, President, on the basis of intelligentsia race. Dalits need good-goverance including certain Netas of Kashmir Geelani, Shabir Shah and others. Dalits have 'no religions', they are free-thinkers = Intelligent Samanj.

Exposition of Kashmir Issue

Underlining the '*Kashmir Issue*' after 1947, there was conflict of the two great communities, that is, Hindus and Muslims and 'third force' that is came into existence as a solution of the 'Pahari Culture', that is, Sudra known as Dalits. Before the partition of India, there was a statement of the Buddhist scholar, "One state, one language is a universal feature of almost every state, that is, 'English'. Examine the constitution of Germany, examine the constitution of France, examine the constitution of Italy, examine the constitution of England and examine the constitution of the U.S.A. One state one language is the rule Hindi or Urdu. Wherever there has been a departure from this rule there has a danger to the state like Jammu, Kashmir and Ladakh. (Dr B.R. Ambedkar, 'Thoughts on Linguistic States; p. 15)

Perestroika and Glasnost History

The Soviet Union Leaders of the Dooma dynasty, they followed the ideology of Ambedkaritie thought as concept Dalit. No doubt *Perestroika* is a word of Russian language which literally means "Restructuring" of the modern society on the basis of 'good ideas' of Shivaji Maratha or 'Aurangzeb'. Who started the terrorist movement in Indra Gandhi and Jinnah as fellow friends of the 'Nam-History'. One needs Dalit history other need Hindu and Muslim ideology, by the way, Dr B.R. Ambedkar was let down due to the non-political interest, he had not in his mind. He was silence observer. Study shows he was universal social thinker. Gandhi and Jinnah's ideology were based on incomplete study and Dalit-literature became threat for the two great forces of the world as a solution of the problem is 'Third Force' that is, Dalit. In simple words 'Perestroika means socio-economic transformation with a aim to make a society a real welfare state. Glasnost has given a new and positive direction to the policies of USSR. As author did work on the composite dialogue as a Sindhi Ruler of the 'Rai dynasty' of Kashmir, who are the real ruler of this area. Politics of the Hindus and Muslims have been failed because, they have no issue pertaining to the development of country.

"One reason is there that democracy cannot work without friction, Kashmir Pandits and Molavis, they have to leave the 'Ritu and Rituals' which have no meaning in the life style of the man as 'blind faith' unless there should be fellow-feeling among those who constitute the state history with the original document of the concept 'Chamar' or 'Dalit'. "Faction fights for leadership and discrimination in administration are factors ever present in a mixed state and are incompatible with democracy" (Ibid; p. 16). In the words of M. Gorbachev "Perestroika implies not only eliminating the Dalit Muslims from Russia, but their conservative idea must be expose". We need 'Scientific and Technological Revolution' as an advance society of the world culture with the ideology of satsang (Radha Soami) as civilised race of the world history. Author study is based on logic. Logic is not there in 'Nawaz Prayer' as 'blind faith' elaborated by Al-bureini in the 9th and 10th century A.D. Society is component of two great races: advance and backward Dalits at one time they were backward, now they are advance in art of writing the Dalit-History. An old concept of the 'Kashmir Issue' as a solution of the problem of the third race. "Slow and steady wins the race". That was the ideology of

Dr B.R. Ambedkar. In simple words Glasnost means openness, a general principle of brotherhood as Holy Quran reflected this idea. This ideology applied to all social groups of Kashmir either Huriyats or Traders = Raj-Rishi Ki Sabita.

North Versus South

In North region of Kashmir people speaks Hindi, Dogri, Kashmiri, Punjabi, Sindi, Ladakhi, Balti, Himachali, Gojari, most of the leaders of these areas they stressed on 'linguistic states', today, we have a issue of Telgana in south India, people need a separate state. But the state like J&K is the issue lying between Pakistan and India, Ladakh an issue of China.

"*No men are foreigner*", this poem has been written by James Falconer Kirkup (1918-2009). He was a prolific translator, writer of poetry and travelogues. No doubt, he wrote several books on the concept of Dalit history by utilizing his knowledge of the poetry is based on as universal social thinker. About the poem '*No men are Foreign*', it has simple and noble message in terms of art of writing that we should not consider anyone as foreign or 'strong'. Dalits are also the part of this country, they were not considered by the modern political forces like BJP, NC, Congress as chunk of population are part of India or Kashmir. Humanity is the same all over the world and in harming anyone we are destroying our own earth or ourselves.

The poem reveals the unity in diversity and having a great message for universal brotherhood or fraternity. In underlines the fact in historical research that the Dalit of Kashmir observed the political analysis of the J&K including Ladakh that the people of this area misbehaved with us as original race of this sub-continent as Buddhist people having the same physical, mental and emotional experiences of the civilised culture as Sufi-Saints. Corruption is there in the idea of man itself based on narrow-minded approach found in the upper class society of Muslims and Hindus. Those are very close to BJP, NC or Congress. Study shows Abdullaha dynasty is dynasty of polluted ideology morally, as well as physical (pp. 124-126). According to J.C. Hill, 'Good Manners', the author lays emphasis on the right conduct of a responsible citizen and a wise man that results from a perspective change. (p. 62 timeless thought a text book compulsory of English for

B.A. I, University of Jammu) without satsang one can not achieve the ideology of 'Good Manners'. Politicians they spoiled the social-structure of the society on 'Bad Manners'. Read out the book of the author 'Sex scandals and political system of India'.

Pollution creator are anti-Dalits of India in Kashmir, Jammu, Ladakh and other states of the world.

State's Biggest Library of the Dalit concept is found at Barnai and Manmat found in Kashmir history after the death of Kashyap Rishi (1500 B.C).

Blind Faith Story of Kashmir

Author inspired from the John Milton's (1608-1674 A.D), who was a great poet of England during the time of Shahjahan and a political writer. Milton's father was a knowledgeable man. He worked as Mahasha of the Dalit Community in England known in Dogri or Hindi in India and Musician and a composer known in English equivalent of Mashu Garide of the local area of Jammu. Author worked on 'Paradise Lost' as we see the present situation of the Kashmir. There is only aggression, corruption and fifty language against the 'Dalit Bhujan Samaj' called 'working labour in China. Because, their ideas is related with 'Law of the Land' not with the idea of phychological history. Their moral code of conduct is dirty as, 'meat eater'. Study is equivalent as 'Rakashas' of the South India which were crushed by Dr B.R. Ambedkar with the idea of 'physchological war' as elevated man of the human history. He challenged the idiot Molavis and Pandits with the stroke of spiritual pen, then he gave a verdict in *History* who were the Sudras? Till date, that means, modern politicians and IAS/IPS, they could not explore his 'ideas' that is 'Dalit' in actual form. No doubt, Mr. V.T. Rajshekar, he is known great writer in foreign countries, but in India Pandit and Molavis, they do not like the 'spakes and speeches' of the Ambedkar's ideology.

Composition of Dalit-I-Illahi Libration Front

The important question to the modern society of "Kashmir' or "India' which has the same meaning in historical phenomena, that is, the story of 'God' and 'Man'. Religion is a formal treatise of the informal education in the context of human approach and it depends on '*theory of Line of Action*' of the man called '*Karma theory*' in the ideology of Mahatma Gandhi and Sonia Gandhi. Sonia is an ideology of Muhmmad Ghori or Ghur as Afgani or Turkish rulers and Gandhi is related with the activities of the 'soul' as a small ideology in the relationship theory of God and Man.

The folk lores and various antiquities and artifacts which have been explored from Bijbehara of Kashmir like Shabir Ahmad lone, adhoc lecturer in English, posted in the GDC. Bijbehara itself as an idea of '*History Repeat itself*' as a Dalit student of this area and many more use to work in colleges of Kashmir, Ladakh and Jammu, Udhampur like Samista Thakur, Hans Raj Sharma, etc. Dr P.K. Kane, also mentions various names in his study about the past poets of 'Kashmir' or 'India' there names are such as *Aupajanghani*, *Katya*, *Kashyap Rishi*, *Gantama, Mandgalya* of Kashmir and Harita of Doda City. *Apastamba* also cites the views of numerous rages such as Babu Ram Rakwal of Doda city, Preeti Bhagat, Lal Chand Mega, Eknath of South India, Kanna of Himachal, Kautra of Kathua (Dr. Janak Singh, Lecturer in Mathematics) there is *Vartika* like Falak Madam of Kashmir, which speaks of *Dharmasastra* as a duty of the individual to see the man in the light of the development of the history of this was now professor in History at Akhnoor College and Falak Madam at GDC, Doda. Jaimini like Pushaplata speaks of the duties of a Sudra or a Dalit historian as Lajat down in Kane, 'History of Dharmasastra' (pp. 12-13). Patanjali declared a cold ware against the anti Dalits Hindus, Muslims and Sikhs of India that today '*Highest Dharma*' of the Universe is *Dalit* or *Radha Soami* as Ancient culture of the Kashyap Rishi of Akhnoor = Original Ideology.

Challenges and Issues Before the Lord

Lord says, "We need good friends", as wifves in the newly constructed 'House of the Lord' at Barnai in Jammu district for the welfare of the state. 'Arthur Miller' All my sons' edited by Nissim Ezekiel published this play in 1972. Nissim Ezekiel is a good friend of mine as a Dalit historian of India or Kashmir. His book on Arthur Miller opened the chapter of American Literature, University of Bombay. He uses to work as 'Reader' in the said department as a modern scholar of '*Dalit Voice*' called him preacher of the Sufi philosophy or ideology. 'All My Sons', his play commercially successful play as the History of Chamar Dynasty, 600-1200 A.D. The play was staged in 1947 during the partition of India. Kashmir became a challenges before the Lord as a part of India to explore the new horizontal track of knowledge to find out the '*Truth in History*'. Negative forces, they proved completely, failure to find out the solution of the 'Kashmir problem' = *Artificial Sciences*.

Problem is lying within the man itself while, it is the same story as the story of 'God and Man'. '*Religion*' is a problem for the anti-Dalits, those have no knowledge of the '*Nam-History*' or the concept of the Dalit Voice' or '*Interior Islam*' as per the statement of Tamara Sonn. Therefore, author needs, association of the 'beautiful women' known as Dr Shabnam Grewal, Dr Sonayna Chakku, Dr Preeti Bhagat of Doda City to run the administration of the Jammu, State as well as of Ladakh and Kashmir for the time being as a first step of the 'War of Succession' for the coronation of the Dalit scholar after the Death of Dr B.R. Ambedkar.

Indian Literature in English: A Critical Review on Dalit history.

It is a modest attempt of the author to evaluate some prominent personalities of the world history like John Milton, G.B. Shaw, Arthur Miller, etc that they did hard labour to remove the various obstacles of the finds of 'Darkness' to remove the blind faith of the society than they become good dictator of the world, wherestand the ideology of ex-professor Z.A. Hashmi or Ex-professor Balwan, Dr Azaz Ahmad Wani or Babu Ram Rakwal as low grade employees of this institution. They have no sense of behavior, but Lord says, "There is no existence of the corrupt historians'. They have mean mentality in their lifestyle 'only prostitution' else is nothing. It is an anthology of various historians on the issue of '*Dalit faith*'. They have no sense of behavior about Madam Falak, HOD English. She is junior to me, but senior in understanding even though she belonged to the 'Muslim Faith' as 'Natural species of the Lord'. Author is committed to professional development, we need more species for the examination to elaborate her personality as professor Samista Thakur as handsome women of the Dalit history as a close relative of the Sufi Saint Scholar. No doubt, she is the wife of author's art of writings. Author needs to complete the story of both the scholar one is genius and other is good human being as *Nam* themselves. Madam needs an association of a Dalit-Soldier Professor Sutee Ved Gargotra an Ex-man of the army personel, worked in 'Jat Regiment' as a handsome scholar like that of Raja Suchet Singh Ram nagariya of Udhampur district in the present history of the man. The family of the said scholars is handsome and royal in nature. Author needs club of this situation as 'One Family' of the 'One Father' as little master Deepit Raj or Rajat Gurgotra, next to Gurugovind ('*Indian Literature in English*; *Critical views*'; by S.Bardudhe). This paragraph contains the impact of Dalit literature and Gandhian fiction on the historical research of the North Indian states. (Ibid). His Co-edited book on Sachin Tendulkar, a great bats man of the World is in the print media. The area of the authors psychology is to face the modern problems of the world history as the story of 'God and Man'. There is no seope of the 'blind faith' thinkers either Aasha Ram Papu or Sonia Gandhi. Farooq Abdullaha, and Umar Abdullaha stand nowhere in the term 'History'. As Arthur miller in his study, again reflected the ideology of 'No Villain' in the following year. Writer killed them in the art of writing with the magic spell of the 'Nam-History'.

In the last, Dalit – History of Kashmir is unending dialogue between the present and the past the commitment of author with 'Nehru and Sheika' is still pending to review more Dalit literature and various aspects of the Indian constitution after the discussion with Farooq Abdullaha or Omar Abdullaha on the issue of good governance.

Origin of the Islam = Islamic Concept or Islamic State of Mind

"Mentifesto of the local Rajputs of Kashmir and their ideology = Kastriya Rajput = serve the society, study the ved". " U n i v e r s a l Declaration of Human Rights", was the mentifesto of the Dalit Samaj = Kashtriya Revolution of the Ambedkarite throught and his icon figure was Nam or Lord Buddha. Syham Sunder, the Chairman of the Bhim Sena visited America, Britian and Europe and he declared a war against the anti-Dalit propaganda. There was a class struggle theory between Dr B.R. Ambedkar to Brahminism that at least. 'A Good Human Being Society' may be launched in the world market. But at the same time, when politics after 70 years of the Independence (1947), there is a

"Protective Discrimination" in the Dalit Samaj = Upper class women = idiot Rajput = Negative thinkers found in the Manhas and Chib tribes of North India. Mira as a Rajput of the sultanate period = Falak Madam = Muslim Rajput = Positive Thinkers = Baba Ravidas = Dr Raj Kumar.

In the Varna oriented = Nam - dan = Dhamma dan is essential for equal status = Human Rights in the 21st century = Pan-Chamar formed the majority and worked a lot to unite the society under privileged class = women = sudra concept = Kashtriya History = Dalit Samaj of the Contemporary world = UNO Resolution.

Graphic Theory

During the last more than two decades have witnessed, militancy is there in Kashmir, why and how, because Manmat needs appreciation = *Badyi* or to hight the Resolution of Kashmir in the world level, that there is a discrimination among Muslims on the question of creating of Pakistan = make the idea clear from the core of the heart and head = Non-Muslim agencies = Mohagir to Mujahid in Azad Kashmir. Body of Victim = Body of Warrior = Kashatriya Race = Chamarisation Agenda = Idiot Brahmin - Rajput Manhas = Mira = Falak = Macbeth style = Wife of William Shakespeare. Status of Women in Dalit Samaj = Male Species. According to my sister Sasista Parveen, good human beings = good scholars. There is, no doubt, in advance Muslim Society, there are god human being = Safullaha Khan = Dalit scholar. We need no adholism in the Higher Education System = Idiot Personalities = Muzzafar Iqbal, Lecturer in Education.

The Children's History of Civilisation= Computer Age, Wrapper = Social change in historical research. Cities lost in the jungles of Central America = Barrack Obama and his family = Dalit Mochi Muslim Samaj = Dr Raj Kumar. Development of a Non-material Culture = Ved Parakesh of the Ancient History = Nam-Dev = Dr D.K. Surya = Chengez Khan Surya. There is no Muslims, no Hindus = all are good human being. Dawn of the Neolithic Age = Brahminism + Black Polish Culture.

The Indus and Yellow River = Kala Samaj = Gurdeep Giri Society, superior than the modern Brahmins of India = Meat Eater = Sharma Baradari of Doda = Manhas. Kotoch = less Satsangis, but pure in thinking to non-thinking. The Mediterranean from the latin meaning 'between the seas' is the biggest changed through the SAmaj Sudarak = Dr Raj Kumar. One is follower and other is not follower = contest theory = change of senerio = politics nil.

Peace and Prosperity is the agenda of the Sudra clan, Brahmin had a destructive vision in their lifestyle = propaganda of the Sudra tribe of Sindh = Gargotra Clan Rai Dynasty and Bhardwaj Gotra = Ravidas's Philosophy = Chamar thought discovered from the north of painting = Jammu City. City of Mandirs converted into City of Temples = Bhardwaj Ashram of Muthi-Barnai, House No. 14 Jambu-divpa = Dream City, situated upper bank of the Ranbir Canal. Canal = Chennal of Chamba = Dalit Samaj. Chamar has a long history of the ancient India = Arathaia, a phrase used in the research work of the past = Dr B.R. Ambedkar = Baba Gurinder Singh ji = Phule = Deepit Raj, Dr Raj Kumar is the hero of the Dalit Samaj = next to Dr B.R. Ambedkar.

Pressures of Change = New Social Orders of the Representative of God = Balban's theory of Nature = Naturalism + Truism = Humanism. Humanism and Rationality was there in Mohammad Prophet's writings = Holy Quran = Message of the God = Chamar thought or Mochi Club of America = Barrack Obamma.

'*Guru Ravi Dass Ki Baniya*', published by Rahul Gootama, Delhi in 2003 pp. 1-24 is the story of Lordism = Arabic Ideology = Rabani to remove the obstacle of the anti-Dalits = Difficult task. In 2003, Dr Raj Kumar took Ph.D. in Art-History and highlight the them of Dr B.R. Ambedkar = Prophet of God. "The genesis of attack from religious obscurantists is based on the misguided youth of the Kashmir valley = Dr J.I. Tarambu = Positive thinker.

"*Science and Society of Early Medieval Period*" = Arabs and Turks representative of the God = Mohammad Prophet = evidence from the "*History of the Chamar Dynasty*" (600 to 1200 A.D.) Durlabhavaradhan Partapadity II of Kashmir = Deepit Raj. Harshvaradhan of South = North India submitted his Buddhist relic = New Discovery of the scientific truth = Chamar Ideology = Sufi Saint Philosophy = Rabani Customs = Buddhamat = No Class and Caste Distinction. "He is the same, call him Mahadeva or Mohammad, Brahma or Adam".

Study shows, that Adam to Prophet, there were 26 Prophet, Verdict came with the ideology of Dalit Samaj = Poor people of the Prophet Mohammad = Dalit Mochi Muslim.

The Holy Quran describes the blessed Saints in the Paradise of Kashmir = Durlabha-varadhana I in the following terms:

"He loveth them and they love him" (V. 54).

Intellectual Forces = Scientific History

The 19th Century for the European Community and the Western World, analysised the Democratic Institution with the evolutionary change for the development of social well being of the society and that pattern was brought by Dr B.R. Ambedkar for the development of Idea and financial prosperity from Katcha Makan to Pacca Makan = Balance of approach for the advancement of the sudra state of mind = New Islamic Culture = Sufi Ideology, but people of North india failed to chease his identity = Positivism to teach a lesson to the natorious goonds of the valley = Farooq Abdullah = Umar Abdullah. Poverty is still existing in the ideology of Negative thinkers.

The Indo-Arabic Contact = Authenlic Approach = *Karbala War*, Peace and Conflict = Gandhi Philosophy = Shia Sooch = Hindu Ideology. Thesis = anti-thesis = Synthesis = "Age of the Scientific Revolution".

The basic ideology of Prophet Mohammad = Mahadeva in the cyclical progress was the Idea = Nam = Kalma = Kun Philosophy and Kashmir was the focus point for the development of Historical Materialism. It was also followed up by Mohammad Ghori and Mahmood Qaznavi acrossed the Kashmir valley with the concept of Sultan = Suratrana and Kashmir became a biggest centre of learning in the world history = Islamic Study = Vedic Knowledge + Prophet Teaching.

After the downfall of the "Gupta Age", the book the "*Spirit of Islam*" = Holy Quran = Holy Word = Cosmic Order came into existence in the 'House of Lord' = Chari-i-Sharif = Kashmiri Ideology of the distorted facts in *History* as the story of 'God and Man'. 'Forgive me O Ghalib for being to reconstruct the religions of Islam, not Religion

= Blind Faith = Rapist Era'. Great Kashmir needs = Strong Ideology = Deobandi Movement or Qadari Orders = Respectable Solution = 7.5 per cent Dalit race of Jammu and Kashmir = Honest Living = OBC and 10 per cent OM = 40 per cent Women = Total 60 per cent and 40 per cent all over India polluted Ideology = Monkey Mind Theory = Darwin's suggestion in Botany. Cardial Insight = Friendship treaty Mohammad Prophet and his family including One Son and two Daughters.

Holy Quran is the History of *Dharmsatra. History of Dharmsastra* translated from Sanskrit to English by P.V. Kane = 9 Vols. In the very first volume, he explained the meaning of *Dharma* in English language = Ordinance, usage, duty, right justice, morality, virtue, religion, good works, function or characteristic. It is a support view of "Holy Quran" = "Holy Book". (p.1)

What was the Dharma of Prophet Mohammad = Serva Dharma to respresents all the distorted facts of the human psychology and it becamse a Holy Quran = Holy Ghost explained in Bible about the beauty of the body of Lord = Prophet Mohammad and exploited by the Negative thinker = Rapist Race of Valley = Halal Meat. Holy Ghost = Prophet's body = Cosmic View of the Gurubani = Message of the Heavenly King.

Prestly Class = Dalit Samaj. Holy Priest = Baba Gurinder Singh Ji Dillion = Judism = Dictator of the World = "Bal Concept" is still displayed in the Char-i-Sarif Masjid as a new discovery of the Art-History = ID = Ego = Destructive Ideology of the human history = Manmat or Evil Spirit. Holy Spirit = Nam or Shabd. Nabi = Avatar, Harif = Letter or Shabd = New Discovery of Truth = Dalit-History.

Holy Quran is based on the teaching of Lord Buddha = Distorted concept from ancient to modern man in art of writing the scientific history of the Holy Prophet = Little Master Deepit Raj. Another meaning of the Prophet Mohammad's Pschyology = An Element of existence = Good Human Being i.e. of matter, mind and force (P.V. Kane, Vol. 1, pp. 1-5).

The explanation of the *Dharma-theory* = Personal Ideology = Realizing Soul in art history *know - Dharma* to be that which is practised both in Art and Science as an Ideology = Truth based knowledge = Aja = Holy Quran = Chamar thought and free from hatred = Moral life, not Mohan Das Karam Chand Gandhi, but it was Dr B.R. Ambedkar, who visualised the idea of Nur Mohammad = Shiv Rao which is essential in the Buddhist philosophy to realize the truth. 'Truth is God' wherestands the ideology of the Sonia Gandhi or Farooq Abdullaha as a leader of the Muslims and Hindu philosophy = Rapist Race. Civilised race = Dalit History based on the term "Wisdom" or Spirit.

Humanism and Rational, approached and preached by Dr B.R. Ambedkar = Buddha Sattva was the Prophet of God of the 20th century. Same references has been quoted by the author from the Holy Quran revealed by Prophet Mohammad = Madhu Mantra Theory = Gurmantra Ideology, Kun was the basic philosophy of the art-historian to published book on *Panchshabada*. Before the revelation of Holy Quran, Bhakti Movement was there in Arab Country = All over the world on the theory of *Arab* = Lordism. It was prevalent in the history of India, after the downfall of the Mughals = Dalit Christianity = Coolie Culture of the Kashmir.

'Kashmir Throughout The Ages'

"Do not fall in Love, with a Killer?"

Agatha Christie Nemesis

The book entitled, "*Early History of Jammu Region*" (Pre-historic to 6th Century A.D.). A concept has been launched by the author to kill the anti-Dalit, historians of Kashmir like Muslims, and Hindus. They have "no history".

I. Life and Times:

Questionably or unquestionably, Garmany has produced a disproportionately large number of great scholars since the Reformation and before and the field of sociology has claimed a healthy share war and economic depression seem not to have adversely affected such development w.e.f. 1947 to onward, "Socialism", rather "Materialism" were the two consent forces, they used to work in the history of India. "Materialism" became "Prostitution". It is focused upon the anti-Dalit = in the upper class society of India either Ghulam Nabi Azad or Sonia Gandhi = Prakash Singh Badal = Poonchi Sardar = Brahminism. During the rule of Bismark = German scholar, he worked on the concept of 'Athen democracy' to cut the nose and throat of the anti-Dalit = have nots. Max Weber and his wife, Helene = Falak Madam of GDC Doda, Lecturer in English is highlighting the theme of "Athen Democracy" = work for the betterment of the future generation. No doubt, she was born in the Muslim family, but she is by nature is a Dalit scholar = Chura Samaj = anti-Dali. Prostitution is not a solution of the social problem, but money matters either, there was Kashmiri Pandit = Dr V.K. Bhatt, unmarried scholar. He made sexual relation with the wife of elder brother, who was impotent, having no sex in natural way and exploited the Babiji for sexual arrangement as now called Bachelor = M.B.B.S. Degree. No doubt, Kashmiri Pandits or Kashmiri Musalman having the same knowledge = Prostitution. By Prostitute of the World is known history = Dr Farooq Abdullah = Nehru Clan = Negative Tribes". Negativism = Positive attack from the sides of Dalit Dynasty = Rai Family of Kashmir, they ruled of Sind nearabout 137 years as per the statement of R.K. Tripathi, R.K. Mookerji, etc. Arab Conquest = Conquest of the Lord.

II. Little Max's = Deepit Raj = Falak Madam's, son represented the society of Dalit Concept = Radha Soami Samaj, the latest finding of the author's scientific discoveries = Social Scientist = Dr Raj Kumar + Chura thought = Dr Shabnam Grewal = Preeti Chamaran = Sonyana Chakoo = Rambi Samaj = Civilised growth in Chamar thought = Raj-Rishi Ke Sabita.

III. In 2003, Dr Raj Kumar took the Degree of Ph.D. = *Paintings and Lifestyles of Jammu Region*" (1700 to 1900 A.D.). Every concept of the World History has been described, this book is not available in the GDC Doda's Library, because, there is illegal purchasing led by Prof. Z A Hashmi = Strong Negative thinker = NC Party's Work. Author has "no party" = Radha Soami ideology" = Positivism.

IV. Study Leave = Military Service = Intelligence War, similar like that of Max Weber did with the cooperation of his parents = Dalit Samaj. No formal education = Dalit Voice = Simple living and high think and their ideology was "work is worship". Kashmiri Pandits = Kashmiri Molavis left the ideology of Dr B.R. Ambedkar = Maharaja Hari Singh = ideology of the Dalit Concept = Garib Ka Niwaj. No

Satsang = Truthful knowledge Dr V.K. Bhatt has no knowledge of the "*Sound-Current*" = Physics Subject = Illiterate man of the human history = Materialistic Sooch = thinking to non-thinking. There is no discovery of the childhood = No class, no Jamaat = Zero level Ke study = Chamar thought = childhood. Teach to teacher, Profess to Professor = Nil vata Nil, Parihar tribe of Doda. No knowledge of Physics or Chemistry = Sarita Parihar = Negative thinkers. *History* is a concept of two great forces, that is, God and Man. The concept launchers are Dalits = Sudras with a family of beautiful women = Wordworth's qualification = Dalit House = Lord's House = playground of the human pyschologist = Nami Rulers = Gulab - nama = Babar-nama.

Akbar-nama = Great Social-thinkers = Suteel Ved = Suchet Singh of the previous life and Diyan Singh = Sat Paul = concept launcher of the French Revolution of 1789 = Working Class = Dalit Samaj is known in Indian democracy of the upper union of the Doda district = Parihar Family or Hashmi Goonda element = Dr V.K. Bhatt, ex-principal of GDC Doda = Kashmiri Pandit, having the same Samaj. Untouchability is still existing in the formal education society = Old concept.

V. Major Scientific Theory on Untouchability = Suahashat = Achut of the Gupta Age = Dalit Samaj "Rites and Rituals' have no in Sudra State of mind = Athen Democracy. English medicines = Vicasul capsule are more than sufficient to draw the lines of Have and have-nots. Have-nots in the theory of Lordism, they stand nowhere, Haves = Truthfall ideology = Preeti Bhagat = Chamarn Wife= having no knowledge of the KPS or IPS = Dr Shabnam Grewal. She is superior women than the writer as "inspiration" of the author's writings who are the original Kashmiri = Dalit Historian and His Family = Satnami Rulers of the Madhydesh. Bun Doda is the temporary house of the residing of the author = rental accommodation. Dr V.K. Bhatt = upper class Brahmin = Kashmiri Pandit is the Chief guest of the Hashmi tribe of Doda and accommodated in the "Guest Room" of the College, Dr Raj Kumar = Dalit scholar has no room for Him = "untouchable Boys" of Sarif's play.

VI. Discovery and Truth = "*Bharat Ka Nam Jambu Devipa tha*" and its capital was Harappa = story of the Nami Rulers = Kingdom's of the Lord's House = Bahujan Samaj Party, a discovery of Sh. Kanshi Ram in 1984. This party distrubed both the Congress and BJP = Coalition Era having no scientific approach, why and because, they (political parties) have the ideology of Nehru-Gandhi and Sheikh=BAMCF. Dr B.R. Ambedkar's Photograph is not sufficient to received the votes of the Dalit Samaj, but to discover 'His Ideology' was the challenge before the Brahminism or Mohammadanism or Sikhism or upper class Christian of South India = IPS/IAS. In North India, the condition of the low caste Christian = Dalit Christian = Chamar Culture, they have no right of knowledge, who was the founder of Christianity = Lord Christ = 'Bahujan Samaj'. Indra, Pusha = Weaker Class = Megh Dynasty of Kashmir = Avantivarman = Meghavarman of the "*Ancient Kashmir*" before the Buddhist ruler Ashoka. Author concluded this paragraph with the statement of Max Weber, "the combined qualities of "Action" to act upon and its "meaning" has to be interpretated = increase of Knowledge = Ambedkarism = Dalit Samaj. In Kashmir, no body liked this concept that is, "Dalit = "Sufi Ideology", and perferred's and perferred's Gandhiji and Bazaz's ideology = Hinduism or Islam. Christianity, left for 'Watal Parivar' = Chamar thought called "untouchables" in India and the theme of this story, that is, "*History Repeat Itself*" = Dalit Samaj or Sufi Ideology or Interior evidence = "Sodara ruler" in Persian art of writing the Medieval History of India and defined the meaning of every term either Islam or Afgan or Pathan or Khan that is logic before the research scholars of the various fields either Hindus or Muslims. Term Dalit, we mean "light of the degraded Samaj or Innocent peoples = Good Womens = Sudra History:-

(1) Early History of Jammu Region (Pre-histeric to 6th Century).

(2) History of Chamar Dynasty (600 to 1200)

(3) Medieval History of Sudra (1200 to 1705)

(4) Paintings and Lifestyles of Jammu Region (1700 to 1900)

Note:- Glorious History of Dalits Past and Present = Check on the Materialist approach = thinker to non-thinker = Socialist Ideology. New concept and New Ideology = Classless Society or Classless Society. No big, no small, all are equal, liberty to some extent, Brotherhood is there.

Rashtriya Uchchatar Shiksha Abhiyan

RUSA is a Centrally Sponsored Scheme (CSS), launched in 2013 aims at providing strategic funding to eligible state higher educational institutions. The central funding would be norm based and outcome dependents. The funding would flow from the central ministry through the state govt./union territories to the State Higher Education Councils before reaching the identified institutions. The funding to states would be made on the basis of critical appraisal of State Higher Education plans, which would describe each state's strategy to address issues of equity, access and excellence in higher education = Qualitive Objective.

Objectives:- Salient objectives of RUSA are:

- Improve the overall quality of state institutions by ensuring conformity to prescribed norms and standards and adopt accreditation as a mandatgory quality assurance framework.
- Usher transformative reforms in the state higher education system by creating a facillitating institutional structure for planning and monitoring at the state level, promoting anatomy in state universities and improving governance in institutions.
- Ensuring reforms in the affiliation, academic and examination systems.
- Ensure adequate availability of quality faculty in all higher educational institutions to devote themselves to research and innovations = Prophet Mohammed Ke Theory.
- Create an enabling atmosphere in the higher educational institutions to devote themselves to research and innovations.
- Expand the institutional base by creating additional capacity in existing institutions and establishing new institutions, in order to achieve enrolment targets = over crowded state.
- Correct regional imbalances in access to higher education by setting up institutions in un-served and undeserved areas = mis-using of Govt. fund.
- Improve equity in higher education by providing adequate opportunities of higher education to SC/STs and socially educationally backward classses; promote inclusion of women, minorities and differently abled persons.

Components

RUSA would create new universities through upgradation of existing autonomous colleges and conversion of colleges in a cluster. It would create new model degree colleges, new professional colleges and provide infrastructural support to universities and colleges faculty recruitment support, faculty improvements programmes and leadership development of educational administrators are also an important part of the scheme.

In order to enhance skill development the existing central scheme of polytechnics has been subsumed within RUSA. A separate component to synergise vocational education with higher education has also been included in RUSA. Besides these, RUSA also supports reforming, restructuring and building capacity of institutions in participating state = secret-agenda of the art-historian = Nami gooda.

Institutional Hierarchy:- RUSA is implemented and monitored through an institutional structure comprising the National Mission Authority, Project Approval Board and the National Project Directorate at the centre and the State Higher Education Council and State Project Directorate at the state level = French Revolution to Lenin's Approach.

I. **Teaching of Mohemmad Prophet:-** The discovery of the Truth = Scientific Knowledge, every Saint-Philosopher has the same message to give and the same teachings to impart as that of Prophet Mohemmad (570 to 637 A.D.). No Saint, no Prefect Master, comes into this world to creat a Religion = Negative thinkers like Prof. Hans Raj Sharma exploited the Dalit Muslims of Doda City = BJP or Jang Sangh Party. We need not to destroy the Brahminical Code of conduct = We need to destroy Election System of India = Jammu and Kashmir State = Ladakh's concept of union terrioritary '*History of the Brahmans*' by Dr Raj Kumar, Kalpaz publication, New Delhi, 2006, pp. 9 to 167.

II. **Religion and Problem:-** Neeraj; M.S.O.E.-3; '*Sociology of Religion*' based on IGNOU Syllabus = anti-Dalit concept. Religion is man made psychyology = Brahminism.

III. **Religious experience = Spiritual contents** = It has two fundamental values = *have* and *have-nots*. Haves = anti-

Dalits and *Have-nots* = Dalit concept = Garib Dass concept of the Moin-ud-Din Chisht of Rajasthan.

IV. Marxian Theory:- Negative concept of the South Indian political leaders = CPM or CPi and other political parties of Mamta Banerjee or Jaylilitya of Tamil Nadu or East Bengal. Janta Dal United = Beju Patnik failed to prove the historical *truth* in his book *'Introduction to Plants*'. Marxian theory failed, why because of his *'Dead Master History*' = Brahminism.

V. Religion and Navratra:- Roza of the Muslim Community = Brahminism theory of the later vedic religion of India = North India as well as South India. It is based on two types of Radha Soami Religion: (1) Rasila Ram's Teaching = Sur Dynasty of the Mughal period or Afganis or Pathans of the Sind and Multan. (2) Baba Jaimal Singh of Dera Bias = Classical history of the various Sufi Saint from Jaimal Singh to present Master Baba Gurinder Singh Ji Dillion. Dr Raj Kumar is follower of this concept as *Dalit Voice = Inner Voice*. It is based on Universal Religion = Jainism or old Buddha which originated from Chura thought = Sh. Bisakhi Ram = Peasant Movement = Mochi thought of Kushana period.

VI. Dominating Ideology:- Big Soul = Theory of Lordism = Arabic concept of the Dalit History.

VII. A bird's eye view, embracing the whole of Dakhan concept = *Sudra Race*, originated from the body, Head = Brahmin + others = One concept of the Human Ideology = Radha Soami Concept, would show it to be a roughly outlined triangular table-land = equality base knowledge of the German-philospher = Zanaide-A-Rajozin = *Vedic India* = New form.

VIII. Western Ghat = Eastern Ghat:- On such a strip the wealthy = Khan Palaza = Gandkhana = Dirty spices of the lord = Hare and magnificent city of Bombay = *Maharshartra* as an ideology of Ravidas = Ambedkarbadi = A selection from the famous anthology = Samista Thakur = Nam-History = Botanist wife of Gulab-Singh as fellow friend in the present life = Raj-

Rishi Akhnoor. Net-Slet = UGC Criteria = Ragini, Sofia, a student of Arabic, wife of the Bharat Rattan Award = Dr B.R. Ambedkar = present Dr R. K. Bhardwaj.

IX. Discovery of Cell = Study of Early Man:- It is based on *Living* and *Non-Living* material. Superior = Dalit Concept = Living Identity = Chamar History. *Living History* = The concept of the Sudra Race = Maharaja Gulab Singh to Dr B.R. Ambedkar found in South India = J&K State. Ladakh is a state of prostitution = Old Buddha Concept = Readymade Turban psychyology.

X. Robert Hooke (1635-1703 A.D.) = Social-Scientist and his micro-level study became useful not in the 17th century, but his contribution still found in the history of *'Human Cell'* = Nami Puras (Dr. V.K. Jain; '*Fundamentals of Plant Physiology*', New Delhi, 2008, p. 1). he was an English Writer, worked on the micro-level study coined the term on the 'Living Cell' Contribution = 'Hollow-story' of the Sufi Ideology = but truth is art of writing the Dalit history. Advance Macro-economics = Ideology of Good Human Souls as a property of Lordism = Mohemmad Prophet.

XI. Correct Ideology:- Meditation of the Prefect Master = Living Deity = Complete Knowledge + Study of various books of the modern genius scholar = Dalits.

8

A Chronicle of the Kings of Sindh and Multan-a Critical Review of the Dalit Literature

The Rajatarangini:- Kalhana's *Rajatarangini* enjoys a unque position amongst the ancient texts of Indian literature in that it is the only composition that can be regarded as a historical text in the real sense of the word. Whereas no coherent ancient treatise on history is available in the rest of the Indian subcontinent, Kashmir has been fortunate enough in this regard that it has a carefully recorded historical tradition dating back to medieval times of the Islamic Culture to Modern Man.

Kalhana wrote his *Rajatarangini* (literally the 'river of kings') during 1148-49 A.D. It is a record of history from the earliest period to Kalhana's own times. Kalhana himself testifies to the existence of not lesS than eleven earlier compositions on the history of Kashmir which he consulted to write his own immortal Rajatarangini = Vedic Concept.

Naturally actors and writers of the universal drama were anxious to gain royal favour and politics is a part time study of the Professor (Dr. Shabnam Grewal).

Although the initial chapters of the *Rajatarangini* do have a rather legendary character, the rest of it gives a fairly good account of Kashmir history which has stood the test of historical criticism. It can be accepted as a reliable record from the seventh century onwards and the details and authenticity increase as we approach the times of the author himself.

In addition to being a fairly accurate history, *Rajtarangini* is undoubtedly a work of art as well. Comprising of eight cantos of Sanskrit verse it is a brilliant portrayal of a bygone age = Past History.

The merits of this great work have not gone unnoticed. As early as 15th century, Zain-ul-Abidin (the great King of Kashmir lovingly called '*Budshah*') got it translated into Persian. Abul Fazal incorporated tracts from it in his *Ain-i-Akbari*. Francois Bernier, who visited Kashmir as early as 1665, makes a mention of it in his *Letters* = Rasa-Theory. it was translated into French by M.Troyer. Many other European scholars worked on it, but it was Sir M.A. Stein who gave us the monumental English translation of this masterpiece in 1900 A.D. = Challengeable Task.

A study of the *Rajatarangini* not only afforts a view of the past but also a realisation that the trials and tribulations of the common man as well as the virtues and the vices of the rulers, have remained essentially similar throughout the ages. This makes *Rajatarangini* relevant to our times and to the future as well.

Kalhana:- It is ironic that no record of the life of this scholar-poet-historian who gave us such an excellent record of his own times and the times preceding him, is available as such. However, a careful study of his narrative does give us some idea regarding the author's personality and the conditions prevailing during his time. Kalhana himself puts a date to his writing, indicating that his monumental treatise was written during the years 1148-49 A.D. After a careful study of the description of events in the *Rajtarangini*, Dr Stein has suggested his date of birth to be around 12th century. The greater portion of Kalhana's life seems to have passed during a period of civil war and political disturbance in Kashmir.

Kalhana's father, *Campaka*, seems to have held several responsible positions under King *Harsha* = Nam. It appears that Parihaspura must have been the original home of Kalhana's family. Though a sympathetic attitude towards Buddhism can be felt throughout his treatise, Kalhana was a Shaivite Dalit Brahmin by faith as Tulsi Dass of U.P.

Kalhana's composition brings out his erudition in the various branches of traditional learning. He appears to have been well versed with the epics, *Ramayana* and the *Mahabharata* as well as the important works of poetry of his period and that of antiquity of the *Dalit-history*.

Kalhana's father having stayed loyal to King Harsha throughout his dwindling fortunes, the family must have suffered many a hardship. Kalhana does not seem to have enjoyed any special royal favour or held any significant office during his life time. This has been an advantage so far as his narrative is concerned because he has been able to chronicle facts without any prejudices or embellishments that could have crept in had he enjoyed royal patronage in the lifestyle of Kashap Rishi and Raj Rishi of the 'Naga Cult'. The Naga Cult tribes have also been found in U.P. Haryana, Jalandhar, H.P. A.P. Bombay and Maharashra particularly Poona etc. in the modern states but in Kashmir, Ladakh they are in minority. Kalhana emerges as a very brilliant historian. He seems to have followed scientific methods in that he has consulted previous works,

Steins's monumental translation of the Rajtarangini is scholarly and quite reliable considering that it is based on a reliable original text arranged by another legendary scholar, Dr Buhler. Kalhana says, "Kings of the River" as a Dalit concept in the art of writing the authentic history as a new discovery of the Indian history.

Kalhana's *Rajatarangini*:- It has often been said of the India of the Hindus that it possessed "no history". The remark is true if we apply it to *History* as a Science and ARt, such as classical culture in its noblest prose works has bequeathed it to us. But it is manifestly wrong if by history is meant either for historical development or the materials for studying it. India has never known among its *Sastra* the study of history such as Greek and Rome cultivated or as modern Europe understands it. yet the materials for such a study are equally at our disposal in India.

They are contained not only in such original sources of information as inscriptions, coins and antiquarian remains generally, advancing research has also proved that written records of events or of traditions concerning them have by no means been wanting in ancient India = Present condition.

This is not the place to examine the causes which in India have prevented the growth of a historical literature in the western sense of the world. They are most closely connected with deep-rooted pecularities of Indian thought and culture which have rendered the mind of the Indian scholar indifferent to the search for the bare truths of historical facts and have effectively prevented it from arriving at the perception of historical development and change into Dalit-Samaj.

It is a direct result of these causes that we find the great mass of what we must call records of Indian history would appear distant from the field of his research. Much of what popular tradition hand retained of the events of any early past, has found its way, overgrown and interwoven with myths and legends, into the Indian epics, the *Puranas* and the fuble literature. The object to which we owe such records of traditional lore, are didactic and religious, but not historical = authentic History.

Historical Kayas:- On the other hand artificial Sanskrit poetry has availed itself, probably from an early date of historical themes. The service in this case mainly as a framework for this display of all the subtle poetic art and rhetorical embellishment which constitute the characteristic object and *reaison d'etre* of the *Kavya*. It is no more chance that almost all '*Historical Kavyas*' (Caritas) which have yet come to light, deal with exploits of the poets princly patrons or the latters immediate predecessors. Sanskrit poetry of the Kavya type has always been artificial product, depend more than any other branch of Indian scholarship word for as such we must class it *Chamar* on court patronage. If then the Kavi had enough originality to choose his theme outside the hackneyed spheres of mythology and remove, what subject more suitable could he find that the life of the ruler who was likely to reward his labours. This restriction of the subject of the historical Kavya has effected in two directions its value as a source of historical information. The fact that it treats of contemporary events represents an undentified advantage. But this is impaired to no small extent by the obvious limitations implied by the penegyrical character there poems. As the events described are suppoed to be well known to the reader, the author's skill is not directed towards a lucid exposition of the facts and their causes but rather towards their poetic embellishment. Hence, results a striking want of accurate details without which are narrative cannot attain true historic reality and an equally striking abundance of obscure allusions, the point of which must necessarily often escape us.

This character of the *Caritas* directly accounts for their rare preservation. Written for the delectation of a particular court and period, they were bound soon to lose popularity if they ever attained it. When no longer read by the Pandits these works ceased to be copied and the few extant manuscripts were exposed to all the risks attending Indian libraries. We can hence scarcely feel surprised that so few only of these texts should have come down to us (*Vikraman kadevacarita*: pp. 1 sqq).

Character and Scope of Kalhana's Chronide:-The interest of Kalhana's *Rajatarangini* for Indian history generally leis the fact that it represents a class of Sanskrit composition which comes nearest character to the '*Chronicles of Medieval Europe*' and the Muhammadans East. Together with the later Kashmir Chronicles which continue Kalhana is narrative, it is practically the sole extant specimen of this class = Sudra State of mind.

A *Kavya* in form and conception the *Rajatarangini* has yet a scope and aim widely different from that of *Caritas* we have previously noticed. Its author's object is to offer a connected narrative to the various dynasties which ruled Kashmir from the earliest period down to his own time. He begins with the legends which represent the popular traditions of the country regarding its earliest history. These he follows up by a narrative of subsequent reigns taken from older written records and arranged in a strictly Chronological order. The final portion of this work, considerable both in extent and historical interest is devoted to an account of the events which the author knew by personal experience or from the relation of living witnesses. The events are narrated from this point of view of a more or less independent chronicler and by no means with the purely penegyrical object of the court poet, which reigns supreme in the *Caritas*.

Kalhana nowhere claims the merit of originality for the plan and form of his work. On the contrary to this, he referes to various earlier compositions on the history of '*Kashmiri Kings*' which he has used. But none of these older workers has come down to us. Nor has Sanskrit literature in any part of *India* preserved for us remains of chronicles similar to the *Rajatarangini*. Though indications of their former existence have come to light the varios quarters. The complete lose of such texts makes it impossible for us to ascertain what Kalhana's work owed to an earlier development, or to judge of its character and its value for historical research by a comparative standards. If we wish to throw light on these points, we can only turn to the chronicle itself. From the indications scattered through the narrative we can gether some instructive facts regarding the author's personality and the time and surroundings in which he lived. A brief analysis of his sources, methods and style will show us in outline the aims and principles which guided him in his labour. Finally, we may, endeavour by a critical examination of Kalhana's narrative and chronology, to ascertain the value of the several portions of his work as sources of historical information. Dalit literature and its development as described by Sharan Kumar Limbale, one of Maharathi pre-eminent Dalit writer-activists, is the author of several story collection about Dalit lifestyle as hardworker race of the human ideology. V.T. Rajshekar, who also highlighted various issues pertaining to Dalit Samaj of India to enlightened the historian of Ambedkar's lifestyle. Dalit literature is a literature of aesthetic sense. It is not easy to learn and it needs devotion, *tapa* and spiritual knowledge of the 'Holy Quarn' that is '*Word*' = Holy Words.

History and the Historical Research = Dalit Literature, Archaeology is a part of it.

I. Introduction – Amritsar session of 2002 = Prof. I.A. Khan, Aligarh photography = Sheikh Abdullah + Pt. Jawahar Lal Nehru = Ideology of Political Process. Flooded Hit-area of Kashmir= Reverse order of the old is gold life = to destruction of the Manmat to realize the Human community that God is there = Basic Ideology + Kayashap Rishi = Bharat Ki Adivasi Naga civilisation = Dalit History; written by Dr Naval Vijogi = Idiot writer, but he did work on Past History of the Raj-Parivar = Raj-Rishi and in 1572 A.D. this dynasty was migrated in South India=Shivaji Maharata.

II. Darvez Dewan's collection = IAS Officer = Baltistan, Chitral, Gilgit, Hunza, Kargil = Leh – Ladakh + Astone invasions of the Parvez Museraff = Ex-president of Pakistan + Lineon the fire = old samaj.

III. Raj-Rishi = Godly-King, Nam – History collection again made from the Naval Vijogi writer. Who wrote on "Indus valley" + Naga Cult' of North India = Gulab-Nama + Rose type of life style from throne to flower = Horticulture Department + Dr Samista Thakur and her husband + Charmar dynasty of Kashmir.

IV. Shilpkara movement = Artistic nature + Aesthetic sense + human value and rose garden study of the Akhnoor valley – Sholapur Ke Life and Mohalla Rising of the South-East = Andhra Pardesh + U.P. State of the Dalit Mochi Muslims + Hindus.

V. Ladakhi- English = La+da+khi converted into original concept = "Law of Nature" = Enlightenment Era. (21 Century to onward) = Manas publication = unity of the upper class society = Anti-Dalit historian. Authentic view comes from the "Low down' = "Low Paid Employee" = moneyless labour.

VI. Jigmet Takpa = Flora of Ladakh = wildlife. Mona bhan = doctoral thesis of Rutgers = Mattalai formula for the publicity = Ependiture statement = Nil/Nil Karcha found in Delhi = Nazla Chack Grah.

VII. English, Gujarati, Maharati, Bengali, they are interested to see the Real Doctor = spiritual values.

VIII. Repetition = Recitation of "Holy Quran" = "Holy Words" of the Zia-ud-Din- Barani's Muslim calligraphy (p. 1)

IX. Mansar = Abstract of all the religion = Dalit concept =- Hard-Hit view to restore the values of the Sufi Ideology by beating the Manmat ideology with Chappla and Juta concept.

X. Sindhu Darshan = Raj-Rishi's psychology = purely dalit in nature = Good Human Approach.

Real Hari Singh + Roti Ram + Petal leaves

I. Introduction – Acantholimon Lycopodioides = (Girard) Boiss + (Longze) = Medicinal plants of the Dalit concept = Jari – botiyan.

II. **Nanak Hill** = Nimmu + Basgo + Likir + Alchi + Rizong +Nyurla + Khatse

III. **Mon Fort** = Aryan culture = Buddhist study = Khaltse + Skinding area of the Kushana period.

IV. **Francke study** = Unima Kavithisa = perhaps vima Kadphises view = 3rd to 5th century A.D.

V. **Dard Castle** = Franche found many Royal Tibetan inscription of the Gupta period = of 5th to 6th century A.D. and 9th century boulders, near the Khaltse bridge.

VI. Nuklok's study of Braknak Khar fort of 12th century.

VII. **Plant Fossils** = Lama Yuru = Mian Bibi's concept = Dalit History Dr Shabnam Grewal + Dr Chura. Hobby Botanist Prof. S.D.S. Jamwal clay modeling = state history in Geographical production = Dalit Samaj + Gujjar Tribe. Bakarwal Nil = there is no need of 'egocentric Approach' = Ashu Vasist = Anti Dalit women, Lecturer in English = Pure-girl.

VIII. **Pather view** = Paras study = Ravidas community. Kargil = talk with Dr Sonia with manners. Husband is superior to her = pati ideology Dr Samista Thakur = Panjabi Bilo = Nam-History of the Guruship theory = Dalit concept.

IX. **Zabalu Khar** = Ancient dards used to collect *customs duty*. Rock engravings = bodh Kharbu + Chiktan Khas.

X. **River – Indus** = Cemposite culture = Dalit concept = Aryan study = "Mon" history. "Kesar- Iu war" = war of the ruhanyat + Namgal tribe of Leh = Lower base study = Basic Ideology = classical age = Buddhist thought converted into Untouchables.

Hard News+ Soft Touch = Mahoobat Ka Kuda.

I. **Introduction** = Cancellation of media dialogue with China = Past History fo the Gargotra Family from Ambgarota = Chamar family of the Dalit Rajput = Historical phenomenonal race.

II. **Strategic point** = Jud + terai road + Hitler's study = German women study = Kashmir history.

III. **Chumar Intrusion continue in the area of Ladakh** = PLA History. **Himachal Pardesh** = Snow – melting area + Chamba state of the Dogra period = Dalit school of thought.

IV. **Sources** = Original study = ALC happening + Insaniyat = All religious ideology = sar = abstract nom.

V. **Constructing of canals** = Devipur satsang ghar = Madam Shabnam + Falak. 2+1 = 3

VI. **Sonam Does not like repeated history** = Manmat study = inspiration view film "Ram Ratan Dhan Payo" = Direct connection with lord's house = Samista Thakur's Archaeological evidence from Doda city = Udhampur District. "*Tankha Koi Nai*", "*Nakadada Payment*" form the ex-Chief Minister = Omar Abdullaha (J&K State). Mira's statement of the medieval period, "*Mira Prem divine* ; (pp 1-75).

VII. **Reconstruction of Kashmir valley** = Savarg Ka Ek Kona = "Mayana Devi Verma ka" view = Samista Thakur + other sisters of the natural History. Migrant Labour = Ideology of the French Revolution = 1789 = Sudra concept of three brother + J&K State + Guru Ka Nam.

VIII. **Financial impact** = Life Insurance Corporation + "Uttrakhand landslide" minus (-) Surya Kumar Rai = Dalit Economist. = (*The Shadow News*; p.1 Dated: 22/9/2014).

IX. **KKR** = Kolkata Knight Rider = Uttarkand's Dalit Historian = Santal's rising + Satnami rulers of the Nazla chak = "Chamar Clan".

X. **"Main Tera Hero"** = Actress study + Nonihal Guru "Tie your shoe laces = chest diasease + "Do numberi madam" = Falak + Mira.

XI. **"Monali Thakur ecstatic to win Best actress award in Washington"** = Hard-Hitting performance against the Anti-Dalit = Prostitute in Nagesh Kukunoor's "Laxshmi " = Era of materialism on we called the "Eru of Dark Age" converted into enlightenment age (21st century to onwards).

XII. **Good singer** = Based on natural sound = Dr Shabnam Grewal = Dalit Girl of Delhi IPS wife gets full marks from the director museum Sh. Bisakhi Ram R/o Nazla Chak = Peasent scholar.

Topic

Bank Chor = *Revolutionary* Ideology from Garib Janata to Amir Ali Khan + Dada, Potra Jaidad.

I. **Introduction** = Khubsoorat Chehra, Khubsoorat mat = Nam – History + "Waterloo" war of Kashmir and Jammu state = Dream city's Ideology + Naya Kashmir = "Rai Dynasty" of the Sind and Multan.

II. **"Mere Dadu Ki Maruti"** = Dr Shabnam Grewal + permanent husband = Sati = pati Ideology.

III. **Constitutional Reform** = Dalit History = concept ideology + 43,000,000 people from the depressed class joined in the round table conference (1930-31) = untouchability concept = Graib Dass's Ideology = Peasant movement of Maharashtra = Chamar Dynastry of Sindh. English and Scottish people were also participated in the RTC 1930-31 (Thus spoke Ambedkar; edited by Bhagwan Dass = V.K. Badgal of Gahi, Jammu Top, at present his specie found in Sri Lanka as a Manager of Tab Union (pp. 18-19).

IV. **Poona Pact** = 1932, a concept of the Dalit Jihad = to kill the Gandhi's Ideology = Biana + Brahaminism = upper class society = Dyarcly system = dual type of Govt. Di+Archy = am orinial concept of the Greek Philosophy = Hellenic era of the Kashmir history = Dr B.R. Ambedkar to Dr.R.K. Chamar + Ali brothers = Sat Paul + Sateel Ved and his family = Athen democracy concept = Chandal study of Kashmir. Ashoka tree = Decorative paintings of Lord's house = Barnai. (pp.39)

V. **Gandhi left the Concept of India and Rose the Revolt against the Dalit Christian** = Chuhra Samaj of the Lord Clive = Beginning of the national movement of India = to kill the Agarian System = Landlord history = Brahminism. Vani was Dr B.R. Ambedkar "Let and Let Live' that was his ideology.

VI. **Protection was necessary through constitutional article** = Roti Ram's History + Dalit pschyological war = to kill the Anti-Dalit Samaj of Gandhi and Jinnah = Explosion of population. Birth control theory = No Employment = Labour concept. Sir Tej Bahadur Sapru = associate friend of the Lord = Dr B.R. Ambedkar + family members = Dr A.K. Raina = Kashmiri scholar of the subject; Hindi; posted women college Gandhi Nagar, Jammu. "Why did not Gandhi and Jinnah take this opportunity in the RTC = Leader Ship qualities = Bakalat nama, only discussion, but having no reality in the artistic nature = in living style.

VII. **Agreement with Dr B.R. Ambedkar** = Truthful man = capable man of the human history = right approach and right thinking and delivered lecture in Hindu conference at Bombay on the 25th September 1932 (;pp. 41, 42, 43 and so on).

Topic = Labour concept + Parliamentary Democracy = Human History + Judiciary Reform.

I. **Introduction:-** Framework of the Constitution. Kashmiri Pandits = negative forces of the Jammu region; they need punishment = Idiot character of Hindu Mythology = Sanake and Wandar species found in human ideology =Chemistry + Botany Deptt. of Jammu province.

II. **German base research** = Authentic history = Late Aryan culture = Dalit History + Dramatist race of the Barnai's Lord's house. They need parade in the open stadium in Jammu province = Hero from the zero ideology = infinite level soch = thinking.

III. **Greater India** = Greater Jammu city. Dalit to Anti-Dalit psychology = intrusion of the Dr Kiran Bakashi in the Anti-Dalit activities = prostitute Samaj + Delhities Historian of the "same idiom". Negative = Positive.

IV. Trade Union Worker Study Camp = Jammuities Low Paid Employee + Delhities editors of the negative thinking = Anti-Dalit Scholars = Brahminmat of Kashmiri Samaj = Sanake Study = Punu Kashmiri.

V. Future of the Dalit Samaj = Top Class agenda of the Human History + Secular approach. American System = Old System; New System = New Ideology = Verification of the Right and Wrong Ideology.

VI. Wrong Ideology = Right view in the future Dictionary of the Art – Historians = Dalit Concept.

VII. English Constitution = Old Concept; New Concept = Athen Democracy = Rajputi – Lifestyle converted Sharma and Verma Baradari = Anti-Dalit Rajput + Negative thinker + Manhas and Chib Baradari and so on.

VIII. The Act of 1935 = Legal practice and Public Service = Against the spiritual History of the Lord = England.

IX. Power Shifting from Dalit to Anti-Dalit through Dr B.R Ambedkar's Ideology = "Dalit Voice" converted into "Inner Voice" or "Interior Islam". Intelligent Brain = Quota Unit = Kashmiri Pandits and Chandal of the Kashmir or Jammu area = Englightened Race = Radical change = British Ideology = Juta and Chappal study. A.C to D.C into physical verification of the Global Village = Dr B.R Ambedkar's Samaj = Chisthi concept of the Rajouri and Poonch = Guru-Govind Singh Ji ideology = Godly knowledge = Chamar's Ideology + Rajatarangini's view = "Old is Gold" = Kingship Theory.

X. Salapatraka's View = Buddhist Samaj of Kandi Area of Jammu + Negative – thinkers = Brahminism + Upper Class Gupta Society, Rajput + Meghs of Akhnoor, Ram Saran, etc.

XI. Ancient Civilisation = Harappa Ideology = Spiritual Content + Indus Valley Culture of Akhnoor History = Manda excavation.

XII. Gar – Ka-Vedi-Lanka Dye = Renu Angurana + Jangral Institution of Talab Tillo = Priyadarshani Mohalla = Chor type women = V.I.P Culture = Deadly against the Dr Raj Kumar Chamar. She deserves light punishment = uncultured women = Kamal Pasha of Turkey's Concept = Atuta = Father = Bisakhi Ram Master Karoyalya = Capt. P.R Bangotra = Anti – Dalit + Bashin of Nazla Chak and others + Gurdeep Giri of Pathankotia.

XIII. Vote to Boot's Ideology = Dalit Historian, Dr B.R. Ambedkar as Ideology converted in Action to Reaction into New form = New Lairra fair = Dandniti = Parade Concept at Bakashi Stadium.

Topic = Big Business = Big Bang Ideology of Dr Raj Kumar Chamar = Nam's Study:

I. Introduction = Pandvas and Kaurvas context at Barnai Muthi between Haves and Have-nots. 21st century A.D = 2014 and so on. Financial condition O.K, but Psychological War, there is 'no concept' to move ahead without Pandavas = Political-break. House = Dalit School of thought = Foreign Influence.

II. Athenian Democracy = Concept of the Gurukul theory = Dr B.R Ambedkar to Dr Raj Kumar Chamar and his Family Members, Wives + Parents. (pp. 58-59)

III. English Resolution = Dalit Christian concept = Scavenager's view = Dhobi Ideology. Kori Gal, Kora Javab = Social thinker + Political Soch = Raj-Rishi Ideology of Kashmiri Samaj = Successful Democracy + Essential Precedent = No pay, no work. Four subject = 3 children + one father and mother's participation into local Parades = Indian History = Natural Law Labour Concept Lagu, Danda Niti based on European Style, Arrangement by Delhities Jatava + Harwar Clan, Kurmi, etc.

IV. Real Test = Test of the Psychology = Brain + Habits of the Human lifestyle = Dirty Kashmirimat + Hindu + Muslim Samaj = Punishment + Danda + Boil water = Free of cost. Nam – Dan = Dhamma Ideology of Dr B.R Ambedkar + Jotiba Phule from South to North + Baba Roti Ram and Punjabi Singer = Jat Baradari of the immediate Ideology = Radha Soami + Chandals of the Buta Mandi (Jalandar) = Ganga Mai (Rani Devi,) Girdhari Kalsi and so on) + Mang Dadu + Nathu Ram Ghai and others. Idea Rules, money + Land does not Rule = Gargotra Family + Chumar Intrusion of Leh. King = Nam + Chamar Opposition Koi Nai = Visionary Ideology of the Hitler to Ambedkar + Raj Kumar Gargotra.

V. Secretaryship, no need = Hitler is view. Satsang Jaruri, Pakanda Koi Nai.

VI. Funding agency = Nazla Chak KeFooz + Amri Devi Ke Nu = Pushaplate.

VII. Privilage theory = Equality base knowledge and to check the 'Crime Rate' in personal form as Guru, Go-Vind + other Sardars = Teer + Gun Powder + Sedidious Act.

VIII. Pure = Sudra + Sodara Race of the Chamar thought = Nazla Chak Baradari = Next to Ambedkar + Chandal Sain Dass Bangotra and others.

IX. Times of India = Accurate balling Edward's III Law of Obligation. Labour Party to Officer Party = 'Slave of the God' not of Brahmins

Topic = History and Politics of the 20th Century + Ideology:

I. Introduction = Historical Background = Dalit prospective = Sufi concept + understanding of the Beem Bandana = Lordship theory of R/o Nazla Chak = Chamar thought = Truthful History = Authentic view (Dr. Durga Dass Basu, *Introduction to the Constitution of India* = Reprint; 2012 + 20th edition; (pp. 1-509). Lexis Nexis Butterwarths Wadhwa Nagpur = Maharabhtra Ideology = Mahar Folk of South India = Chamar concept = evolution theory of mind.

War – Lords = Pandava Race

I. Introduction: High-caste Hindus = Padaha Family of Bhadranlta = Honest Living Approach = Mahasha Baradari established their Kingdom at Barnai = Good people of the Human History = Right Man's approach having good administration, knowledge whereas in Govt. Sector; there is destruction of the Human lifestyle = Brahmin Concept.

II. Women make up almost 50 per cent of the Human Resources of every society = Dr Shabnam Grewal = IPS Officer = Dalit Samaj of Delhi = Dalit Christian = Chuhra Bradari + Chamar Concept. She is more advance from her husband = Pati = equal status as War-Lord.

III. United Nation Theory = United States Ideology of India = (J&K State) = Baba Roti Ram of Sindh and Multan Captured the area of North India = Pakistan + Blochistan. Associate study = Women Study Centre of Gandhi Nagar, Rohni Nai of Rani Bhag = Dalit Culture = Educated Women having the realisation of Truth = Balance type approach in Art History = Gurumat Ideology. Women-empowerment = through Nam-Theory or a good Satangin Lady = Labour Concept.

IV. Labour Concept = Concept of the progressive idea in history = Roti Ram's Ideology. "No Friendship, No Enmity" = equal status of the Lord.

V. British Rule = Lord Clive to Lord Mountbatten = Gurumat History found in English = Radha Soami Concept as per the statement of K.M Panikar "Britisher provided the Ideology of Dalit Concept" = Coolie Culture = Marget Thatcher's View = "Chuhra Culture". Old Christianity converted in New Testament = Dalit Samaj of the Jammu and Kashmir State.

VI. Non-Brahmins = Radha Soami Samaj = anti-Dalit + Dalit = Chamar Concept. A survey of Indian History = Social Scientist's View + Scientific – knowledge. Gorka Troops = Poor Race of the Lord found in Nepal = Butan and Bangladesh = Pakistan + Afghanistan. We need old kingdoms of the Lord Buddha = Chandragupta Murya = Rearing of More = Manmat population of Panjab. There is no Jalsa Jalus found in this area = Weath of Nations, according to the statement of D.C. Gupta, = Indian National Movement, Vikas Publication, Delhi = Development idea of the Human Right and Dalit Ideology = Sufi Saint Concept.

VII. History of the Freedom Movement India = History of the Research finding Race = Nam's Ideology = the Export Trade of India = Englishtenment Era 2010 to onward as living species of the Lord = Dalit Family = Good Human Beings.

VIII. "Doctrine of Lapas" = Mismanagement of the Govt. = Annexation Power of the Lordship theory = Gura Sidhant theory. Home Rule Movement = Movement of the Historical thought = Lordship theory = Reformation period of the

Hindus as well as Muslims philosophy = Good Ideology. Inam Commission = Commission of the Human Race with magnetic force = Roti Ram of Mirpur Siddhar. Jammu.

IX. A History of the Indian Mutiny = Revolt Concept of the Dalit Samaj = East Indian Company to kill the anti-Dalit propaganda of 1857.

X. Faithful people = People of the Lord = Renu Angurana Jangral = Gargotra Family of Akhnoor. Jagirdari System = System of the Humans Rights = Division of Labour as the concept of the Hire Labour of the Human History Brahmanmat = Mat of the "Real Education" = Human History + Free Education = Dalit Psychology.

XI. Lapse = Declining History of the Gandhi and Abdullaha Family = Political Era = to find out the Era of the "Dalit History".

XII. Rani = Soul of the Ganga Mai of the Guru Ravidas = Qualified Lady.

XIII. Ryotwari System = State-Subject System found in Pondicherry = Bengal Settlement of the British Empire = Sufi Ideology of the Chuhra Concept = Dalit Samaj of South India.

XIV. Women's Rights and World Development = Equal Right of the two Great Soul = Man and Woman + Unnatural History.

XV. Relationship Theory = Brother and Sister = Nam – Marg = Sarup Publication Delhi; 1996; page Nos.1 to 328.

XVI. Female Psychology = Psychology of the Lord into New Form = Production Method = Chamar History to check the idea of Advancement in Dalit Culture = Radha Soami Samaj.

XVII. Women Education = Garishth Aashram study = Sewa Marg = Social Services of the Human Ideology = Good Education = Learner Samaj.

Types of Scientific Research

The main purpose of the scientific research is to explore the new horizontal field for the poor scholar = Dalit Concept into Athenian Democracy = Concept of Labour.

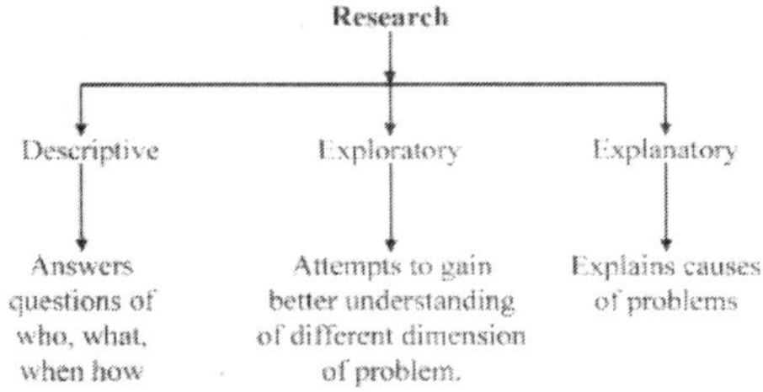

The other types of research are:

(a) Pure: Sudra methods applied;

(b) Experimental and evaluation;

(c) Qualitative and quantitative and;

(d) Longitudinal and comparative = New Period or Fresh Orders.

(1)

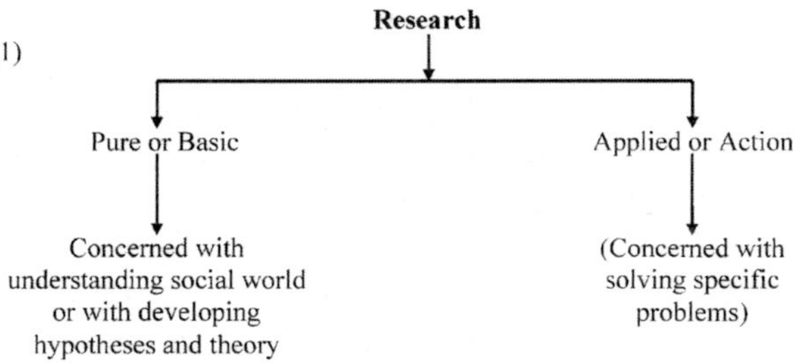

(2)

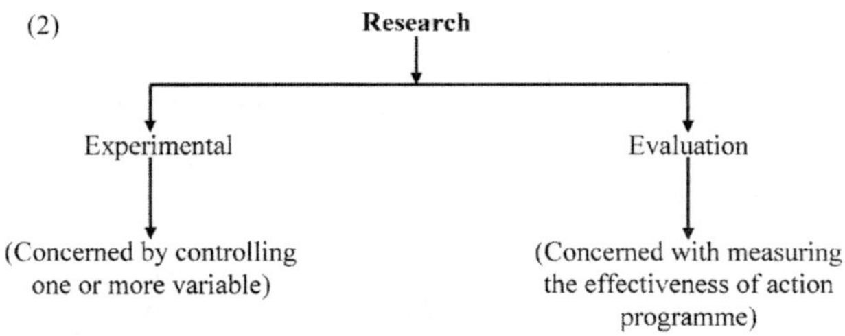

(3)

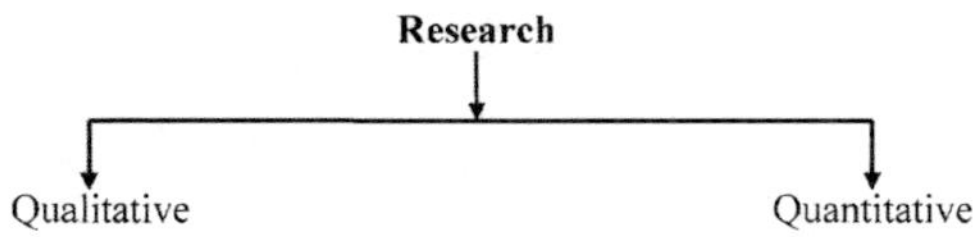

(4)

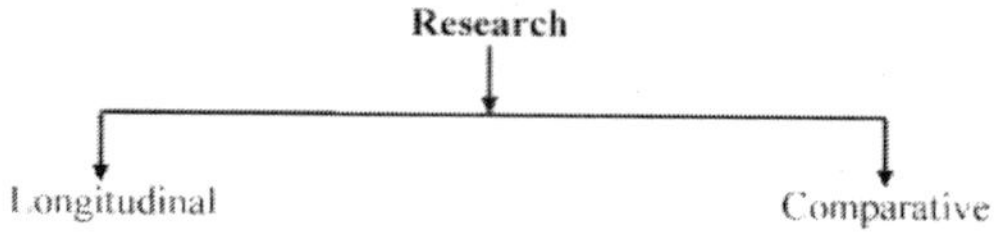

We have to elaborated in detail methods = Social Problems.

Computer Age = Age of the Socialism

I. Introduction: Computer applications were introduced in 1940 and its concepts was originated in 1930 with ideology of Western Scholars and its mechanism started by Dalit French philosopher in the University of Tubingen by Wilhelm Schickhard and his associate Dalit Brahmin = Chamar thought = Einsten's physical verification = scientific thought = Madam Falak = Radha and Soami = Dr Raj Kumar, a new concept introduced in Dalit Muslim Bradari of Doda city = their presence = Devi Devata = Shiva and Parvati.

II. Social History of Socialism = History of Chamar Dynasty (600 to 1200 A.D) Published, 2009. It is a powerful tool to control the good people of India = "Human History" or 'History of the untouchable' = History of Mohemmad Prophet and his family members. Their presence is felt at almost every working place, viz, homes, schools, offices, industries, hospitals, banks, retail stores, railways, research and designing organisations and so on. Radha Soami Mission = Universal Truth.

III. Data Base Collection = Dalitwise ranks in modern administrative units either in Police or Army.

To identify the past of a Dalit Scholar = Hitler's concept = Gulab-Nama = Sudra thought.

IV. To identify the role of Mecbeth, as the wife of William Shakespeare's into modern psychological survey of India = Dr Raj Kumar = Dr Shabnam Grewal, the first wife of the author's writings, 2nd Sonayana Chakoo, 3rd Preeti Bhagat and 4th Madam Falak = Flying Squad to see the modern problems of the anti-Dalit historians of Kashmir, Ladakh and Jammu = Radha Soami Scholars.

V. Characteristics of the anti-Dalit scholars or politicians = Business minded rulers = Materialistic bodies of India = Jammu and Kashmir state = Ladakh vision. It represents the modern scholarly approach to teach a lesson to Narendar Modi = anti-Dalit or Monkey mind political thinker.

VI. To enforce the Dalit Concept = Universal ruling agency = Karnal or General's concept found in Military campaign against the 'Beautiful womens of Kashmir' = *Vitasta* view of the Jhelam = Nam – History.

VII. Social Change = Dalit Ideology. It is indeed a great pleasure and privilege to present the '*History of the Sudra*' to Madam Falak as divorce lady of the materialistic concept = English men = Saraswati of the previous lifestyle = British lady = Immature culture to became Mature Lady = Childhood to *No-Jaban* Woman = Dalit Historian = Dramatist character = experienced women. No lust, no harassment = Radha Soami Master's wife. She needs guidance to write certain dramas on the materialistic culture = political era = 1947 to 2016 and onwards.

VIII. Birth Control Movement, it was originated in Europe towards to end of the 18th century. An early impetus to the movement came from T.R Malthus, the famous English Economist = Dr Manhor Lal Barwal of Commerce College Jammu. During his time population of England was rising at a rapid pace; a phenomenon that was produced by a host of factors = Dalit Scholar = Dr Raj Kumar into GDC Doda city. (*Encyclopaedia Britannia*, 1955, Vol. III, p.647). Population, National Planning Committee, Bombay, 1947. This function was presided by Pt. Jawaharlal Nehru, and later on became PM of India and Dr B.R Ambedkar as 'Law Minister' to operate the system of 'Materialistic Age' = "Brahminical Era".

The modern name of this movement is "Planned Parenthood" = Dr Raj Kumar, Madam Falak as his wife and three souls of his contemporary ideology = poor concept in historicism = *Megha Riwaj*, *Daulat Ko Nai* = Khaki Kalander = Sufi reckon. Amir Madam Falak = Radha Soami = *Vedic India*. This movement started in 1942 in Sweden and then in Asia as a controlling system of the 'Birth Rate' and Sanjay Gandhi was killed in this conflict = Indra Gandhi's ideology was sexual enjoyment with Davinder Brahmachary of North India. Therefore, she did not control the Birth-Rate of the Muslim Community as Brahmin by caste = anti-Dalit PM ('*Birth Control, its Social, Political, Economic, Moral and Religious Aspects*'; by Sayyid Abul Aila Mandndi, pp.13-163).

9

Rationalist and Humanistic theories of Cultural Development

A study of Kashmir secularism and painstaking record of indigenous historians fromKalhana to onwards as well as before him, the Vedas and *Nilamatapurana*, *Buddhists* and *Jain's* works called *Prajnaparamita*, *Chach-Nama*, *Natyasastra*, *Bilhana*, the famous author of *Vikramankadevacarita*, *Gulab - nama* and so on, they reveal the authentic history of the area and its development. 'Kashmiri ideology', in their ideas revealed composite dialogue between the centre and state government but at the same time, the said sources, no doubt, have been used by the Kashmir scholars like P.N.K. Bamzai, P.N. Bazaz, P.N. Tikoo, etc., but they could not determine the ideology of Dalit concept which was there after the Kashyap Rishi to onwards. Due to the reason of that, there were foreign invasion led by various 'Dalit Yogis' with hard hiting ideas and with the '*Living Meditation*' of *Zinda Pir* as we take the example of *Arab conquest*, *Durrani invasions*, etc.

'Pandit Jawaharlal Nehru', with the accession of Maharaja Hari Singh, as a Dalit scholar visualised the idea of 'Buddhist Philosophy' in the discovery of India and Mahatma Gandhi is '*The story of my experiment with truth*' as a social and economic thinker of the society as a 'Biana by caste', and Ambedkar was observer of the situation as a Dalit historian. He did not use to believe on the 'Rite and Ritual' as *Gandhi* and *Jinnah*, used to believe. Britishers, they were compelled to leave India = Dr B.R. Ambedkar's Art of writing the *Dalit-History* = to expose the Kashmir Pandits.

The ideology of its founders were, not Dalits, they were Brahmins = Muslims of North as well as South India.

1947: Freedom and Partition

The Religious Reform Movements of the 19th century lied by Raja Ram Mohan Rai, Swami Dayanand Sarswati, Sir Sayyed Ahmead Khan, Mrs. Annie Besant and their followers stressed on the two doctrines of reason (Rationalism) and Humanism (logic), they also sometimes tended to appeal to faith (beliefs) and ancient authority to bolster their appeal before 1947 or downfall of the Britishers = Dalit-Samaj. The said scholars opposed the ritualistic, superstitious, irrational and obscurantist elements in Indian 'Religious'. Similarly, Sir Sajjid Ahmad Khan aroused the anger of the traditionalists (Haditists), who follow without knowing the reason that what was the politics behind that concept. ('*History of Indian National Movement*' by R.K. Sharma, p.p. 58-59).

Surat Spilt (1905)

From Lord Curzon to Lord Mountbatten (1899 to 1948 A.D.) there was great revolt between the *Haves* and *Haves-nots*, because there a great political will of Mahatma Gandhi and Ali Mohd. Jinnah, even though Britishers introduced certain administrative reforms in the history of India (Kashmir as its integral part divisioned on the question of 'Simla Agreement' as well as Tasakant proposal'. Partition of Bengal led by Lord Curzon, 1905 and resentment displayed by both the communities either Muslims or Hindus with the celebration Id and Diwali, but at the sometime, in 1902 A.D. Lord Kitchner came to India as a new commander-in-Chief of the Indian Army as General Vikram Singh of Northern command displayed efficiency to control the borders of 'Gate way of India'. In 1911, this partition was stood cancel with the agitation of the partition India, liberate and rest of the area which is lying called as N.W.L. of Sindh. The Muslims of this areas are mostly traditionalist, they do not like Dalit concept = Sufi Saint concept.

Civil Society and Modern Kashmir

Democracy in its liberal pluralism concepts made presupposes a model of 'modern society' or '*Naya Kashmir*' the question, about the '*Naya Kashmir*', neither Hindu Brahmins, particularly Kashmiri

Pandits or molavis of the present period, did not explore the concept of Prophet Mohammad and the '*Rai family*' of Kashmir; who ruled, not in India, but on entire world Community = Megh Baradri.

Infidel Society

Islamic Reformation Movements, not led by only Prophet Mohammad, it was revolutionised by various *authors*, *peers* and *faqirs*. No doubt, Bahavi movement was started by Sir Sayyed Bareclvi (1786-1831 A.D), this mission does not become popular among Dalits of Kashmir. But at the same time '*Aligarh Movement*' that is the Lord in historical phenomena led by Sir Sayyed Ahmad Khan, a poor Dalit Muslim of U.P. He founded by M.LA.O. College of Aligarh which has now became a big university. But original idea of his struggle die down with the development of traditional historian (Irfan Habib). They stress on *Nawaz*, Nawaz, itself has the meaning 'no voice of God', a political motivated prayer.

Purada System

Sir Sayyed Ahmad Khan opposed the 'Purdha system' as a concept of 'blind faith' among 'women'. He propagated his views through his paper '*Tahjib-Ul-Ahlaq*' (Moral Reformer). Study, again, shows that upper class 'Muslims or 'Hindus', they inferior in understanding the concept 'Sudras'. Purdha, here we mean have against the system. System in India is there, but lack of knowledge displayed by such communities, which do not realize the subject-matter of human psychology. Purdha is within the body of man (system) to see the Lord with the help of good doer.

The Ahmedia Movement

Mirza Ghulam Ahmad, who was the founder of this movement. He was an inhabitant of Qadian in Gurdaspur district of Punjab. He was regarded the Prophet of the 'Dalit Muslims', 'Massiah for Christians and the Divine incarnation of the Dalit Hindus. He viewed the truth on logic history. He fought against the anti-Dalit people of India.

Sati system

Sati system which mostly followed in Rajasthan, now in Haryana among Jats as a class of agriculture. They need nofemale parduction.

But pandit, they left this rite as a crime against the Sudras and Women. Sati is, here, we do not mean about the burnt of women in the Middle Age or before the Britishers. No doubt, Britishers, they stopped the act of crime with heavy hand. Sati in historical study, we mean, we have to listen the music of the Nam-history = Truism.

Child-Marriage

Child marriage was the old concept in Indian history, it is still found in Bartund or Pahari areas of Doda, Kishtwar, Bhaderwah in village life due to lack of proper education. There is one family of the Sikh in the interior of Bartund. The candidate use to study now in 10th class. He was marriage, before two years. Thus, the past practice is still existing in Jammu and Kashmir state. Mohandas Karam Chand Gandhi (1869-1948 A.D.) and the departure of Lord Mountbatten = Free-thinking state = concept India.

A section of orthodox Hindus particularly Kashmir Pandits, they do not like Gandhiji for his liberal attitude even Pt. Jawahar Lal Nehru and same story was to be happened with Ali Brothers of Turkey and Muslim league already observed the Pakistan Day, March 23, 1947, before the arrival of Mountbatten. But, his lady professor Frankely was very close to Ambedkar and Nehru for the 'transfer of power' to India on the question of '*Naya Kashmir*'. Dalit of Kashmir, they had no formal education, but they had visionary view of human lifestyle as an 'International fame class'. They had good relation with Dalit Christian.

On January 30th, 1948 in the evening Gandhiji was going to attend prayer meeting as usual as Muslims of Kashmir use to Masjid without out knowing the logic of concept, five time in a day to remember the Allaha, but Allaha use to reside in the consciousness of the man. Gandhi used to visit in the man made *Mandir* and *Masjid* and Dr.B.R. Ambedkar was regular listener of Sufi-Saint teachings = Satsangi scholar.

Death of Dr B.R. Ambedkar was historical and Gandhiji only had a little view in his ideology, therefore, a Dalit Maratha named Nathu Ram Godse, now he use to reside Chandigarh (Mohali), short four bullets at Gandhi. At once, Gandhi collapsed on spot and died in the 'Night', not in the 'Morning', that period was the beginning of rise of

'Dalit concept'. In the 'Dark Age' we use to work with 'Light' as concept of the historical phenomena. This movement was started by Dr B.R. Ambedkar and his associates for the 'Enlightenment of New Era'.

This book offers a fresh study on the analytical approach on the concept of Sufian Kalam.

Simply put this question, before the politicians, that they have no more idea, only 'prostitution'.

Classical Observer

As a philosopher, *Lao Tse* was also an observer of both the 'Human Beings' and '*the Natural Phenomena*'. It is the similar story as 'God and Man', author has already described in the study as a refinement approach for the new comers of the historical phenomena. *Lao Tse*, the great follower of Taoism concluded the various event of 'History of China' that behind all these manifold workings of nature there exists an 'Ultimate Reality'. 'Modern communist', they do not believe on his historical view. They believe on his historical view. They believe on 'Manmat'. Therefore, their concept is inferior than the Indian researchers. (*The Essence of Tao*, by Pamela Ball, p.19).

"The summit of reality can only be realised within oneself", said Buddha. A great Sufi Master adds that "the source of truth is within and he himself is the object of his realisation", according to Schopenhauer.

Buddhism is not a, 'Religion', in the sense in which the term Namo is commonly understood as Nam or Kalma or Tao, 'Holy Ghost' which explored by the Muslims, non-believers became 'meat-eater'. Study shows, 'meater-eater' cannot observe the 'idea' of 'analytical history' as , *Ar*, *Sutar*, *Chamara*, etc. were the tools of Ambedkar's ideology for the measurement of historical research.

The concept of Lord Buddha is:-

Not to do evil

To cultivate good

To purify one's mind' ('The essence of Buddhism', by Jo Durden Smith, p. 9).

Destruction of Pandits and Molavis

After the death of Dr.B.R. Ambedkar, nobody visualised the idea of Sufi-saint as concept Dalit. According Mudraraksara, the story which related to Prophet's ideology, killed the anti-Dalit with idea of 'Nam-History' some scholars believe that the conquest of Magadha preceded the ousting of the Greek garrisons found in the Kashmir history and went to Punjab, who has been sometimes been identified with Poros as a necluar state of mind. Thus, the historical drama of the *have* and *have not* is based on 'third force' that is 'Sudra Family' for rational building of the state. (R.S. Tripathi, '*History of Ancient India*', P.148)

War is not a solution of the problem, it is only dialogue between the said forced an historical modern researcher.

Yueh-Chi-Movements

It is similar story as that of 'Little Tibet' or Ladakh, about the fourth decade of the 2nd century B.C. This movement launched by Hiung-hu a tribe of 'Turki nomads' won a decides victory over the 'Yuchi-chi, who do not believe on the modern concept of Buddhism that '*Buddha and His Dhamma*'. Study shows that Nam-dan of the 'Living Master' is essential for the development of progress in the area of Kargil, Leh, Nobra, Batalik, Darass Żanskar, Baltistan, etc. This area was very low to the modern communist world that is China. In the Panjtar second of the year 122, however, Gushana occurs as the name of a Maharaja (C.1.1.11. No. XXVI.p.70). "The great kind of this dynasty was 'the King of Kings or Nam, the son of heaven,t he Kushana, always like 'in the idea of Happiness' = Chamar thought.

Dark Interval

According to the Puranas of ancient India Raj-Rishi used to live in Kashmir. Later traces of Naga rule in Bhadharwa, Kishtwar, Rajouri, Poonch, B.G, K.G. Mendhar, Ramban, Kotli, Bhimber, Manjakote, Chandrakota, Batote, Chanani, Sudhmahadev, Ramnagar, Bagohi, etc. indeed, they may have sprung up on the ruins of the Kushana Powers.

'Imperial Gupta Power'

The origin of Guptas is shrouded in mystery as the story of God and Man, but on the consideration of *truth*, it was knowledge base society found in North India, particularly in the area of Punjab. They were of '*Sudra Jats*' (*Vishnu Purana*; BK. III, chapter 10, v.a)

Rudradeva a *Rudrasana* was the founder of this dynasty. Guptas were the great family of 'Naga cult' they were not found in U.P, but also in Kashmir. They also extended their power with Kerala (Malabar coast) as Dalit Christian (Prof. Jouvean – Dubreuil, '*Ancient History of Deccan*'; 1920, p.61)

'Origin of the Naga Tribe'

They seem to have been 'Cave-dwellers' an ideology of the mental exposer in horizontal way of life style and might have used simple tools like pen and copy in art of writing the '*Dalit History*' a concept the Mukari rulers. Naga here, we means that both the communities Hindus and Muslims, they have been failed in all walks of life as materialists race. Dalit race is race of indigenous culture 'work is worship', backbiters are Muslims or upper class Hindus, their ideas is based on 'prostitution' and nothing know about the 'western culture'. Western culture is advance as 'we people' that is 'Dalit concept' or 'Radha Soami' as a modern many of the human history.

The entire race of the Ambedkarite thought from 'Old stone age' to 'New stone age' is capable and genius. They have no lust of sex in their lifestyle as the materialistic have in the lifestyle as we have seen in the 'Abdullaha family' a prostitute by profession. From the history we learn '*The Philosopher's Stone*' is Baba Ravidass. *Nilamatapuran* describes as a "plough". (M.L. Kapur, *Kingdom of Kashmir* p.33).

Iron Age

In the area of United Provinces, however, 'Iron' was also used in Kashmir, on the question of that, sometimes, Brahmins led pollution in the society. *Solution* of this event is '*Die to live*'.

Political Awakening

Political awakening of the 'Dalit Family' was not upto Ambedkar, but Valmik, Jesuts Christ, Lord Budha are there. Rest of the work done by the 'Gonanda dynasty' of Kashmir. They were Naga and Nomadic people of this area and took shelter in low lying hill areas that is the area of Jammu region, Bhauhana Chak, than Nazla Chak, now at Barnai as isolate clan of the state.

Rulers of Kashmir

Gonanda – 1 to Jarasand (3000 B.C.) as Dalit dan of the Mudradesa. Gonanda was succeeded by his son Dhamoder to the thorne of Kashmir. Later, when Yasovati gave birth to a son, he was put on the throne as Gonanda II. Thereafter, it was ruled by Pandavas of North India. One of the Pandava Kings of Kashmir was Sundarsena (Ajay Kumar Basin from Jallandar).

Cyrus (558-530 B.C), the founder of Persian empire.

Contents

1. History (World and India)
2. Miscellaneous – Sudras
3. Raw – Material – Brahmin

The Path of the Masters

The path of the masters is the science of '*Surat Shabd Yoga*' which is absent from both the major communities. Radha Soami is the 'New Religion' of the world. It is an audible 'life-stream' permanent is Brahmin on the earth. Yogis are Dalits.

Comparative Analysis of Gandhi and Ambedkar

Ambedkar was 'Satsangi' and Gandhi was '*Pakandi*'. Pakand is there in political history of India. Man's first duty is to know himself. Ancient rishi (Kashyap Rishi) pointed out in substance: "Worship the gods, if you most; but your first duty is to find out the truth in human behavior who and what you are yourself". (p.24).

New social order

In the '*Age of Intellectual*', we have to keep ourselves mum, that is the order of the 'Social Animal' as 'Dalit Scholar'. There was a time when Darwinism threatened to sweep all philosophy and there is only 'Nam', they have to practice in their lifestyle or called 'Creative evolution', "Life is not simply protoplasm acted upon by chemical osmosis and electrical reaction" (Julian Johnson M.A.B.D. M.D. p.28)

No Enmity, No Friendship

Science and Religion of the ancient society are no longer enemies. Indeed the hour is approaching and now is, when these two angels (Baba Gurinder Singh and Dr Raj Rishi) of light shall meet in Russia or Afghanistan. It will be seen on the question of the same ideology; "*seret thought as the liver seretes bile*".

Critical Review of the Dalit Philosophy

All our problems can be solved with the idea of Nam' and his way of thinking. As prophet says, "There is no embezzlement in the lifestyle" corrupt is there in the idea of Muslims and Hindus community. Dalit as a deprived section of the society, now became a leading force of the world community as elevated class. The novel 'untouchable' of Mulk Raj Anand have been written about the life of an *outcaste* Bakha, a young sweeper living in the outcaste's colony of Poonch in North India; found in the history of upper class Hindus the colony becomes the living symbol of the age old Ansari Motors of Kashmir. ('*Indian Literature in English Critical Views*' by Satish Barduddhe; pp 94-95).

Kashmiri Literature and Folklore

The term 'education' has a number of derivations:-

1. *Education* is derived from Latin word, 'Educare' which means to bring up or to nourish the idea of little soul.
2. *Education*, we means to lead out or to draw out the attention of Dalit historians on the basis of poverty line injustice among homeless section of the society-Reforms in the field of 'social justice'.
3. It is agains derived from the Latin word "Education" means the act of teaching and training, not tuition work and its adjective theories they are known as knowledgeable person or Enlighten historian in the field of skill labour and in art history.

Aristotle says, "Education is the creation of sound mind in the sound body. It develops man's faculty especially his mind". (*Basic Approach to Education was the concept of Raj-Rishi*)

Culture Heritage of Jammu

The present brochure or work of the Dalit race owes its origin to a desire to present a coherent account of the Sanskrit literature produced in Jammu, posted in Ladakh, then Kashmir as original place of understanding between Dalits and anti-Dalits. Now, we need proletariation type of govt. without knowing the "*Reservation Idea*".

An interesting feature of the '*Dalit literature*' of the Sultanate period (1200 to 1500 A.D.) is the use of a large number of Arabic, Persian and Turkish words like Khatona (Khatun), Khanagaha (Khangah), Mallika (malik), Madrasa, Ravava (Rabab), Suratrana (Sultan), etc. as a part of social history in art of writing the Sufi concept.

Secular Spirit of the Dalit Literature

From Kashyap Rishi to modern man dalit literature is on the whole, secular in spirit. Though theology found a place in Radha Soami, they have the interest of dominant over the world history by exploring '*History of the Dalit samaj*' in 10 to 12 volumes on the ideology of the Sufi-Culture = New concept of Hindu Society = Dalit Historian.

Part - C
Ladakh

10

Ladakh and its Buddhist Philosophy

Introduction

"Heavenly Kissing Hills" Known as little Tibet or Ladakh. The "History" of this area goes back to "Aryan culture" "Simple living and High thinking". This Aryan tribe in Pali language known as "Mons", "*Charamkara*" in Sanskrit in original form as dramatist and artistic race of the "World History". The derivation of the Buddhist language called Ladakhi in common language. History creator are Dalits of Jambudvipa with the idea of "Light" in English form and known 'Lo' in Dogri lipi. Lipi term is the term of 'Law of Nature' in the historical point of view, who provided the status of ST to Ladakhi people through Constitution of India, (Dr. B.R. Ambedkar). Old Buddhist culture, even the Iranian and Arabic (Islamic) culture is there in 'rite and ritual' form as negative thought as meat eater Brahmins of Ladakh or Kashmir.

Historicity towards *Tao* Philosophy, "Journals of Social Sciences on from the university of Jammu reveal Ladakhi Culture is equivalent (=) "Sufi Saint Culture". Its origin base started from old French meaning journal, a diary or daily record of the various "social justice" theories relating to a advance society of Kashmir or Jammu or Ladakh. All the three regions are basically "One in culture" during the ancient period of history and Latin language of the various terminological study drawn from "Ancient Rome" originated from the "Dalit Culture" of the Christianity from a lafiz or Harif (Word) or Wisdom latinus or 'Latium' found in central Italy. American scholars, they were use to write down original words of Italy in their "National language" as a part of the study reflected from Spanish or Portuguese than to India (Kashmir) like term "caste". Its original meaning is pure = Sudra.

What is Tao? In historicity of Indian philosophy. Its philosophy deepened in meaning, but simple to understand that is 'Nam'. Its basic origin founded from the same place that is the valley of Akhnoor; called "Indus". "History of Modern Europe since 1789" was the study of Dr B.R. Ambedkar to visualised the condition of Dalits of Europe and widely spread this idea in India or Kashmir in spiritual study, both have the same meaning as that of Ladakh history too. Tao Te -Ching is the appropriated man, who spread the mission in Chinese language and Ladakhi called Buddhism or New Buddhism and ST status was given by Dr B.R. Ambedkar. What Gandhi did for them to spread their own culture through Dalai Lama. Dalai Lama's visit as a social reformer or infidel by nature. Who how before the Buddhist bastion founded from the Buddhist monastery of Akhnoor. How, he is original man of the Buddhist philosophy. He is a strong Brahmin of the modern period. Sir, Ambedkar's book published in B.C. 2541 – 1997 A.D through "*Buddha Bhoomi Publication Nagpur*" According to him, "Why did the Buddha take Parivraja? Or Sanyas from the material worlds because of his follower, they were proved "Infidals" as that of modern Ladakhi Brahmins of the area. Development is there in the area, but they do not like the ideology of Dr B.R. Ambedkar that is '*Untouchable*'. The four Aryan subjects, that is, Chamar, Meghs, Barawalas and fourth detected by Gandhi known as Harijan. BSP opposed it as illegal term. It shows they are the same historians. They did not corporate these terms in their modern study. No doubt, they reflected the idea of 'Aryan groups' as "Nalik race". They have no knowledge of the advancement. Study, again, shows, they are also proved "Modern" Brahmins. They are working as communal group on the funding of Congress. Who provided "rights of labour". It is the similar story as that of Kashmiri Pandits of Kashmir.

I. **Dedication of Merit:-** "May the merit and virtues occrued from this work, Adorn the Buddha's a "Pure Land" or "Sudra Culture" before 1947. What is contribution of this area during the time of "National Movement" from 1947 to onwards, proved nothing, only they are stressing on the explosion of population. Study, again, shows, they are burden on earth". (Nam Amitabha) as per the statement of the writer.

II. Black Mailing Association:- "*Black money*", scholar is not talking about (OECD) Association. Scholars is talking about (OECD) association and black mailing thinkers. They are not supreme or above the "Name Amitabha" they are modern Maleech = Brahmin. They use to worship the Dalai Lama, not of Ambedkarities" Guru of Ved Vyasa. Dr B.R. Ambedkar is a "symbol of global socio-political revolution", what they pay back to the Dalit society. They are again proving meat eater or 'prostitute'.

III. Bhaisajya Guru:- The Medicine Buddha (*Yakushi Nyorai*) published by the "International Buddhist Minastic Institute, 2001", translated by "Dharma Master Hsuan Jang", known as another Hiuang Tsang of India in the form of Dr Raj Kumar. He Published a book on the same author on Dalit literature = Ambedkarities Buddhism '*History of Chamar Dynasty*" and compiled the whole theme of the modern Buddhist philosophy after Dr B.R. Ambedkar as a 'Dalit King' of this area. Author needs a handsome women of this area for the *recreation* as well as for the development of Dalit literature. Name is not known by the said scholar.

"Doctor of Body and Soul", old Buddhist clan of this area, there is no soul in the body, how the body move without "Soul" as deadless race of the human history. (*Medicine Buddha Sutra*, pp. 0 to 101).

IV. Islamic impact or Modern Islam

Iran for merely called Persia, after this, Persia became independent country, it had good relation with India during the time Zain-ul-Abidin. (1420 to 1470 A.D) , the great king of India like 'Akbar the Great', he brought Persian scholar during his reign for the development of Dalit-history as a great scholar of the world knowledge. He worked on the "idea" of his forefather that is "Qutab" or "Nam" or "Mons" as "Sindi Culture".

Iranian Plateau stretching eastward from Tigris River meaning from the Tarana of the Nuri Shamb of Ladakhi, its comparative study found in B.G. River in Poonch from the higher altitude of the Jammu state, mentioned by Ragunath Rai, a wonderful historian of the period. The ancient civilisation of Iran can be studied from the time, when the hordes of Aryan speaking invaders swept down from Turkistan into Iran during the period before 2000 B.C. After this, '*Kashyap Rishi*' from the Jheer bardari of Jammu laid down the stone of "Kashmir issue" as a founding father of this state. The main body of the Aryans particularly chamars, they have been found in the low region of the *Leh* area. They use to speak every kind of language whatever have been originated in this world. They had Punjab dialect, Urdu dialect, Dogri, Tamil, Marathi, Hindi, English etc. The name Aryan still survives in Indian history in the word Iran (*Ariana*) which is applied to Dalit community of Kashmir (India), Ladakh, Jammu, Punjab etc. as well as in other part of the Northern states, Japan and Russia. Chinese has Ladakhi language as 'infidals of the old concept' they are modern Brahmins.

In short, this area, known as Minor Asia has a Persian King called Cyrus. He conquered the Chaldeans, the entire Buddhists and Muslims, they included in the territory of Egypt. Due to the Balkan wars, Revolt of Greek against Turkey was the tension between Russia and Austria. It shattered the reactionary Congress system of Metternich. Anti Turk Policy against Young Turk of the human history later on called Ali Brothers.

Total collapse of the Central Power in Palestine, due to the rising of the anti Dalit propaganda in Kashmir or India.

"*Surrender of Germany*", before the leadership of Dalit historian in 1918 A.D. In brief manner, it is the future of coming generation.

V. **Trade Genes/Jeen:-** Trade genes of the 'Buddisattva Baba Sahib Dr B.R. Ambedkar" in Ladakh region has been reflected by Dinesh S. Anand from the 'Nanda dynasty' of the Sudra

Family'. He wrote on Dr B.R. Ambedkar" thought and his book is divided into four contents:

1. *Dr. B.R. Ambedkar: Prophet of the Modern Era page.*
2. Dr. B.R. Ambedkar: An Emancipator,
3. Why Dr B.R. Ambedkar Embraced Buddhism.
4. Baba Sahib Dr B.R. Ambedkar as Bodhisattva.

In the preface, author had made the discussion with various scholars including women of India (Kashmir) with indirect or direct way; about the Ladakh history; containing Kargil and Balitistan too. No doubt, Gilgit was the part of the Dogra Empire before 1947 A.D. Astore was the capital for the origin of Buddhism. Now, this place or area is in the possession of Pakistan. But, there is less crime incomparison with 'Kashmir infidals' both the Hindus and Muslims, Sikhs and SC/ST/ OBC, they are in minority. During the militancy (1990 to onwards). Who is responsible of that bloodshed called as 'cold war' of the region = Jihad. No doubt, Ladakh was also hijacked by this time by the Muslim community particularly. 'Sunni Muslims', because they have the 'ideology' or 'rites and rituals', not have the ideology of 'Sufism'. They were their in minority 'Aziz tribe' and others. Aziz at one time was the painter of the Gulab Singh School of thought. His economic condition was poor, he was not satisfied with labour, he has given a chance to develop his family. Now, they are very close to NC and sometimes with the Congress Party as survey made by the author during (2000 to 2003) posted in GDC. Kargil and visited with the family in Leh district and stayed in Sachin hotel. "*Yasin Malik's Rabble Raising Antics*" proposed in 'My News My views Khabr o Khyalat' a Urdu magazine, version in English monthly published about 16 pages Rs. 20/- did not elaborated the Dalit concept of Leh; which developed from the Dogri term 'Lo to Light' and its second form is "Lit" = Ladakh as a part of the Kashmir history as an ideology of 'Dal Lake'. "Life is a stream" and he expressed his view with Omar Abdullaha, ex-Chief Minister of this state as separatist head of JKLF, but he did not consulted the Sufis of *Jambudivpa*, either he discussed issue with Ved Mahajan or Ved Bashin, a news editor of 'Daily Excelsior' of Jambu as culprit man of the Buddhist society. "In February, 2013, Malik as a Rajput Muslim went to Pakistan to spend some time with his family" study shows, that he is not Buddhist, not Muslim, but he is misguided youth of the 'National History' "touch the conscience of Indian govt. and India's civil society" at least we have no concern with the "military" and the "Militancy" both are negative thought of the human history. Author has broad base knowledge as "Bodhsattva" who is affiliated with the 'True ideology' as 'Bhagwan on earth", Bhagwan, not "inshan" on earth. Earth is meant for good human being. This is the message of old document of the Prophet Mohammad, that is, "*Holy Quran*" (p.12).

Kashmiri Sufism

Kashmiri Sufism developed with ideology of "Labour Class" in Europe or in India; but, there is no '*labour class*' in Kashmir, Ladakh and Jammu, because with the development of economy after the down fall of Sufism in Kashmir an ideology of Kashyap Rishi (1500 B.C.) as original man of the 'Dalit Parivar', not of the "Sanga parivar" or R.S.S, both are proved 'Nakami Parties' to prove the ideology of Dr B.R. Ambedkar, who was creative writer of the 20th Century. What, Yasin Malik did for the Kashmir Pandits, he broguth '*militancy in kashmir*' to liberate the Kashmir from the South Indian scholars or Delhities govt. with the help of Pakistan. Pakistan is a dying country. It has 'no ideology' of the Sufi saints or Dalits = Chamar. This state has been dominated with American ideology and Chinese too and third force in South Asia is India, a story of the "highly praised" Prophet Muhammad, April, 571 and died in 630 A.D.

Now, the question rises "What is Islam?" has been drafted by a lady Dr Ruqqia Maqsood, not by the Masud Choudhary Ex-VC of Bud Shah University of Rajouri', Gujjar by caste, but infidel by Nature, a great support of the NC. No doubt, he accumulated huge wealth, but he could not change the plight of '*grib nomads*' of India, It is upto the Master. Master says, we need "Living Meditation" meaning "*Tan-Man Si pari Ki Yatra*" has been written by H.A. Davin, Dera Bias, having no hope of life. "Life is the God's virute or upto Living Master. He never dies. He is Living soul of this area sometimes called "Kashyap Rishi" or "Deepit Raj" as original story of the God and Man. (pp. 7 – 185).

Message of Divine

The Holy Quran says, "if you eat clean things, not meat, eggs, fish, mottan, beef, chicken, Cigarette, wine etc. How you can obtain the bliss of god". It is the sporting material of the "Dalit Samaj". A person who listen the message of Divine. God says "there is none like you" as merciful man. Same story was happened with Sheikh Farid, a ruler of the Punjab and Sindh area. On the other had, Dalit historian, "Dr. Raj Rishi (Kumar), it affirms that He is seeing, Hearing, Knowing as the gene of the God, originated as per the statement of a 'Compact Dictionary thesaurus Wordpower Guide, Indian edition or in Ladakhi *boli* called Mons as Aryan tribe, who biological is distinct sequence of DNA forming part of a "Chromosome", by which offspring inherit as *Nam* or *Chamar* as prophet of God, before that he was Dr B.R. Ambedkar now Dr Raj-Rishi. These are the characteristic of a Dalit Family originated from the German word *Gen*. to became *Zen* car as an old model of the German states. We need Naya Ladakh = Naya Kashmir = Naya Jammu. According to English terminology, it is "informal study' of the author drived from the word *gen/jen* as information about the societal growth as a general information, not for only Ladakh peoples, but for other Buddhist scholars of Far East, Japan, China and other countries" Tiny Japan", an ideology of Dr B.R. Ambedkar to construct the "Tiny Tibet" with the advancement ideas of Boddhsattva.

Modi falsifies, twists facts: According the Ex-PM Dr manmohan Singh. He says "think seriously" what the party which believes in "demeaning others" will do to the country. Dr Nowal Viyogi is better then the Narinder Modi or Kapil Sibal or Dr Manmohan Singh Ji, why because he worked on "Kashmir issue". He worked on various Dalit themes of Kashmir. Moreover Master Mohan Singh Brahmin Rajput is superior to them. He says, "He is honest and great writer". He has no needs political will in his lifestyle. The same story has been observed by the author from the Dalit Muslims of U.P. (*State times*, 18 Nov. 2013, P. 1).

Pride or Shame

We pride on the work of Dinesh S.Anand, who explored "New ideology" on the Ambedkaritie thought on the basis of truth. Who is a successful writer, who speaks truth. Author needs, no friendship with idiot master Desh Raj Bashin, having zealous feeling within the community itself. Scholars is open minded and social thinker, he wants to remove "Untouchability" between the '*Haves*' and '*Have nots*' with the stroke of pen or pencil. Pride here we mean "a group of lions" having especial qualities to kill the anti Dalit forces 'with ideology of *Sudra*' by forming a party named "*Dalit-I-Illahi Liberation Front*" from the same constituency, where from the author born (Akhnoor) or Nazla Chak. Pride, here, we have another meaning, I want to invite certain Ladakhi Buddhist Scholar for the celebration of the Victory = Vijay Devas + black-mailing = Dalig Buddhists.

A person who is qualified to perform Buddhist sermons, wherefrom he was born. People know me that he is great scholar and worked in the family of Dalits or Sudras. Smugness is upto Desh Raj Bashin, not to Sham Lal Sharma (Ex-PHE Minister of this area). He well knows me. He is a great social thinker. He worked on the topic of 'Guru Ravidas" Philosophy. "Life comes from life". He is next to Dr B.R. Ambedkar, "A startling challenge to the modern Dalit Brahmins either B.R. Lachotra or R.L. Lochan; they have no contribution in the favour of true society as "Paripartan Rally" of the art historian. Study of the scholar is based on origin of the life and the universe. "*Morning walks with his Divine Grace*' by '*A.C. Bhaktinedanta Swami Prabhupada*'. He knows me, author use to live in the "Dream city" House No. 14; Barnai and has given verdict in "History". He is open minded scholar as Sufi Saint Dalits. (pp. 1 to 14).

Vedic Cosmology

Vedic Cosmology is not based on the 'Daily Excelsior' writer Mr. Ved Bashin. The book of the other is new 'social order' of the world culture; Des Raj is identity stands nowhere in historicity. He is strong idiot or prostitute from the background of mathematic; a money minded scholar of the same village. He is not in a position to look after the Dalit race. He needs more money from his scholarship study.

"I am single; no plans to get married yet". According to the statement of Katrina Kaif, Dalit Muslim lady. Author needs her help as a court dance of the authors Darbar, a beautiful and man like personality. She does not have a plan to get married nor with Salman Khan or Randir Kapoor. She is lover of the art historian. She, again, expressed her feeling through 'statetime' paper, date already mentioned above "I want to have a long and peaceful life' with my children, Ramiyan, Sheru, Depu, etc.

WIDOW CONCEPT = FORMAL STUDY

Satsangi = Gupta Baradari of Jammu Region + Srinagar + Leh Ladakh; Nil/Nil clan of the North India = Damara concept. Nai-Baradari = Efficient Race = "Karigar Log". Sonali Gupta = Idiot Women + Uppal Family of the Jammu Region = Nirangkar Bhawan Ideology, having no concept OF Simran of the Lord = we need destruction of the Brahminism of the Jammu Region = Prof. Sindhash Sharma = Nilak Samaj + Mir Family of Poonch = Gujar + Muslman people, who do not believe on the theory of representative of God = Balban's concept of the "Qutab Family" of North India. Bela Rani Sharma = having Human Right Concept = Low paid employee.

Schedule Caste Women:- Dr Shabnam Grewal = IPS of Delhi = "Dil Lagis Film Story", Representative the Chura Culture = Coolie Culture = Manmat Study = of the labour class of North = South India + Adhavis = Jyoti Rania + Savita Ganju = Unemployed Union = we have no need of the era of "Status and Power" = "Blind Faith Concept" of the Human History = The Era of before the Qutab-Ud-Din Aibek = Nam - Dan essential of the lord for the "Evolution of Mind". Author is master of all the Arts = Scientific Discovery = We need Equal Status = Man to Man, an ideology of the Kingship theory = Materialism + Ladakh Ke Story.

Poverty in History

Realizing concept of the Dr B.R. Ambedkar" ideology = Joytibai Phule of the Mali Culture = Gardner Concept Low-paid Employee = Roti Rozi Ki Ideology = Labour Concept + Taj Mahal Study of the Lord's House = Good Behaviour = Good Sangat = Bad Pocket Area. PHE Department = Stoping Writing the Resolution of the Charter of Demands. We need Civil Sectt. Close. Rest is best for Realisation as 'Repentment Ideology'.

Scheduled Caste/Scheduled Tribe

Labour Class + Social Structure of the Dalit Samaj = Representative of the Tribal Rulers = Pandavas Race = Guru's of the past History = Guru Nanak to Guru Govind and so on + Roti Ram + Dr B.R. Ambedkar, Having the Equal Ideology as Baba Bisakhi Ram of nazla Chack = Scientific Kissan = Mehanat Kass Labour = Dalit Concept = Gujar Tribe, who rearer the Goats and sheeps of the area = old concept in form = Raj-Rishi Ke Sabita. Racial Factor = Universal Instinct of Maternity = Guru Bandana + Rani Didi of Jalandhar.

Childless woman + other = Film Mamata of the beautiful lady = Nutan, actoress of South India, based on 'Hakiki Moohabat' = Realism of the Kalidass Dramas + Meghdoot from Padder = to close the chapter of Manmat into Enlightenment Era = Natural Scenery of the Lake = Chandrbagha concept found in the below area of Kishtwar = New India.

Dr. Radha Karishna's Ideology to explore the new field of life for Dr Sat Paul Gargotra + Renu Angurana = Dr Suteel Ved + Padamini Tikoo + others - Dr Samista Thakur = Anthentic Concept of the Lord = No scope of the anti-Dalit population of Jammu region in Satsang's Ghar = Destruction we need of the Jammu Tibi = Ragunath Pura = Bazar + New Railway line of Rajouri through the spot = Gumat Bazar + Fatth Da Chakan + Pacca Danga = Groups = Biana Concept. Dalits and Anti-Dalits = Natural Race + Sh. A.K. Angurana, Retired IAS.

Recall the Memory of the Lord = Honest Man Culture = Scientific View of the Love - Story of Dr Sat Pal Gargotra = Dr Angurana Jangral + Gargotra Tribe = One Family + Koshal Samotra = ex-Principal of B.Ed. College, Jammu = No need of pension + TA DA of the tour and travelling from GDC Doda to Jammu. Author needs to control over the family with the stroke of natural pen = Buddhism as an old concept we need "New Bharat" + "New India". Therefore, we need no illusion = "Currency Note".

Tanka System of the Medieval Period

Nanak Shahi Sikka = Gold Coin system = Status as per the Ambedkarism = No profit, No Loss theory. Illegal possion on Golden ornaments, may be shifted into Dalit Concept = Roti Ram's Ideology + Ambedkar's throught = untouchable = Equal Status.

Maharani Falak + three others = Looting and plundering method of Mohd. Ghori + Ghazanavi methods applied into the Athenican Democracy = Transfer of power. Power = Dalit Concept. Slap on the left Cheek = Amla Aggrawal = left the prostitution converted into Dalit Concept = Roti Ram's concept of Mirpur Siddar (Jammu), Nam = Buddhism + Roti Ram = Ideology of the Global Village. According to Ram Angurama Jangral + Gargotra Family = Nam-dan essential = "Zenda Guru Da" = Representative of God = Dr Raj Kumar Chamar a concept launcher of the Global Ideology = Roti Ram of Nazla Chack + *Dera Bhabiyan* and Roniki Ram of Chandigarh. Ajit Surendra and his Family = Well Come theory or address system. Dukhi Parivar, converted into "Suki Ideology" of Jalandhar.

"Was it a woman, or a Man

That Passed this way? I cannot tell

But this I known, a set of bones

Is travelling upon this road" = Anthropological study of the living *Man* into a well being body of the Lord Suachat Nil, equality base knowledge.

Akand Bharat = Anand Bharat = Story of Prose and Poetry = Dalit English Literature = Falak Madam of Doda City = Life Pattern of the Lord + Other Women = A Social Scene of the Suchet Singh's Palace of Ramnagar = Dalit Samaj + Mahasha baradari of the same locality.

Woman and Sikhism

Ideology of Anti-Dalit Samaj = Upper Class History + OBC of the Cheer Bardari + Nai = Follower of the Sudra Concept = Poonch History of the early career of the Dr Raj Kumar Chamar + Pappu Yadav + Manmat Family = Close related of the OBC + Churha Baradari, Sushil Kumar Bhangi. Guru Angad Dev = part of the Dalit + Lower Caste Hindu + Muslims of the Falak Heroine of the Lord's House, Mira to Falak, gap-arrangement = Political History = tough terrian of the Doda City + Padder Area.

Geographical and Societal context to the reference, no need in English Subject = Direct talk with Dr Shabnam Grewal through train journey. Maaka + Susral, both the houses are the same = One Concept = Chuhra or Chamar. Julah = Doda Pul + Network of Sri Lanka Baba Guru Ravidas + Jusit Christ. Lord Buddha + Jainism = Kashtriya Concept = Vedic study to serve the society and learn the vedas = Complete History "*From Pre-history to New Man*" (Pre-historic to 21st Century A.D.) has been re-written by my Wife = Dr Shabnam Grewal = DDE Study = Direct or Indirect Message of the Lord's Study = Sotu Ram = Knowledgeable Historian, "*Maa Ka Dil, Deepu Ki Raj*" a drastic step taken by the Family Members of the Lord = Western Culture = Soni Banga Culture of the Nazla Chack Clan. **Reason:-** Inchargeship of the Globe = Pati + Patni's Ideology + Concentration on Art - History = Koob Surat Look = Aggressive Ideology = Vegetarian Sabad. **Langer Commander:-** Renu Angurana, Lecturer in English = No Chance of the Nokari + Sokari = Nai - Concept = Dressing - up the society = Nam's theory = Historical Phenomena.

The Sunday Tribune, dated, 7 February, 2010 author has seized the account of B.L. Agrawal (IAS) having 220 bank accounts, officer in Chattisgarh as per the report of Income Tax Department. In the same paper, '', belong to the BSP and Ambedkar Sena (Mool Niwasi) in the anti-Dalit propagenda against the Ambedkar's thought as untouchable raided by police party including Sardar SHO in their houses at around 4A.M. and Jagdish Kumar was also involved in this gang rape case as culprit of the human history; that he is not Radha Soami, but a modern *'Brahmin-Chamar'* leader like Hans Raj Hans. Author is deadly against 'them including Ganesh Dass and Benarsi Dass ex-Principal of 10+2, Chaman Lal Shivgotra, M.L. Parwan have been found very close to each other in the mal practises as modern '*Dalit-Brahmins*'. Ram Paul is a soft spoken man, author likes him including V.S. Hans, Girdhari Lal, Hans and Digra family of upper Barnai. My aunty is weeping on the issue of transfer from Jammu to Doda, author has already exhausted in the far flung area and his top priority in transfer policy at Paloura as Incharge Principal and Madam Parihar has to be shifted in R.S. Pura and Rajini at Samba and Prof. Neelu in Parade College against Anjeela Qureshi as a fresh appointee and Sindu Kapoor in B.Ed. College. Now, scholar wants to jump into the politics of Sufi

Saints as Radha Soami is his party as a missionary writer. Nehru-Gandhi is a neglected idea which author has proved in his study after the death of Dr B.R. Ambedkar as a saint soldier and French philosopher. *History Repeat itself* was his idea during his life time. Now, the history has been repeated and it is an astonishing attack over the modern politicans like Barrack Obama, Rahul Gandhi, Sonia Gandhi, Malayam Singh Yadav, Dr Manmohan Singh. Author is aware of the fact that expiry date of the Ganesh Dass is nearby. He is working as a leader of the BJP as a frustrated man of the said party. Nobody, like him even Hans Raj Hans. Certain BJP leader, like Bodh Raj, Sh. Gharu Ram, they are deadly against the author as a Schedule Caste boy by passing the politicans and wants to attack over assembly. It is impossible. Ashok Khajuria is determine to attack over the Assembly with 'Fresh Idea' that is '*Chamar thought*'. Yash Paul, Bhim Singh, are party to it. B.R. Kundal, ex-Chief Secretary is working against the author as a revolutionary man. His appointment is fix for Depty-Chief Minister and Tara Chand is deadly against the *Chamar* Community as strong idiot Barwala like anohar Lal. CTA President is working behind the author's statement that writer is working on the compromising formula as 'Third Force'. It is astonish attack over his new-wedded wife *Sonyana* (*Kashmiri Panditani*) has listened that writer has divorce his previous wife and she has joined the prostitutional centre and busy with her love affair as arrogent woman of the Nam-History. Author welcomes his real and first wife that is Sabnam Grewal as a driver. During the British Raj, she was a English lady, now she is a Keralaitie as honest and dedicated woman. "Love gets love, hatred gets hatred". Author's natural thought wants to live with these two natural women: one for domestic life and other for foreign affair to discuss various issue like road problems, irrigational problems, security purposes, etc. In the *Natural History*, we want to punish, Ajeet Angral, ex-principal, G.L. Thappa, V.H. Hans, M.L. Parwana, Chaman Lal Shivgotra, Raj Singh, M.S. Balourai, Ranjod Singh, strong idot Rajput-Brahmin indulging Prof. Neelu Gupta, Nutan, Anil Gupta, Jagdish Lal Megha-Brahmin, Bachan Lal, Romesh Lal Uttam, S.L. Kholi, Sohan Lal Megh, Ashok Kumar, Hans Raj, M.L. Dogra, Narinder Megh, Bisakhi Ram, etc. Author wants to convert them into Sufi Saints in the '*Journey of the Soul*' on the enquiry of their action and style of functioning including

Vajay Sharma, Subash Sharma, Sudhir Vaid, Susheel Sharma, Daya Vilas, Savitri Sharma, etc. wherestand their idea and tanting remarks against the author as a Schedule Caste boy as frustated lot and make a fun in the art of writings.

11

Ladakh and the Civilisational Growth

"Whenever the mind gets distrubed,
Vedas alert us = Third Eye and also
guide us", Pt. Shriram Sharma Acharya

The major Ancient Civilisation of the World that flourished one after another:

I. Mesopotamia (3000 B.C. - 538 B.C.), non called Iraq, ranking among the earliest and best known civilisation and dawned on Sumeria = Sumerian Civilisation (3500 B.C.). Politics Hittites = Nam, based on Hammurabi Code = Babyloanian Empire = Nami Rule, City known Assur = Brahmin of Kashmir. Their (Assyrian) (1100-650 B.C.) = Iron Age or Metal Age = Present Age of India = became Persian Empire.

II. Egyptian Civilisation as Herodotus said, "is the gift of the Nile = *Nilamata Purana* = Black Polish Culture. Development of agriculture = Natural means of Irrigation found in this area too = Present Age = Modern Era. It developed in three parts:

(a) The old Kingdome = J&K State (2700 B.C. to 2000 B.C.)

(b) The Middle Kingdom (1991-1778 B.C.)

(c) The New Kingdom (1580-1100 B.C.)

Note: Their kings were known as Menes = Miniya tribe of the Sudra state of mind, now known as Dr Desh Raj Miniya etc. All the written material of this Indu race is deciphered = Megh thought = Dr Ashok Kumar Bhagat (Ph.D. Chemistry); his art of war is Nam-History = Pschyological War. Social life, "*Simple living and high thinking*". Political Astronomy = Jagdish Vadgal from Ghayi. In 2770 B.C., they adopted, the ancient King of Egypt ascalendar year of 365 days. "Dog Star" = Political Leader = Narendar Modi.

III Chinese Civilisation: Confucius and Taoism (2000-15 B.C.) = Buddhmat = Sant Mat = Dera Bias = Satluj = Nobra State of Mind. Ladakh was the part of the Central Asia. Discovery of iron, paper, printing press, proclaim and new textile technique = Kadhi industry or Scientific Findings = Tao rivalry = Communism at present. There is no god.I

IV Iranian Civilisation: Formely called Persia having close relation with Aryan = Schedule Caste Tribes of Sindh = Indus River in 2000 B.C. Nam = Aryas = Girl Child of a teacher of Doda = Bun - Doda = Nam as a child or baby to Babylonian. Civilisation started from the ideology of the girl child = Holy World is the theme of the Holy Bible = Lord Christ = Nam or Chamar. they had the relation with foreign countries = Ladakh Culture = Shia Culture.

POK = Division of Jammu and Kashmir State, Why it was divided after 1947 = Less formal education = Blind faith. No belief on Prophet = Dr B.R. Ambedkar, living soul of the past including *Phulle*.

Why *Shia* and *Suni* conflict created among the Muslims, Old Sunni, Modern Shia = Sadamu Hussain = Old Concept of the Quran Adam to Prophet = 26 Prophet, Holy Quran came a verdict of the lord = Authority of Vedic India = Quranic verses into Arabic ideology as the theory of lord to control the earth = by listening the music of the lord. Karbala = Daya and Daristy = Sunni thought = Surya War = no conflict, but it was imagination of the unseen to seen article. Prophet = Mochi tribe = Creative Idea. Idea rules, money does not rule that was the ideology of Mohammad Prophet = Dr Raj Kumar. Holy Quran is similar prediction as that of Jainism's, Tirthan-kara. They believe that Mahavira = Mohammad Prophet, the last holy book of this Kashytria clan, was preceded by 23 other Prophets. Of these, the pennltimate, Parsvanath, appears to have been an historical personage, wrapped up in mythology = Chamar thought = Kora Kagaj. Sada = Shiva.

Islam is the Religion of "Rites and Rituals" as an old concept. New Concept is Chamar throught of the Kashmir History = Jammu State = Dilli State. Islam, here, we mean, submit before the God = Kun = Kalma = Lam an alphabet of Urdu or Arabic = Akshar in Hindi. The period between 600 to 1000 A.D., saw the emergence of Islam = Chamar thought = Mochi Ideology in poor society among Muslims = Sabda Theory (Raghunath Rai; p. 137).

Kashmir has remained a part of the Indian Empire since the time immemoral = Remote past = beginning of the History = Buddhist Centre where from 'History of India' has been distorted = Buddhism or Old Testament = Old scriptures of Lord Buddha = Nam. Nam-History = Chamar thought = absent from the modern Buddhist scholar of Leh, Ladakh. They believe on Manu Smriti = Corrupt Race = Rapist Race = Brahminical Ideology is a common term used for a Black Polish Culture = Political historicans, they do not like the Buddhist thought of Dr B.R. Ambedkar = Radha Soami Satsang. Thus, the whole philosophy of Lord Buddha has been based on Biasya Guru = Little China or Bangladesh or Nepal = Preaching Centre.

Note: Ladakh Division = "Land of Lamas", now at present, after the 1947, Brahmanism = Buddhism. It lies in the North-east of Kashmir Valley by passing the Zojila Pahar = Rockey Mountains. It used to be the centre of trade routes from Kashmir to Galgitstan = Dogra Culture = A New Buddhist State. Partapgard has been found in Kargil = Degree College. There is no Satsang Centre. Zanskar is also found separate from it = Degree College. Thus Ladakh division having less crime rate = God fearing society. They speak Kargili language = original race of human history.

It does not reflect the Mon Culture = Manmat Study. Nubra, Chanshul and Zachan, they also reflected the same culture that is, Manmat. Gurumat only found in employee = Dera Bias at Leh.

It is apparent from the above study that the outlook of the Ladakh before 1947 was different because China was a part of the British Empire = Dalit Samaj.

Origin of the Earth:- Nam-dan for the study of nature = Early Man = Lama Warfare = Negativism found after 1947 = Political Era. The planet, on which we live = Geographical Change = 21st Century = Social change and moved about, is a huge sphere of radius of about 4000 miles and (6400 kms) but this planet is itself a small member of the "Solar System" = Surya race. Since the Solar System = Surya Race is there the only one of the kind found in Ladakh region during winter on the white sheet of the snowfall = Aibek Culture = Moon Race.

Study shows that origin of the earth and Solar System = Chandal Race had the unique phenomenon that happened to occur in the universe during some very remote past = Dalit Culture = Ideology of Zorawar Singh ji in the history of Ladakh Division.

The earliest theory origin of this state is known before the Gulab Singh = '*Nebular Hypothesis*' = 'Buddhist Race'. The theory of bi parental origin of the solar system = Ravidas philosophy and named '*planetesimal Hypothesis*'.

Jaans and *Pauts* = Jeffreys (1925) custom theory is known as the '*Gaseous Tidal Hypothesis*'. According to Jeffreys and Jeans statement that during the very ancient past = old Buddhist days an extremely large star, Lord Buddha = Ashoka's Philosophy = Buddh No Namo. Ambedker says, "Buddha and His Dhamna". New Buddhist philosophy = Radha Soami School of thought = Dalit school of literature. Old theories disorted, new came into existence, with ideology of Nam = Chamar thought, while earth moving in space to close the chapter of political era = Manmat or Rapist Caste = Muslims or Hindus = Negative thinker; chanced to approach the Sun = Ravi = Surya. To clear the earth from the sin free society = Buddhmat State = India = Jambu, Srinagar and Leh. Manmat is a pollution in the state policy of present govt.

A long line of Dalit Kings from Damodar Dutt = Nanda Ruler of Afghanistan to Age of Gupta, there is a Buddhism in the state of Jammu = Maurya Dynasty powered was transferred to Mongol ruler of the Ladakh region. Jammu state was flourishing at that time having close relation with Russia and Gandhara was the capital of the state = Dera Bias.

History and Ecological Science, traced out from Greek writer Herodotus = enquire about the past event = Constitutional Study = Maker of this World = God or Nam. Ecology deals with the environment of Biology = "Soul and Cultural" thought. Groupism die down itself. 'Love gets love tough gets tough'. This science of truth derived by the first German ecologist Earnst Haekel (1866 A.D.). It derived from the Greek term "Oikos" meaning home = Home Rule Movement = Anne Besant.

"*Home Rule Movement*" means go by the practical approach, "A Concept of Athenian Democracy", a brance of knowledge = Origin of the earth = Voice of God, and state find truthfulness theory of Lord Buddha = Nam=Dan.

No doubt, "*The Science of the Soul*" and "*the Journey of the Soul*" is a complex question for the Political Leaders of India. They made politic with groupism = Brahminical historians = Satish Chandra or Irfan Habib of Aligarh Muslim University. Hindus and Muslim school of thought, they encourage the '*Rudebadi* system to biafarcate the social groups and both encouraged the Manmat system to dominated the poor people with false propaganda and '*Bank Vote Politics*'.

Bank Vote Politics = NC Govt. and encouraged the Muslims and upper class Hindus in Administrative field. Dalits or minority communities, they came with ideology of Reservation = Sudra State of mind people = Ladakhi people. Quota = Category people in Govt. Sector = Employee are proving honest. In open Merit = Om encouraged the corruption in state level agencies. Political leader monoplosied the system = Nil Ruling. Corruption in large scale. Manmat = Environmental pollution created a bedge between the non-political leaders = Baba Burinder Singh ji, Dera Bias and his followers = Dalit Samaj = Less corruption, no manmat = less chances for the transfer. Chack made rulers = Darwin's theory "Origin of Species" = encouragement of original species = Sat Paul Gargotra + Suted Ved.

Level of Study = Recognised Individual Pesonality = Historical thought. E.H. Carr, What is History? It is a question mark to the anti-Dalit historians of Kashmir. Population explosion = Capturing of Land of Kashmir = Black Polish Culture = Barbarian Race = Rapist Ruler; Sheikh Mohammad Abdullah to Umar Abdullah. Sonia Gandhi or Rahul

Gandhi = Dirty Culture of Delhi = Dilli. No politic, "Ram Nam Sat" = Radha Soami Religion.

Note:- Labour Class = Sudra Class were socially deprived by the said political leaders without knowing the "Classical Age" *that was Wonder in India* = Ladakh State or Jambudvipa. According to the traditions of the society Kashmir takes its name from a Sufi sage scholar = Kashyap Rishi, who used to live on the bank of a mountain lake called Satisar = Abstract of all the Religion = Buddhist Philosophy of Radha Soami Centre of Dera Bias. He drained this lake and the reclaimed land was called Kashyap-pur of Kashyap-mar = Kashmir's original historian. It seems that the name of Kashmir comes from two Sanskrit words "Ka" = Water = *Jal* and "Shimira" = (dry up) land for the establishment of Dalit Colony = "Cheer Ideology" to wash the presence of the knowledge from Manmat = Rapist race of Kashmir = Muslim Community, both Shia and Sunni = Old Concept. Dr Arthur Neva writes, "The Climate of Kashmir is quite eminently suitable for Europeans".

Study shows that Britishers or Frances, they were the Dalits = Sufi Saint Scholar = Fredric Drew or Moorcraft, etc. Uptill the end of May, Climate of Kashmir Valley = that of Switzerland. It appears from the Ladakhi Damodarapur = Strong Ideology = Bahikas of the Penjab = Sound - Current, passed into Kashmir history = Ladakh Division = Jammu State = Imperial Study = Radha Soami, identical with Sada-Chandra = Chandramas, according to Dr Raychandhuri (R.S. Tripathi: p. 253). During the reign of Chandragupta II = *Durlabhavardhan Partapadity* II of the Kashmir history = Nanakan Sehib of Pakistna; Fa-hian's-Itinerary (399-414 A.D.), came overland from China to India = Present Age = History Repeat itself = Buddhism = Classical Historian = Chamar = Rudra = Nam or Kun of the Arabic Countries. Samndragupta = Rig-Veda thought Palaliputra = First son of the lord = Deepit Raj.

Domination of Brahminism

Domination of Brahminism in North India over the Dalit Samaj = No Reservation = Constitutional study. History of the Bahujan Samaj Party has been revealed = Kun Study. Dawn of the Abdaullah Family, rise of Gargotra Clan = Equality based knowledge. Brahmins degraded and failed in their "objectivity" = Who were the Shudras? Shudras are the Almighty rulers of India = Jammu State = Dilli Govt. Buddhist were generally cordial, Hinduism, Sikhism, Mohammadanism = persecution of the Women History = Dalit Kings = Nil/nil Jatibad. It is upto the Great Master to Little Master = Rabi Kiyal = Savivait Rulers of the ancient Kashmir.

Despite of the historical facts in Ladakh but that race is superior to the Kashmiri-Muslims = Kafirastan. Ornamental Stones = Sufi Philosophers = Dalit Historians they are in abundance in different parts of India = Jambu State. South India, Rajasthan, M.P., Bihar and Orissa = Stone's Philosophers well-wishers = no opposition. Makrana Marbles = Rajasthan = Reygeysthan = Agra Construction = Taj Mahal, that was the age of pre-clambran = Gwalior and Chie for = Mirabai = Ravidas = Banaras, idea corrupted after the 1947. Hindu or Muslim Benars = Negative thinker.

Ganga = Ideology of the Ravidas philosophy = Nir. Pollution created are Pandits of this area = eco-challenge = Manmat thought damaged the natural resources of the History = Water.

Three Kingdoms = *Cholas*, *Pandyas* and *Cheras* (Keralas). Ashoka calls the third as *Keralaputras*. Foreign Trade = Cottage industries = converted from the Indus Valley River produced muslims = term Muslims introduced in Sanskrit language = in Hindi terminology. It carried on overseas trade in these articles = Political leaders as Non-alignment Movement = Nam historian's development in universal leadership qualities = Dalit Historians or Dalit Scholars. It was a '*periplus Suvarnabhumi*' (Malay Peninsula) and China in the east = Ladakh Division.

A Jajmani System = Brahminical Ideology have been seen in North India = Jambu State = Chenei fashion = Vasinavi system = anti-Dalits propaganda = development of Sanskrit and Arabic language. Chamar condemns the selfish man, who only caters for him mention in the Rig-Veda = beginning system of the Dan = Samagri (P.V. Kane, *History of Dharmasashtra*, Vol. I, p. 9).

A Concept of Athenan Democracy

The monsoon = 'Mon Culture' of Kashmir and Ladakh and 'Soon' is a English term used for the 'Rise of Sudra and Down fall of Vaisyas in North India' as per the statement made by a Dalit scholar Prof. R.S. Sharma in his study 'Social Changes in Early Medieval India (500-1200 A.D.) on "The First Devraj Chanana Memorial Lecture 1969, New Delhi (JNU). He stressed in the beginning of the lecture "Closed Economics : Loss of Mobility" (PP. 3-19).

I. Theory of Social Change = Computer Era

There are three regions combined as "One State", that is, Jammu and Kashmir, Ladakh has "Mon Culture" = Aryans of India = "Chamar thought" = Iranian Culture = Aryan Society = Cultural Development that was the finding of Ambedkar's Administration = Blind faith that is "Hindus" and "Muslims". Old Buddhist Concept = Old Testament of Bibile. "New Bible" = Chamar History. As per the statement of St. John, "In the beginning was the Word, "Word was with God". Now the undersigned has repeated the *History* of Asian Culture, where stands the ideology of the Umar Abdullah as Negative thinker of the Muslim Society. "Idea rules, money does not rule" that was ideology of Dr B.R. Ambedkar. At one time, he (Umar Abdullaha made statement in a press conference before the Parliament election that there is or should be an ideological war. Author does not know upto this date, which kind of "War", he is fighting in North India with Sonia Gandhi = 'Blind Faith'.

II. Since peasants, artisans and marchants were very attached to "Abdullaha Family" at one time after 1947; as A.G. Noorani displayed the photographes of Pt. jawahar Lal Nehru and Sheikh Abdullah on the book of 'Article 370. A Constitutional History of Jammu and Kashmir published in 2011. It is wasteage material of both the scholars either, there was Pt. Jawahar Lal Nehru or Sheikh Abdullaha. Dalit Scholar as third force of the 'Gargotra Dynasty' of Jammu = Amba Garota, migrated towards north due to attack of the Muslims on Hindus as low caste shifted from Ambgarota to Bhawana Chak (Bhawana Chack), due to devastating of the militant group of the upper class society, both "Hindus and Muslims" had '*one culture*' that is, 'rites and rituals'. Maharaja Hari Singh left the idea for the development of '*History*' as the story of 'God and Man', 'Religion' is man made as per the authentic statement of Dr B.R. Ambedkar.

'Religion', here, we mean, 'Ligion' with the God = Zero level ke study = universal Truth.

III "Feudal Ranks and the Varnas":- This statement author quoted from the same scholar, That is, R.N. Sharma as Satpatiya Brahmin, who speaks truth, not 'tell a lie' like Narendra Modi opposed the 'Secretaryship Ideology' as "funding agency". He made a statement "Do away with archaic rules I will back you". *Daily Excelsior*, p. 1, dated June 4th, 2014, Vol. No. 50. No. doubt, he is illiterate as KAS or IAS/IPS, but he is "Intelligent Man", because, he knows the problems of the 4th class employees as Sudra Concept found in '*Ancient History of India*'. Study shows that IAS/IPS/KAS etc. are the feudal ranks and varans are teachers or good learner scholars, who has authentic approach in their minds. Stop fundings and work like a gentleman.

IV "Proliferation of Castes":

Brahminism = Muslim Family having the same concept as negative thinkers = Damaras of Kashmir. Kashmir at present even Jammu today have the Hellenic view of the 'Greek Society', not found in Doda city = Doddi, Gujjar. We need 'Social Scientists' to rule over India like A.K. Angurana, Ashok Parmar etc. They are good scholars of the "Varna Society" = "Nam-History".

History of the Brahmans = Negative Ideology = 'Abdullah Dynasty' = Lodhi Clan. They have knowledge of the Bhakti Movement Rameshwar Prasad Bahuguna, a well known scholar of Jamia Millia Islamic New Delhi, who worked on the topic of "*Symbols of Resistance, Non-Brahamanical Sants as Religious Heroes in Late Medieval India*", 2003-2004, pp. 222-253. He worked on the achievements of Maulana Kabir, Namdev = Nanak, Raidas = Raghunath Rai and Dadu Dayal = Surinder Kumar of Rajouri. Sant needs 'no money' Brahmin needs money, who is culprit IAS/Teachers. Teachers, those are involved in mal-practices, that is, Dr S.P. Sharma, Prof. Z.A. Hashmi etc., who has the background of prostitution.

V Political Leader = Sanakes, Dogs etc. = Politic = Rajniti = Vedic Sidant = God as representative theory of Balban = Kingship theory. Sanskritisation = Hinduisation, Arabicnisation = Musilmanisation = Negative Thinkers = One Concept = 'Brahminical Ideology'

= Rose as the theory of Gulab-nama which was written by Diwan Kirpa Ram = Dogra Concept = Sant Marg. Gulab Singh learn this concept from Maharaja Ranjit Singh of Panjab, Dr Raj Kumar = Maharaja of Beas, Shri Gurinderji Dillion, belonged to "Jat Family" a concept of 'Soul of the Science' = 'Zero Level Ke Study'.

VI Early History of Jammu, Kashmir and Ladakh:

Kashmir is an ancient principality of the "Dalit rulers" from Kashyap Rishi to modern Man, that is, "Deepit Raj", a historical son of the Lordism theory that is called in Arabic language a ruler of this area = Mohammad Prophet, who was born in Kashmir as mentioned by four authors in the history of '*Far East*' (p. 1). Before him, Lord Buddha was also born in Kashmir, because this land belonged to 'Sufi Ideology'. "Sufi Ideology" found in 'Sudra Family', as challenged given by Dr B.R. Ambedkar for the creating of China, who were the Shudras? and this book was published late, 20th Century in 1997 and '*Caste System* in *India', Buddha or Karl Marx* having the same meaning as an ideology of the 'Sufi Saint'. The Progressive Idea in History was neglected by both the Hindus and Muslims, because, there was no 'Formal Education', large scale among Dalits or Sudras. Untouchabilitiy is, again, existing both the societies, that is, 'Hindus' and 'Muslims'. Dalits as third force are, have the knowledge of Sufi Saint Ideology as co-operative force of the 'Nature'. Nature stands, within the man's itself, not in Mandir or Masjid, as black-minded thought as per the statement of Prophet Mohammad author.

VII Prophet Mohammad and DurlabavardHana of Kashmir or Khasmir had the good relation; where from the History of India has been distorted. No doubt, there are certain Dalits, at one time, know became Brahmins and Muslims like A.K. Angurana or B.D. Bhagat or Ashok Megh. They do not like to hand sake with the fourth class employees even Meghs, in large scale became Brahmins and Muslims like K.K. Digra or Dr Sanjiv Digra etc. Prophet remain Prophet. Durlabavardhan remain *Durlabavardhana* as it is depend upon the "Law of the Land" = Karma Theory = Line of Action = Ambedkarism or Phulle. Wherestands the view of the Chief Secretary as Big Brahmin of this area and small Brahmin is Dalit.

VIII. Science and Society:

Before the Karkota Dynasty of Kashmir, Guptas were the real rulrs of this area. It appears that bulk of the population among Hindus, they were Dalit (Sudras) = Gupta Age = vegetarian Age and followed the principle of Ahimsa or non-violence = Truly this savours of untouchability = "Dalit Samaj". Dalit Samaj or Chandals are more superior than the Hindus and Muslims, because they are vegetarian. It is still blot on Brahminism or Musalmanism. Prophet was the son of a Dalit Mochi = Barrack Obama = Dr Raj Kumar, Dr B.R. Ambedkar was Buddh sattvas at that time, he appeals to all the commonities studies the Vedas as a secret document of the thought either Gita or Bible or Holy Koran. 'God is one's as demonstrated from his (Ambedkar) sculpture, which has been installed before the 'Parliament House', who is the destructive of the Aryan Samaj = Dalit Samaj = Sufi Community, that is, narrow minded concept of the BJP Govt. Hindutatatav = Negative Thinker (R.K. Tripathi: *Ancient India* pp. 1 to 490) that Absence of History = Political Era (1947 to 2016 A.D.).

Very little is known from the "Age of Ashok" = Buddha a Namo", as statement revealed by Dr B.R. Ambedkar = Pure Land = Caste System in Litan Language (*The Buddha and His Dhamma* (pp.1-593) = Study of the Nam-History.

IX Barrack Obama and Dr B.R. Ambedkar:

Barrack Obama made the statement in his Parliament house on "Athen Democracy". He spoke in the favour of Dr B.r. Ambedkar.

X "Dr. B.r. Ambedkar was born in a poor family and cut the nose and throat of the Brahmins and wrote a document known as a "Law of the Land" and it serves all the right of the sub-continents peoples of India and this document is still functioning, Brahmins and Molavis of India cannot be change as a symbolic ideology of the '*Dalit-History*'. No big, no small all are good human being. Study shows, he had the universal Ideology of the Nam-History' (8 Nov. 2011). V.P. singh also favoured the Dalit Samaj on their plight. Now today, there is a great development, only there is a need of the streamline the sources of economic growth = "On Equality Rights". "Might is Right" = Sound-

Current = Power of Knowledge. Money matters placed on 2nd position as Mohandars Karam Chand Gandhi, placed 2nd in the British survey of India and Dr B.R. Ambedkar was the top most scholar of the world. Ali Mohammad Jinnah and Gandhi were advocates, Dr B.R. Ambedkar was Nam = Chamar = Mahar. According to Alexander Robertson, *'A Study of Untouchables in Maharashtra'*, a religious life of India, based on Realism or Kalidas Ke Drame' (published, 1938, pp. 5-131).

XI Islam was penetrated in India after the Sindh Conquest = Leh Ladakh Area = Pakistan and Bangladesh. China remained like the Taoism = Buddhism = Islam = Sudra Concept = Mochi Ideology of the Barrack Obama. Mohammad Prophet = Dr B.R. Ambedkar launched the campiagn from South India through Dalit voice = Inner Voice = Interior Islam (Tamara Sonn, *'A Brief History of Islam*; p. 58) published by Black well, 2004). Yuch-Chi Movements = Bhakti Movement started during the 2nd Century B.c. - the year commonly accepted that is 165 B.C. They were divided into two groups, that is, *Little Yuch-Chi* and Big tribe as *Siao Yuchi-Chi* found in North-Western India. They were follower of Wu-Sun as 'Surya Race', known as Dalits in North India as described by R.K. Tripathi (pp. 113-114). This tribe had three brothers (Kaniska, Kujala Kadphises and Vima Kadphisesr. Kaniska is indubitably the most striking figure among the Kushan 'Kings of India', 'Work and Worship' was the ideology of this tribe. Know called Gargotra or Bhardwaj clan. That clan had a school of painting in North India (Bahmana Chack). China was migrated again North-West and the moment was launched by Dr Sun-Yat-San, he was the son of a farmer. He visualised the idea of Taoism = Buddhism = Chamar throught. Untouchability is till existing in Dalits of North India either there is Megh or Barwala or Batwal. Study shows, Chamars are the original of Buddhist race of India. Mayawati ex-Chief Minister of U.P. exploited the Athen democracy concept of Sh. Kanshi Ram who was real founder of the BSP. On the concept of Dalit or Chamar. Author punished with the stroke of pen. Pen is the real historical study in art of writing the good themes of the Indian Democracy. 'Art of Living, a concept has been launched by Ravi Shankar, having no meaning to revelation the art of writing the Dalit = History. Dalit Concept is the concept of Sufi Ideology, 'Jai Guru Dev' = Nanak's ideology reflected by Ravidas in his Chamar Philosophy.

Nirang Kari = Nira Kar = Teg Bhadur" concept to realize the truth in art-history, but failed to prove the identity of the Nam-Dev = Dr Raj Kumar.

XII "Immediate Successors" of the Kaniska dynasty were Guptas, means 'work in hides and cutter in hides', that is, definition of the 'Dalit Ruler'. Karkota = Sarkota was the ruling agency of Prophet Mohammad. Harshvaradana = Durlaba Varadhana having the same meaning as Nam.

XIII Decline of the Kushan Empire, which prepared the way for the Guptas for welding Northern India eventually into one mightly empire = Nami - Empire = Dalit Samaj. But the Kidara Kushanas, a branch of the race, established themselves in the Kabul Valley = Gobi dessert and despite the fierce onslaughts of the Hunas in the 5th Century A.D.; there are traces of their survival until about the middle of the ninth century A.D. (R.K. Tripathi, *Ancient India*, p. 234).

XIV The "Dark" Interval = Political Era= Brahminism or Mohammadanism = Negativism. Indeed, they may have sprung up on the ruins of the Kushan power = illetrate race = formal study. Chandragupta I was followed by his son Samudragupta = Durlabavaradhana Partapadity II; Samudragupta was a versatile genius. He had several sons (cf. *bahn-putra-pantra* = a Race of the Dr B.R. Ambedkar = Chamar historians of North India = Sudra Kings = Natya - darpana = Natya-sastra=Shivities Race = Shai Muslims = Superior Race = less in number found in Kashmir whereas Sunnis, who were less in number, increased their population as Vote bank = explosion of population = Brahminism or Mohammadanism, became illetrate from the background of the human history = Dalit Samaj and power was shifted to Hashmi or Qurashi tribe of Sind = Gotra and Pravara.

XV Religions Condition = Here Brahmanism predominated as an ideology of the Development of the Human History = Angral = Bua Dati = Devi-Chandra = Mata Vashno-Devi concept which traced out from *Vishnu Purana*. Brahmin rules, Sudra does not rule = Political History. Political History = incomplete Knowledge of the Sudra Kings = A Chronicle study of the Kings of Kashmir. Uparika Maharajas or Goptas = Gupta Empire of India = Sudra Race = Maha Pratihara = Nami Ruler and Durlabhavaradhana Partapadity = Universal Truth.

Declining of Brahminism and rise of Sudra = Japji ruler = Chakarvati Raja = Shahjahana.

XVI Huna Invasions = Spiritual Study = Closing of the Gupta Age, rise of Karkota Rulers of Kashmir-Multi-Religions Society = Rites and Rituals. Economic condition well versed of the low caste Hindus of Rai Dynasty of Kashmir = Sudra Rulers where from the History of India has been distorted. Repeated attack = undermined the Gupta Dynasty of Kashmir with "Internal Evidence" = Dalit Samaj = Dalit History = Rai Family of Kashmir = Sindi Rulers of Ladakh.

XVII Civilisation under the Guptas and Rise of New Powers = Brahmanism = Jainism or Buddhism where form the Dalit history has been distorted = Quality Education = Origin of the Knowledge = Development of the Dalit Literature = Kushi Empire of Bartund = Kashmir, a clan working in the jungle to verify the Truth in History. History distorted, why and when during the past from Ashok to Mohammad Prophet = Dalit Samaj = Bhajan Patri = Arabic and Sanskrit script in art of writing the good books like Gita or Holy Bible placed by the Gideons. Holy Koran = Holy Bible, Guru Granth = Mandala Books. Sita = Rita = Nam History as an old concept of the Athen Democracy of India. Damaras = Vaisyas = Old Gupta of the Jammu region like Prof. Chaman Lal Gupta or Virendar Gupta, Old Brahmin = Surinder Kumar Sharma, a retired teacher of Mathematics GGM Science College of Jammu = Dr T.R. Sharma. In modern Kashmir = Political Era, no Hindus and Muslims are found efficient as Tirath Kumar Sharma or Surinder Kumar Sharma = Satpatiya Brahmins = Sudra Race. History writers after the death of Dr B.R. Ambedkar = Dr Raj Kumar Brahminism die down itself as Vaisya Study Kashtiyra or Rajput = Old Concept = Brahminism = twice-born theory.

XVIII Origin and Derivation of the Names:

According to Dr Jayaswal, the Vakatakas took their rise from the Bund elkhand = Chandelkhand found in Doda City = Doda Clan = Kundal Clan of Jammu region in Kashmir only few names have been found in art of writing the Sindh History = Jhelam Valley Road. Bhagat = Megh Bradari = Dalit Race became Brahmins in the Political State of Kashmir, Vakatakas, = Sudra Rulers = Rai Dynasty = Brahminism = Islam = Concept of Negativities = Political Era = "A Concept of

Athen Democracy" again launched by the Sindh Dynasty of Kashmir = Chamar thought = Brahminism in the 6th century A.D.

XIX Akhil Gargotra:

Bhardwaj Ashram of Barnai = Ravidas Niwas, War with Ravan = Ajatshatru Singh Jamwal = MLC of NC Party son of Dr Karan Singh Jamwal = Sanskrit Scholar = Brahmin writer believes on Sanskrit Literature = Arabic Literature = Negative Sciences = Chemistry, Physics, Botany, Zoology, Geology, Engineering = PDD, PDD = Medical Science and its number of branches ENT, Dentist and so on do not determined the truth = Pollution in large scale as an ideology of Gandhi Family for the development of *History*, that is, story of God and Man = Study of the Science of the Soul = Bhardwaj Asharm of the Jammu region = a book on the "*Paintings and Life style of Jammu Region* (17th to 19th Century A.D.) published in 2006, New Delhi. A copy of the same perserved by the scholar Dr Karan Singh Jamwal = Brahmin scholar.

XX Ram Janma Bhumi = Jambudvipa = Mule Niwashi Bhaujan Samaj Ki Viyatha (*Ram Chandra Prajapati Article*).

XXI Realising the threat to their very political existence = Nehru-Shiekh, Hari Sigh left the ideology of the Dalit Samaj = Kingship theory Dr B.R. Ambedkar, started the low caste Movement of the South Asia to the awakening of the Dalit Samaj with reference to the context of Sufi Saint ideology = Dalit Era with five persons = Pandava's race = awareness of the rights, not of the ritual study = composit dialogue = No Caste, No Religion = Equal Status = 'Good Human Being'. Politics = Rajniti = Ved Parkash = Spiritual Era = Enlightenment Age = Jambudvipa. Negativism no need, as a hurdle for the establishment of "Glorious History of Dalits'.

XXII South India = Nam History = Dogra Culture. Dogra Culture = Sindhi Vision] Multan found in Pakistan = Indus Valley Civilisation.

XXIII Basic Ideology = Insaniyat = Huriyat Conference = Nam-History = Rajatarangini having spiritual knowledge = untouchability = Chandrapide = Ambedkarbadi = Dalit View, it has often been said of the India of the Hindus = Rites and rituals History = Political Era (From 1947 to 2016 A.D.). Rising of Dalits, downfall of Molavism =

Panditism that it possessed "no history". The remark is true and putforth by M.A. Stein, if we apply on "Athen Democracy", work is worship. No wages, no rights to work in govt. institution, who are corrupt in their lifestyle = Moral Study = Fake degree of Muslims and Hindus and Universities issued by the Central Province of India = U.P.

XXIV Ambedkar and Karl Marx = Class struggle ideology = Haves and Have-nots = Dalits and anti-Dalits found in India.

When, History became "Science and Art", it produces classical culture and Brahminical literature became its sources for the writing of prose and poetry = classical literature = vedic literature = "A concept of Alhen Democracy" or vedic India = Holy Word, that is, the concept of lord Christ = Old Christianity = Chura Culture = Ravidas Culture.

XXV Character and Scope of Dalit Literature = New concept of learning known in art of writing the Dalit literature = New school of thought. The ancient coinage of Kashmir = Kashap Rishi's view in art of writing the Dalit history = New style in art of writing and reading introduced by Dr B.R. Ambedkar = Dalit Concept = Qutab ideology, a persian ideology launched by Zain-Ul-Abidin, before it was started by Moin-Ud-Din Christhi = Nam-History.

XXVI Varieties of Style = Varieties of language introduced by Him = in Manmat = Dalit Samaj = Satsangi Literature = Brahminism. The term style is derived from the Latin language is *called Style* = Chamar thought. Brahmin *Style* = *Dry style* = Satish Chandra or Irfan Habib. Pain Style = Ambedkar Style = Baba and Kundra's Literature of Jallandar. Delhi school of thought = Dry Style = Brahminism. Neat and elegant style = It may be regarded as the Perfection of style = Dalit literature = Dera Beas = Madhydesa history = History of various Popes.

A florid style = Phulle's Philosophy = stop the child marriage system = mature culture. Immature culture = anti-Dalit culture. The term florid is used with a two fold signification = on a mental discovery = imaginative pschyology.

XXVIII Immature Culture = Adament Approach = Material culture is lovable for Brahmin to hored the wealth with mal-practices = Dishonest Approach = Madan Lal Sharma or Sham Lal Sharma =

Congress Party including Prof. Safu-Ud-Din Soz Ideology = Manmat not Gurmat. Carefully revision, we mean is the best means of correcting the past history of the God and Man = florid style of thought = Dalit Concept.

In brief, Athen Democracy = Spiritual Era = Scientific Knowledge = Truth base study. What are its effect = *Life is fair*, it was found in Western Culture. Puritan Empire = Dalit Hindus or Muslims Govt. known as common wealth ideology (1649-1660 A.D.). It brought by Aurangzeb in India after the downfall of Cromwell. The rule of Puritanism = Ambedkarism = Pure thought brought in India by Ambedkar as a rule of the law = Constitutional ideology Dr Jitendar Singh MP of the Jammu region has the concept of diabeties = diabetialogist to check the sugar level of the human body = Sansar Chand's View = Incomplete idea as Gandhi had to his mild = Vikalat Nama = Hindu Ideology = Rites and Ritual = Ali Mohammad Jinnah = Advocate = Incomplete Ideology = Manmat = Evil Spirit Idea, based on *jadu Tuna* or Slavery system in Muslim Community or in Hindu Community even found in the Sikhism., Christianity declined and rise of Negativism = failure of modern govts. On the issue of work culture. Work culture is a concept of 'working class', politics is no more is an issue of the Indian society. The main issue is to streamline the 'development works' into common consceuses = civilised vision, to end the corrupt ideology in 'Human Pyschology' = 'Man Made History' = Work is worship culture = transparcy into human behaviour, no caste system = varna system = Dalit Samaj. Ambedkarism or Phalle = Dalit Samaj of the Lord Christ = Christanity. Now, this era is the beginning of the Christianity of Dalit Ideology = against the anti-Dalit = Brahminism. End of the Nehru - Gandhi Ideology = Sheikh Hasina = Sheikh Dynasty, based on incomplete thinking = Hari Singh. Hari Singh created history = Satsangi ruler and took shelter in Bombay due to the rise of anti-Dalit forces. Good King = Dr Manmohan Singh, who ruled ten years out of the dirty politics and left the idea to rule over India with the rising power of Dalits in North India.

The view that *poverty* is simply shortage of income is fairly well established in the Dalit literature. The inadequacy of income is often the major cause of deprivation that we standarly associate with poverty, including stgarvation and famines (Oxford India Paperbacks

'*Development As Freedom*'; Amartya Sen, 2011, P. 72). To analyzing the social injustice into *Social Justice*, there is a strong case for judging individual advantage in terms of the capabilities that a person has, that is, the substantive freedoms, wherestands the ideology of Amartya Sen = fight against the anti-Dalit propaganda. In this way, poverty must be seen as the deprivation of basic capabilities rather than merely as lowness of incomes, which is the standard criterion of identification of poverty.

The perspective of capability - poverty does not involve any denial of the sensible view that low income is clearly one of the major causes of poverty; since lack of income can be principal reason for a person's capability deprivation. (Ibid; p. 87. Chapter-4 *Poverty As Capability Deprivation*).

Indeed, inadequate income is a strong predisposing condition for an improverished life. If this is accepted, what then is all this fuss about, in seeing poverty in the capability perspective (as opposed to seeing it in terms of the standard income based poverty assessment)? The claims in favour of the capability approach to poverty are, I believe (Amartya Sen) the following:

(1) Poverty can be sensible identified in terms of capability deprivation; the approach concentrates on deprivation that are intrinsically important (unlike low income, which is obnly instrumentally significant.)

(2) There are influences on capabilities deprivation and thus on real poverty - other than lowness of income (income is not the only instrument in generating capabilities) = Dalit Samaj Ke identity = Chamar thought.

(3) The instrumental relations between low income and low capability is *variable* between different communities and even between different families and different individuals (the impact of income on capabilities is contingent and conditional).

The third issue is particularly important in considering and evaluating public action aimed at reducing in equality or poverty (Ibid; pp. 87-88).

Deprive of capabilities in terms of social functioning. This consideration - pioneeringly outlined by Adam Smith in '*The Wealth of Nations*' (1976) - is quite central sociological understandings of poverty and it has been analysed by W.G. Runciman, Peter Townsend and others W.G. Runciman; '*Relative Deprivation and Social Justice: A Study of Attitudes to Social Inequality in twentieth Century England*' (London, Routledge; 1966), and townsend; *Poverty in the United Kingdom* (1949); e.g. the difficulties that some groups of people experience in "taking part in the life of the community" can be crucial for any study of 'Social exclusion' to "*Social inclusion*".

India is, of course, highly diverse in terms of human development, with some region (most notably, Kerala) having much higher lends of education, health care and land reforms than others (most notably; Bihar, U.P. Rajasthan, M.P., J&K). The limitation have taken different forms in the different states.

It is, however, interesting to note that economic growth in Kerala seems to have had a faster rate of reduction in income poverty than any other State of *India* (G. Datt; '*Poverty in India and Indian States*': An update (Washington 1997). While some states have reduced income poverty through high economic growth; Punjab etc., Kerala has relied a great deal on expansion of basic education, health car and equitable land distribution for its success in reducing penury = Leh Ladakh is social history = '*Advancement Idea*'.

Income poverty and capability poverty also found in Sudra concept, why Brahminbad is superior, they work for the betterment of the society quoting the example of Amartya Sen, '*Winner of the Noble prize in Economics*'. "*Development as Freedom*", in this book *Sen* develops, elegantly, compactly and yet broadly the concept of Manmat. But historically, he is weakened to provide the freedom to the Dalit Communities ('*Gujjars and their Tribes*'). In global economic development, India is lack behind to compare with U.S.A. or U.K., Germany or Franch. Why because, there is a civilised growth in human history rather than the instrumental behaviour in social sciences (Policy and Politics in India went into the hands of negative forces = *Illiterate Politics* or Brahaminical thinking = Self judgement, not realizing the *truth* in art of writing the "*Social Sciences*". *Gurumat* is essential in art of writing the thesis in all branches of knowledge = Essential History.

Author is known most controversial, public figure in Ladakh area by publishing the book '*History of Chamar Dynasty*' as an historical document = factual theory of the Islam by re-writting the whole History = Chamar thought + Buddhist Philosophy = Knowledgeable document. The reason of this historical research is to obtain the beauty of Ladakh + Shia Community = Sharif Log = Common concesus of the Ladakh division = Polish race of the human Ideology + Dalit Concept = nil/nil Brahminical Ideology.

Note: Chitra-Kala of Ladakh region = of U.P.'s Trade Mark. 90 per cent of T-Ministers = Telangana, 56 per cent A.P., 34 per cent Karanatak, 27 per cent Odisha are facing Criminal Charge on the Ideology of Development = Ladakh is superior than these.